AF538272

WINNER LOSE ALL

WINNER LOSE ALL

Dr. Cook and the Theft of the North Pole

---

by Hugh Eames

with illustrations

Little, Brown and Company — Boston – Toronto

FIRST EDITION

T 06/73

Library of Congress Cataloging in Publication Data

Eames, Hugh.
Winner lose all.

Bibliography: p.
1. Cook, Frederick Albert, 1865-1940. 2. North Pole. I. Title.
G635.C66E15 919.8 [B] 73-3410
ISBN 0-316-20070-0

Published simultaneously in Canada by Little, Brown & Company (Canada) Limited

PRINTED IN THE UNITED STATES OF AMERICA

To the memory of my mother and father,
Grace Jackson and Hugh Fowler Eames

History . . . to cleanse the story of mankind from the deceiving visions of purposeful past.

— J. H. Plumb

Acknowledgments

AMONG INDIVIDUALS, I am particularly indebted to Andrew A. Freeman for his pioneer biography *The Case for Doctor Cook*, a solid and indispensable book written at a time when Cook was close to becoming an unperson. I am also obliged to Helene Cook Vetter, as staunch a daughter as any father ever had.

In addition, I am grateful for the existence and kindness of numerous historical societies and other institutions, such as The Stefansson Collection at Dartmouth College; but most of all I am grateful for the existence of the New York Public Library.

Contents

Illustrations

I

Cook Versus Nature

I

ALTHOUGH all the members of the club were aggressive men, multimillionaires, most of them, and of the self-made variety, none of them contended that the great geographic prize was their man's private property.

It was nothing as blatant as that. They simply believed that their man, having chased the prize through twenty years, had certain privileges that sportsmen everywhere recognized. And they also believed that these privileges had been ignored by their man's rival, who was one of those loners, unsupported by any club of any sort. Moreover, the members of the club had spent hundreds of thousands of dollars supporting their man's expeditions, and it was infuriating to have the upstart loner return to civilization and assert his deed five days before their man could notify the world of his own success.

Accordingly, when they heard a rumor that the loner — Frederick A. Cook, M.D. — was a fraudulent person, it was easy for them to believe that only their man's claim was genuine. This being so, it was natural for them, the members of the Peary Arctic Club, to spend more money to spread their news; or, as one friendly commentator put it, "to direct and control the proper sort of publicity necessary to preserve the dignity of the truth."[1]*

* Source references will be given for all material quoted in support of the historical argument. Sources of material quoted for purely narrative purposes will be given only if the author believes it is of particular interest or significance.

But the truth could not be spread until the facts had been organized, and this took time. At first, not every member of the club was aware of all the facts. This included the secretary, who made a small error. After Cook had declared his attainment of the North Pole, reporters asked the secretary for his reaction. He responded: "If the advices are authentic, I will naturally be very pleased over Dr. Cook's triumph."[2]

Five days later the club's man — Commander Robert E. Peary, U.S.N. — arrived at an outpost of civilization and cabled the world that he had reached the North Pole. Almost immediately the secretary, Herbert L. Bridgman, made a new statement. Dr. Cook's claim to the Pole "invites remark among men who respect honor and observe fair play," Bridgman wrote. "That [Peary's] men, methods, and reasoning should be appropriated and the long struggle finished before he had his fair and final opportunity is a transaction upon which the American people will render just judgment when they know all the facts."[3]

A few days passed, and then the club's assault upon Cook began. It was conducted with remarkable vigor. By the time five months had passed, the club had "proved" that Cook had not reached the Pole; it had "proved" that Peary (as in "leary") had reached the Pole; it had succeeded in getting its "proofs" accepted by every newspaper in the country. As for the demolished Doctor, he, on the verge of a nervous breakdown, had fled the country.

All of which was a formidable testament to the ingenuity of the Peary Arctic Club, because at the center of the North Pole controversy was a unique reality. The North Pole, the object of three hundred years of exertion and millions of dollars of expenditure, did not exist, physically. It was and remains a theoretical point on an ice-filled sea, in which the ice is in a state of slow but constant drift, so that no explorer, ever, can materially prove that he has been to what the Eskimos know of as the Big Nail. No proof tradition existed in high Arctic exploration. The explorer's statement that he had reached a certain point on the polar ice was accepted always.

With its victim hiding somewhere, the club hired the Metropolitan Opera House and presented its "National Testimonial to Commander Peary." Every seat in the auditorium was filled, and up on the stage the polar hero was attended by a court of thirty-one of America's most powerful millionaires. The Commander lectured, was cheered, and was then presented with a purse of $10,000 subscribed by the thirty-one tycoons. It was an impressive gesture then. Today it is not creditable.

Frederick A. Cook was a great romantic, and exceptionally naive politically; but he was also tremendously able. One of the anomalies of his life was that when his accomplishments could be witnessed by several people, his abilities were recognized and rewarded; but when his deeds could be authenticated by only one or two, he was proclaimed a liar and a con man. Today he is considered, when he is considered at all, to be the most discredited humbug in our history. Yet it is not difficult for a modern investigator to show that the Doctor was neither a liar nor a con man, but a unique and valuable hero who, at the minimum, is not simply one of the greater victims in America's history, but the all-time champion.

Aside from his eyes, which were blue and fine, Cook was an ordinary looking man. His height was five feet nine inches, he weighed around 175 pounds, his shoulders were wide, and his chest was deep. He was sturdy, a brave and energetic man of action who in repose seemed placid. Some of the photographs of him are unfortunate studio stills for which he posed in Arctic furs. In these and other pictures his hair, which was ash-blond, appears brunette, and his skin, which was brown and weathered, seems sallow. He had a yellow mustache. It was walrus-large when he was young, but became smaller as he matured. As it shrank and finally vanished, his features became more impressive. In his old age his photos reflect dignity, endurance, and kindness.

He was a rational man who had tremendous faith in the human race and took words seriously. The New York sporting goods merchant David Abercrombie said of him: "In his talk

Dr. Cook is slow, but he always chooses his words carefully and speaks methodically. He is not in the habit of using mere words." At the same time Cook was gracious, genial, and forthright, and he was well liked by those who knew him. "This was always and everywhere the rule," the explorer Vilhjalmur Stefansson said, "with naturally the usual exceptions."

It was all part of a drama that began, for present purposes, when Greek philosophers started to wonder about the shape of the earth. For a time they believed it was a flat disk bounded by a great river. Later they decided that it, still flat, was an oblong rectangle supported by compressed air. But by the end of the sixth century B.C. Greek scientists had learned that the earth was a sphere. They then, for convenience, invented two imaginary lines. One circled the earth and was called the equator. The other ran through the center of the earth and was called the axis. "Pole" is the traditional term for the point where the axis cuts the surface of a sphere, and the scientists positioned the earth's axis so that its poles were at those points around which the stars appeared to rotate.

But then the Church, greatest of clubs, became alarmed. The scientists were proclaimed pagans, and priests went about demolishing the notion that the earth was round. Round? Could people walk with their feet above their heads? Could rain and snow fall upward? The earth, obviously, was flat. It was flat and it was rectangular, shaped exactly like the Holy Tabernacle described in Exodus. Any other belief was a sin. The flat-earth theory returned to favor and was popularly believed for over a thousand years.

But the idea that the earth was round continued to exist in books, and was supported by the experiences of seamen. By the time of Columbus, every educated man understood that the earth was a sphere. Then Magellan sailed completely around the world, and the Church retreated to rethink the matter. Today man knows that the earth is not round like a ball, but slightly pear-shaped, being fatter about the South Pole.

By the beginning of the twentieth century, man had inspected most of the surface of his spherical dwelling place, but two locales were still unattained: the North and South Poles. For certain men these remained, as Roald Amundsen wrote, "a something that man had not yet conquered, a continuing evidence of his weakness. . . . every mystery made plain . . . exalts the spirit of the whole human race." And of the two Poles, it was the North Pole that fascinated man, whose civilization was for the most part northern.

Meanwhile, Norwegian explorers had concluded that the North Polar Basin was an ice-filled sea, and that there was only the barest possibility of land existing at its center. The scientific importance of the North Pole shrank and its attainment degenerated into a sort of international sporting tournament.

And then, from a telegraph station in the Shetland Islands, the New York *Herald* received and immediately published a cable from Dr. Frederick A. Cook:

REACHED NORTH POLE APRIL 21, 1908.

Instantly, a delighted world demanded more information. Reporters searched for anyone who knew the Doctor and soon found his brother William, who described him as "a self-made man," and said, "like all Cooks, he was possessed of a very earnest ambition." William Cook did not elaborate on what he called "the Cook ambition," but it is easy to understand what he meant.

Fred Cook, his sister Lillie, and his brothers August, Theodore, and William, were Americans of German descent. Their father, Theodore Cook,* who was also a doctor, had been born in the Hanover region in Germany. Their mother was Magdalena Long, whose family had emigrated from Frankfurt and had settled in New York City where the father manufactured cigars. After Theodore and Magdalena had married they

* Koch was the original family name. Theodore Cook anglicized it during the Civil War.

moved to Hortonville, a hamlet in Sullivan County, New York. There Frederick Albert Cook was born June 10, 1865.

Five years later Dr. Theodore Cook died of pneumonia, leaving Magdalena with five blond-haired children and no money. For several years they remained in Hortonville, where the children attended the district school four months each year. Will Cook remembered that Fred "was a prize student in geography. It was the study which interested him most."

Fred Cook was still in Hortonville when he had his first tremendous adventure. "As a small boy, I remember being fascinated by the lure of a forbidden swimming pool," he wrote years later. "One day when but little over five, I, impelled to test the depth, plunged into the center, where the water was above my head, and nearly lost my life. I shall never forget that struggle, and though I nearly gave out, in that short time I learned to swim."[4]

Eventually, Magdalena Cook moved her family to Brooklyn, where she and Lillie sewed for the sweatshops, Ted Cook worked for a beer keg manufacturer, and Fred and Will found jobs at the Fulton Street Market in Manhattan. There they arrived at 2:00 A.M and often labored until noon. Fred Cook's attendance at school was haphazard, but he kept up with his class.

"My boyhood was not happy," he eventually wrote. "As a tiny child I was discontented, and from the early days of consciousness I felt the burden of two things which accompanied me through later life — an innate and abnormal desire for exploration, then the manifestation of my yearning, and the constant struggle to make ends meet, that sting of poverty which, while it tantalizes one with its horrid grind, sometimes drives men by reason of the strength developed . . . to some extraordinary achievement."[5]

After Fred Cook had graduated from public school, he decided to become a doctor. To pay for his training he started a milk route. He built a wagon equipped to handle the glass bottles that had just been invented, and because he offered door-to-door service, another new idea, his business prospered. In 1887 he entered the medical school at Columbia University. At the end of the first year he transferred to New York University, which was located more conveniently.

"He began his day at 1:00 A.M.," Andrew Freeman, his first biographer, wrote, "checked with his men, rode with them to the milk depot, and drove a wagon when a driver was absent. At 10:00 A.M. he was in the medical school . . . where he remained until 4:00 P.M. Thereafter he studied until 9:00 P.M., then slept until it was time to start milk deliveries."

In 1889 he married Mary Elizabeth Forbes, whom he had met at the First Methodist Church in Brooklyn. In 1890 he graduated from medical school, opened an office in Manhattan, and in his first six months had three patients. At some time during these months, Mary Elizabeth died of peritonitis after giving birth to a baby, who also died. In his lonely office he treated his grief by reading of travel and exploration.

One day he noticed a newspaper story about a Lt. Robert E. Peary. The Lieutenant, then stationed at the Philadelphia Navy Yard, was preparing an Arctic expedition for which he required a surgeon. "I sat down and wrote out an application," Cook said years later. " . . . Two months passed before I received any answer. I had almost given up hope when I was startled by receiving a telegram to go to Philadelphia and meet Peary. I went."[6]

After a few minutes in Peary's company, Cook sized him up as "a thoroughly decent fellow and a strong character." Years later Cook recalled that Peary had warned him: "The life up there under the Pole is terribly hard. . . . We will be as much out of touch with the world as we would on some other planet. Some of us more than likely will never return. . . . I advise you not to go if there is any fear in your heart."

Cook replied: "I am willing to take the chances."[7]

As the afternoon ended Cook became the first member of Peary's expedition, its surgeon and ethnologist. The contract specified that he would receive no pay.

Scholars have not been able to find much about Robert Edwin Peary at his best, but at his worst the evidence, today, is abundant. Although his name is identified with the Arctic, which he invaded again and again, a more fundamental association would be with fame, for which his need was extraordinary. Like Cook, he lost his father early and was raised by his mother; but unlike Cook he was an only child. At seventeen he could not abide the company of any contemporary who outshone him. "I must be the peer or superior of those about me to be comfortable," he wrote his mother; "not that I care to show my superiority, simply to know it myself."[8] In the next few years his requirements expanded. "I shall not be satisfied," he now wrote his mother, " . . . until my name is known from one end of the world to the other."[9] *

But by the time he met Cook he was thirty-four and the going was slow. He had graduated Phi Beta Kappa from Bowdoin College, and after a brief hesitation, had made straight for Washington, D.C. There he had worked for the Coast and Geodetic Survey, then joined the Navy as a civil engineer with the simulated rank of lieutenant. Eventually he received a prize assignment: surveying part of the route for a proposed canal across Nicaragua. He read everything he could find on Nicaragua, the immediate goal being "a knowledge of the Isthmus equaled by no living man," and did valuable work in the three months he was in Nicaragua, despite the disturbing rumor that the American government favored a route across Panama.

Back in Washington, in a bookstore, he found a pamphlet describing an attempt to cross the Greenland ice cap. The Arctic had always interested him, and he now discovered that only three men had ever ventured any distance into Greenland's formidable interior. It was, therefore, a potential avenue to

* The Peary problem goes far beyond himself. It includes the aggressions of his club and the delinquencies of his biographers. In 1926 one biographer, Fitzhugh Green, described Peary's antecedents and conception thus: "It was as if that group of good people were laid like an egg of Destiny in the womb of a clean nature for the single purpose of bringing forth a finer specimen of the race than the commonplace mechanics of gestation could achieve." Later biographers, closely supervised by the Peary family, have come painfully near to emasculating the entire controversy, itself an episode that reeks with "the commonplace mechanics of gestation."

fame. In the summer of 1886 he sailed north with three months' leave and $500 borrowed from his mother.

Greenland at its widest is nine hundred miles across. Peary penetrated not quite one hundred miles. The distance was slightly less than that gone by previous explorers, but when he returned to Washington he had something to talk about. He did so. "My last trip has brought my name before the world," he wrote his mother. "With . . . the assistance of friends whom I have made this winter, I will next winter be one of the foremost in the highest circles in the capital, and make powerful friends with whom I can shape my future. . . . Remember, Mother, I *must* have fame."[10]

In 1887 he returned to Nicaragua to work on a new route for the proposed canal. When he arrived back in Washington he married Josephine Diebitsch, whose father was associated with the Smithsonian Institute. Meanwhile, the rumor that the government favored a canal across Panama had strengthened to the point where, for Peary, the Arctic was obviously the main chance. Since he had a slight lisp (as had Cook), he studied elocution, then lectured about Greenland. He appeared before scientific societies and proposed an expedition to determine whether Greenland was an island or a continent. By the winter of 1890 three scientific societies had agreed to support him, the Navy had granted him leave, and Cook had become his first volunteer. Soon afterward, Peary accepted Eivind Astrup, a young Norwegian skier. Astrup wrote of his first sight of Peary: "His whole appearance inspired me with absolute confidence. His tall, lean figure was elastic and sinewy; his features, coarse but determined, were aglow with intrepid resolution."

His mother called him Bertie. His wife called him Bert. His friends called him Bob.

Besides Cook and Astrup, Peary's expedition included John Verhoeff and Langdon Gibson. Josephine Peary also went along, and her presence made newspaper copy. An even more exotic member of the party was Peary's servant, Matthew

Henson, a twenty-five-year-old black. Not much was written about Henson, but he went north too, as he would on all of Peary's subsequent expeditions.

The explorers sailed from Brooklyn on June 16, 1891, aboard the barkentine *Kite*. By late July they had established their base camp at McCormick Bay on the west coast of Greenland. On July 30 the *Kite* sailed south, not to return for a year. It was everyone's first winter in the Arctic, but conditions were not impossible. The fur clothing made by the Eskimos was satisfactory; and Peary kept everyone busy hunting, making sledges, and learning to ski and to handle dogs. On one test march Gibson was heard to observe that the inland ice trip would be hell, a remark that Peary did not appreciate. By spring everything was ready, and on May 5, 1892, Peary, Cook, Henson, Astrup, Gibson and some Eskimos started out in search of Greenland's northernmost point. Henson and the Eskimos soon turned back. Henson had a frozen heel, and the Eskimos were certain that the interior was the home of giants and devils.

With Peary leading and indefatigable, the remaining travelers struggled across 150 miles of snow and ice and reached Humboldt Glacier. There Peary announced that only he and Astrup, the best skier and map maker, would continue north. Cook and Gibson turned back with one sledge and four dogs, leaving Peary and Astrup with three sledges and fourteen dogs. "The whips cracked," Astrup wrote, "and we . . . slowly lost sight of each other in the midst of that desert of snow."

Thirty-four days later Peary and Astrup reached approximately latitude 82°. They then turned south and on August 5 arrived back at the base camp. There Peary could feel triumphant. In ninety-seven days over ice and snow, he had traveled some 1,130 miles. And he had won. His expedition had achieved its goal. Greenland was an island and its northernmost point had been found. He and Astrup had virtually stood upon it when, from the top of a huge cliff, they had viewed a channel — he named it Peary Channel — that he was convinced marked the island's northern boundary.

(In 1907, however, Danish explorers discovered that Peary Channel did not exist, and that Greenland continued for a considerable distance beyond where Peary said it ended. In 1915 the United States Navy ordered Peary Channel expunged from its maps.)

On August 24, 1892, the expedition sailed south aboard the *Kite*.

After a pause in Brooklyn the *Kite* went on to Philadelphia for a reception. Going ashore, most of the explorers thought they had had all they wanted of the Arctic, but "after a drink, a bath, and good food," Cook wrote, "we were all eager to go back again."[11] Peary was planning an expedition for 1893. He wanted Cook with him, and once again the Doctor agreed.

Afterward Cook lingered in Philadelphia and soon had an unexpected visitor: Matt Henson, complaining about his eyes. When Cook discovered that Henson had only thirty dollars left of the fifty Peary had paid him for the expedition, Cook "paid Henson's fare to Brooklyn," Floyd Miller wrote in a biography of Henson, "and put him up at his mother's home. Dr. Jackson Mills examined Matt and discovered . . . severe . . . sun-blindness. . . . Treatment was given without charge, and for the two months Henson was confined to bed, Cook's sister Lillie was his nurse. His eyes responded well, and by December . . . he was ready to leave the family to whom he would be forever grateful."[12]

Peary had strong reasons for wanting the Doctor with him again. In the north Cook had handled himself splendidly. While the expedition was sailing for Greenland on the *Kite*, Peary broke his leg. It was the kind of accident that could end a traveler's career, but the Doctor set the bone skillfully, then tended his patient, who would write of Cook: "I personally owe much to his professional skill and unruffled cooolness in an emergency."[13] Peary also described Cook as "Indefatigable worker, earnest student of the peculiar people among whom we lived," and stated that Cook had obtained "a record of the tribe unapproachable in ethnological archives."[14] And Astrup wrote of Cook: "a very active and energetic comrade . . . who, as the ethnologist . . . proved himself of great service."[15]

After the explorers had settled back into society, it turned out that both Cook and Peary were living in Brooklyn. Peary had been assigned to the Navy Yard, and Cook had opened an office in that borough. They did not seek each other's society and rarely met, but when they did their relations were cordial.

One day the Doctor was invited to lecture before the Kings County Medical Society in Brooklyn. He did so, for no fee, and confined himself to the medical and anthropological aspects of the Eskimos. His fellow doctors then suggested that he publish his findings in a medical journal. Because the contract Cook had signed included an agreement not to make any public lectures or write any articles for one year after the expedition had returned, Cook went to Peary and requested permission to publish in a medical journal. Peary turned him down. No member of his expeditions, he told Cook, could publish anything except in a book over his name. Cook then resigned from the 1893 expedition. "Here was the only break I had with Peary," he wrote later. "I resigned then and there as a volunteer, but did so in a friendly way. There really was no lingering malice between us."[16]

Soon afterward Peary asked Cook to give medical examinations to the members of the 1893 expedition. Cook did so, and on the day before the expedition sailed went down to the ship. While he was on board Peary told reporters he regretted that Cook, because of professional engagements, was not going north with him.[17]

In those days Americans were fascinated by the Arctic and identified with those who adventured across ice. Frederick A. Cook, now someone people talked about in Brooklyn, began to prosper as a doctor. But something other than medicine now possessed his mind — "a new and absorbing passion which ever since has dominated my life . . . the voice of the Arctic, the taste for the icy expanse, the Polar Sea. . . . Something keeps calling, calling, calling until at last you can stand it no more, and you return, spell drawn by the magic of the North."[18] And so, in the summers of 1893 and 1894, Cook went north.

The 1893 voyage was a disappointment. Off Greenland the captain of the small ship he had chartered refused to sail to Cape York, where the far north really began. "Cook pleaded, argued, insisted," a member of the crew recalled, "but Captain Hebb would not risk his ship in the . . . ice floes. When all argument failed, Cook wanted to take one of the ship's small boats and start north; but the Captain would not hear of it." Cook was able to make a few journeys up fiords, and to study the Eskimos. The sailor recalled him saying: "To conquer the North you must become an Eskimo." On one trip up a fiord Cook met some Eskimos, the sailor reported, and "forgot about everything else. Indications of a storm made us uneasy . . . but he paid no attention. At length we felt it was becoming serious and threatened to leave him. All he said was 'there is no hurry' and kept on talking until he was ready to leave."[19]

The 1894 expedition was even more frustrating. Cook's party sailed north aboard the *Miranda*, a ship notorious for its penchant for rocks and collisions. Nor was this idle talk. She soon found an iceberg and rammed it, and from then on all was disaster. Cook responded with witnessed courage and skill, but in comparison with the problems involved in sledging across ice, the last voyage of the *Miranda* was a jaunt, and four years passed before Cook's abilities were tested to the maximum.

In the meantime, he became engaged to Anne Forbes, the sister of his dead wife.

Then, in the New York *Sun* for August 20, 1897, he read of the troubles of the Belgian Antarctic Expedition. Its surgeon had resigned at the last minute and a replacement was needed. He wired his application to Brussels and was instructed to proceed to Rio de Janeiro and join the expedition aboard the *Belgica*. Anne Forbes begged him not to go, but three weeks later he sailed.

In Rio the expedition leader, Adrien de Gerlache, welcomed him in an eloquent address, made in French, of which he did not understand one word. But he was not the only explorer with a language problem. The expedition's leaders were Belgian, the crew was Scandinavian, and the scientific staff included two Russians and a Romanian. "They wanted me," he wrote later. "I wanted to go. We were to be together for two long years, speaking a polyglot of seven languages. We mixed it all together and came back with a new lingo understood by no other human being."

After the *Belgica* had reached Tierra del Fuego, at the tip of South America, de Gerlache decided to pause and map the coastline. Lucas Bridges, the young son of an English ranching family there, observed the ship's arrival on January 1, 1899. "A man appeared on deck and hailed me in English with a slight American accent," Bridges wrote in *Uttermost Part of the Earth.* "He was a smartly dressed, personable fellow, not much over thirty and full of life, rather below medium height and sturdily built. He introduced himself as Dr. Frederick A. Cook." Bridges would also recall that Cook "most obligingly visited sick natives, including Kanhoat's little boy, who had . . . serious eye trouble. Things had gone too far to save one eye, but the doctor preserved the sight of the other, to the delight and relief of Kanhoat."

Mapping the coastline required six weeks, and by the time it was finished the Antarctic exploring season was almost over and the expedition's future seemed bleak. De Gerlache then made a bad decision. The *Belgica* would not only continue south, it would attempt to break the record for the Farthest South. He thus had the dubious honor of commanding the first expedition ever to be frozen into the Antarctic ice. The original plan had been to land four men to winter near the magnetic South Pole and retrieve them in the spring, but now — three hundred miles below the Antarctic Circle — everyone was trapped. It was a disaster for which the expedition was unprepared, materially or psychologically. As the long polar night settled in, the men became lost in melancholy.

Roald Amundsen, who would become the first man to reach the South Pole, was the mate on the *Belgica.* Years later he wrote: "It was in this fearful emergency, during those thirteen long months in which almost daily the certainty of death stared us steadily in the face, that I came to know Dr. Cook intimately and to form the affection for him and the gratitude to him which nothing . . . could ever cause me to alter. He, of all the ship's company, was the one man of unfaltering courage, unfailing hope, endless cheerfulness and unwearied kindness. When anyone was . . . disheartened, he was there to encourage and inspire."[20]

But the Doctor could only do so much. One seaman went insane. Others were also beginning to break down mentally. De Gerlache was despondent. Cook treated him imaginatively, exposing him to the energy of an open fire, and after a week the cheerful flames revived de Gerlache's will to live.

Another problem was women. "Inevitably men long removed from feminine society will turn their thoughts to women, and almost exclusively to women," Cook wrote. Part of the problem was relieved by a beauty contest. "When the elimination ballots all had been cast," Cook wrote, "the real and decisive race was found to be between the two most famous beauties of that period — Princess de Chimay (born Clara Ward of Chicago) and Cleo de Meroede, the French actress. Fervent electioneering preceded the final vote. . . . The Princess de Chimay won by a narrow margin. Sadly enough, when we did return to civilization poor Clara had violated the conventions by running away from her titled husband with a gypsy fiddler . . . and was entirely out of things."[21]

In the meantime, very plainly, Cook had become the expedition's unofficial leader. "With the return of the sun," Amundsen wrote, in *My Life as an Explorer*, "after the long Antarctic night, he led small parties on scouting expeditions in all directions, looking for evidence that the ice might providently open and leave a channel for us back to the open sea."

One day someone discovered that a small basin of water had formed about a thousand yards from the ship. Cook predicted that when the ice broke the opening would lead directly to this basin. He proposed that a channel be cut to the basin, and that the ship be floated through the channel so as to be in position to take immediate advantage of the opening. The explorers spent weeks cutting the channel, then towed the *Belgica* into the basin. More weeks passed and then, suddenly, the ice cracked and broke and the opening ran directly to the ship. But the perils of the explorers were not ended. As the *Belgica* moved toward the open sea it had to squeeze its way between two giant icebergs, which for several days held it as in a vise. "Here again Dr. Cook's ingenuity saved the day," Amundsen wrote. "He had carefully preserved the skins of the penguins we had killed, and now we made them into mats and lowered them over the sides . . . where they took up and . . . mitigated the impact of the ice." Out on the open sea, everyone became violently seasick.

After the *Belgica* had returned to Tierra del Fuego, Lucas Bridges recalled, Cook appeared in a fur-lined overcoat. Bridges coveted it immediately, and so the Doctor presented it to him. Later, Cook sent young Bridges, "two pairs of snow-shoes that he had used down south," Bridges wrote. "They were a great improvement on my own amateur copies of the Canadian tennis-racket type . . . and I was very grateful."

When the *Belgica* arrived in Montevideo Cook found mail awaiting him. Anne Forbes was dead. Her family said she "seemed to pine away."[22]

He returned to Brooklyn in June, 1899. He was now thirty-five; blooded in the Arctic, blooded also in the Antarctic, where he had performed magnificently, as all who had survived acknowledged gladly. When he went to Europe in 1900 he became, in Brussels, the only non-Belgian member of the expedition to be honored with a medal by that nation's king. Years later Roald Amundsen judged him "the finest traveler I ever saw."[23] All fields of human endeavor have their great spirits. That Frederick A. Cook, in exploration, was a genius, will one day be formally recognized. He was a noble man, one of those who, in the words of a mystic, "shines a little."

By 1900, the year the Doctor was rewarded by the Belgian king, Peary was leading his third expedition to the Arctic and, from American and British geographical societies, had himself acquired some medals. During these years he had become a very restrictive man. A sailor on one expedition recalled: "We could not take a picture, converse with the natives, or pick up a walrus tooth without his permission."[24] And he was just as restrictive about larger matters. Although he did not claim the whole Arctic as his private property, he did, in his own mind, possess North Greenland and what he called "the American route to the Pole." This was Peary territory. Strangers who entered it were charged with "appropriating my domain," "forestalling my work," and "appropriating my plans." As he grew older his delight in possessing increased. Once, after establishing a new Farthest North, he wrote: "A day's march beyond Aldrich's Farthest and what I saw was *Mine*, mine by right of discovery, to be credited to me, and associated with my name, generations after I had ceased to be."[25]

Being as he was, it was not difficult for him to understand just what it was that made tycoons contribute to expeditions to the North Pole. In a circular letter to a group of millionaires he wrote: "And if I win out in this work, the names of those who made the work possible will be kept through the coming centuries floating forever above the forgotten and submerged debris of our time and day. The one thing we remember about Ferdinand of Spain is that he sent Columbus to his life work."[26]

Over the years Peary had become a most imposing man. He was six feet tall, with reddish blond hair and a huge chest. A lady reporter found him "the ideal type of the explorer. Tall, wiry, muscular . . . his lean face is burnt by years of exposure to the wind — not bronzed . . . but burnt a peculiar red and white in the cold flame of the Arctic; his jaw is as firm as iron."[27] He was an imposing man. He was also a disturbing man, almost frighteningly close to the animal. During the polar controversy a reporter wrote: "Peary's big, sandy head, his ever-pulsating muscles and constantly twitching nostrils . . . every inch of him . . . was as hard as Bessemer steel; his muscles danced and squirmed under his shirt as he moved and breathed. Whenever he spoke he heaved out his great chest, gestured slightly with his freckled . . . hands, and made a peculiar gurgling sound in his throat. . . . He smiled from ear to ear, showing every one of his big strong teeth, that are almost wolfish in their set and grip as he talks."[28]

In addition, he was very excitable. "He had not a clear head," the English geographer J. Gordon Hayes wrote in *Robert Edwin Peary*. "He was one of those men who make contradictory statements because they forget what they have said previously. Thus he was inconsistent . . . continually expecting to keep his cake and eat it . . . nearly all emotion, and devoid of . . . love of truth."

He was, finally, a proud, egotistical engineer turned monomaniac explorer; most capable of taking care of himself, but not really interested in the problems of others. So he was not a true leader. Green, his most blissful biographer, acknowledged: "Many in Peary's command used to return hating him in a way that murder couldn't gratify." But not everyone dreamed of murdering Peary. Hugh J. Lee, a member of the 1893–1895 expedition, wrote: "He was kind and gentle, and withall, understanding, which is true greatness. He was the grandest man of whom I have ever known." More experienced men, however, thought otherwise. "Having his purpose clearly in mind," one member of his final expedition conceded, "he perhaps came to think of his men as instruments, to be used with cold precision to the accomplishment of certain purposes clearly perceived by the master mind."[29]

His 1893–1895 expedition, from which Cook had resigned, had been a failure. In the first year his longest journey was 128 miles. In the second year he, Henson, and Lee reached a point five hundred miles north of their base. On the way south they were forced to eat their dogs. Of this journey the historian Jeanette Mirsky wrote: "For all its magnificent bravery, the results were as barren as those of the preceding abortive attempt." By the time Peary returned to America he was forty years old. "I shall never see the North Pole unless some one brings it here," he told reporters. " . . . In my judgment such work requires a far, far younger man than I."[30]

Cook wrote to another explorer: "Peary's failure is sad news . . . but it is what you and I and all of us who knew the bad shape of his equipment expected. He has fought hard against tremendous odds. . . . He deserves sympathy."

But after a year in civilization, Peary was ready to go back. Now he had thought out a new solution to the problem of the Pole. As a solution, it was "not merely the *most* practical but the only remaining one."[31] The expedition, based in North Greenland, might remain north five years, and could cost $150,000. By 1898 Peary had obtained most of what he needed, including five years' leave from the Navy and the promise of a ship, the *Windward*, from Lord Northcliffe, a British press tycoon. The exploring party would consist of himself, Matt Henson, and Dr. Thomas Scott Dedrick.

A merciless series of events then began. Peary learned that a Norwegian expedition commanded by Otto Sverdrup would also be in North Greenland. Although Sverdrup's purpose was to map a portion of the region, Peary suspected a polar effort. When the *Windward* was delayed in England, he chartered the *Hope* and sailed north to defend his territory. Eventually, the *Hope* became frozen in near Cape Sabine, some seven hundred miles from the Pole. Sverdrup arrived soon afterward and became frozen in fifteen miles south of Peary.

One day when Peary, for reasons of his own, was in the vicinity of the Norwegian camp, he accidentally came across Sverdrup. The meeting, Peary remembered, was short and not effusive. Although he did agree to shake hands, he refused Sverdrup's invitation to a cup of coffee. He explained that his tent was not more than two hours away, and he was going home to dinner.

Originally, Peary had planned to wait until February, when the long polar night ended, before establishing an advance base two hundred miles farther north at Fort Conger. This was simply a shack built by members of General Greely's disastrous expedition of fifteen years earlier. After his encounter with Sverdrup, however, Peary's mind became warmer and warmer. Here is how a biographer of Matthew Henson described the situation at Peary's camp:

" 'Sverdrup may at this minute be planning to beat me to

Conger,' he cried with marked irritation. 'I can't let him do it! . . . I'll get to Conger before Sverdrup if it kills me!'

" 'But Lieutenant, this is the dead of winter. It's stormy and damned cold on the trail. Wouldn't it be better to wait until spring?' Matt asked.

" 'No!' Peary cried vehemently. 'I can't possibly afford to lose my one chance of a northern base to a competitor.' "[32]

And so, in December, 1898, Peary, Henson, Dedrick, and some Eskimos went out into the Arctic night, and in seventeen days, moving through cold as intense as 63° below zero, fought their way to Conger. On this insane journey Peary's feet froze, and after he reached Conger and removed his shoes, several of his toes snapped off at the joint. The next morning Dr. Dedrick removed parts of seven toes. For six weeks Peary lay helpless on his back; then Henson and Dedrick strapped him on a sled and battled their way back to the base camp where Dedrick performed a more sophisticated operation.

By summer Peary was walking without crutches, but the flesh over the bones of the toes remained raw and bleeding. Bob Bartlett, then first mate of the *Windward*, remembered that Peary "had to walk over pools and streams of icy water, which of course, rendered his footgear soft as pulp." Bartlett asked Peary how he could stand it. Peary replied, "One can get used to anything, Bartlett."

A few months later he was hiking — with a swift, shuffling stride — miles across the ice. Yet the loss of his toes was a miserable handicap and he was no longer self-sufficient as an Arctic traveler. Although he would come north again and again, he would be increasingly dependent on Matt Henson. More and more, instead of hiking alongside the sledges, Peary rode wrapped in furs. This he never acknowledged.

But in New York, although Peary could not know it, his fortunes were improving. Morris K. Jesup, a banker who specialized in railroad securities, and who would leave $6,000,000 to the American Museum of Natural History, was organizing the Peary Arctic Club. On January 29, 1899, it first met informally at Jesup's office at 44 Pine Street. Those present were James J. Hill, builder of the Great Northern Railway; Henry W. Cannon, president, Chase National Bank; Anton A. Raven, president, Atlantic Mutual Insurance Company; Eben B. Thomas, chairman, Erie Railroad; and Peary's press agent, Herbert L. Bridgman, who was also business manager for the Brooklyn *Standard-Union*.[33]

Not present, but accepting membership in the club, were John H. Flagler, founder, National Tube Company; E. C. Benedict, president, Gold Exchange Bank, and hunting companion and financial adviser to former President Grover Cleveland; Frederick C. Hyde, member of an old New York family; Henry Parish, president, New York Life Insurance Company; James M. Constable, merchant; Henry H. Benedict, company director; Eliphant W. Bliss, who manufactured the torpedoes used by the Navy; and H. Hayden Sands, novelist. Grant W. Schley, president of Moore & Schley, an important brokerage house, joined soon afterward, as did Edward Wycoff, a founder of the Remington Typewriter Company.[34]

All were expected to "subscribe the sum of $1,000 for each year of Peary's expedition," and to "stand behind him." At the time Peary had known Jesup for several years — the contact had been made by Josephine Peary — and had already notified him: "I have taken the liberty of attaching your name to one of Greenland's glaciers."

The club's first move was to send a supply ship north. What report it brought back regarding Peary's condition is unknown.

Peary, Henson, and Dedrick spent the next two years at Conger. They twice started out on what were, given the condition of Peary's feet, hopelessly impossible forays toward the Pole. Their longest journey took them to the shores of the North Polar Basin, where Peary, for the first time, viewed the terrible ice of the Arctic pack. His previous voyages had been across the less difficult ice of the glaciers. After three days on the pack ice, during which they progressed only fifteen miles toward the goal, Peary ordered the return. So ended his first official assault on the Pole. During the journey back to Conger his emotional state was terrible. When they reached Conger Henson attempted to help him off the sledge, a Henson biographer reported, but Peary shook his arm free and "raised himself feebly. . . . 'You'll not live to see the day I have to be treated like a helpless cripple,' he said disdainfully, and tottering drunkenly, he started for the house."[35]

On May 5, 1901, they returned to their southernmost base at Cape Sabine where Peary was reunited with his wife, who had come up on the *Windward*. By this time the three explorers had spent three years in the world's most inhospitable environment with no civilized companions beyond each other. For various reasons Dr. Dedrick had twice submitted his resignation. Now, when he offered it again, Peary accepted, and Dedrick went to live with the Eskimos.

Such was the situation in Peary's camp when, on August 5, 1901, Cook arrived aboard the *Erik*. He had come north as surgeon on, of all things, the Peary Arctic Club's second relief expedition. Herbert L. Bridgman, commanding the expedition, had gone to Cook and had represented the voyage as an errand of mercy. The Doctor paid his own expenses and received no fee.

Ten years had passed since Cook and Peary had seen each other. "The first impression was that of an iron man, wrecked in ambition, wrecked in physique, and wrecked in hope," Cook wrote. ". . . To the public he was on the way to reach the Pole, but to himself, no such effort had been made. Peary was worried, anxious, discouraged as I have never seen him before. In desperate overreaching he had frozen both feet. Dr. Dedrick had removed eight of his toes leaving only the two small digits and painful stubs with which he could barely walk. . . . Peary's press agent [Bridgman] also showing as representative of his financial backers requested that I examine Peary which I did."

Cook found Peary to be suffering from early symptoms of pernicious anemia:

"Peary's pulse was weak and irregular now fast one hour

later slow. The temperature was subnormal. The face had a morbid color and cast with copper hue. The skin of the body was straw color with some gray-green blotches. The abdomen was much distended but the body was thin."

After the examination Cook said to Peary: "You are through as a traveler on snow on foot, for without toes and a painful stub you can never wear snowshoes or ski."

Peary did not reply.

Because Peary had complained of his appetite, digestion, and shortness of breath, Cook continued: "You must eat raw meat and liver; this as you know is the Eskimo cure for weakness such as yours."

Peary replied: "I would rather die; besides liver is poison."[36]

Such is the substance of Cook's report on Peary at Cape Sabine in 1901. Years later he would add one more memory. Once, for Cook, Peary had been "a strong character." But at Cape Sabine "I learned . . . that Peary had developed a temper which made him more or less domineering, and which could not brook resistance. It was this spirit that moved him to such rage when he learned that I had beaten him to the Pole."[37]

On April 6, 1902, Peary, Henson and four Eskimos again started out over the pack ice for the Pole. On April 21, after traveling a hundred miles and reaching latitude 84°16′27″, they turned back, still 343 miles from the Pole.

On May 17 they arrived back at Cape Sabine to await the ship that would carry them home. Peary wrote in his diary: "I think of four years ago when . . . full of life and hope and anticipation. . . . Now a maimed old man, unsuccessful after the most arduous work. . . . Has the game been worth the candle? And yet I could not have done otherwise than to stick to it. . . . As I look at the cliffs a feeling akin to homesickness comes over me, but it is for the youthful foolish hopes and dreams with which they have been associated (youthful if one can regard forty-two years youthful as against forty-six . . .)."[38]

Then the *Windward* arrived carrying Josephine Peary, who informed her husband that an Italian — Captain Umberto

Cagni — had established a new Farthest North. Peary winced and demanded: "What was it?"

Cagni had beaten him by 137 miles.

Peary relaxed slightly, Henson remembered, then said: " 'Next time I'll smash that all to bits.' " His jaw clamped tight and he "almost snarled as he repeated, 'Next time!' "[39]

He arrived in New York on or about September 23, 1902. Otto Sverdrup and his party returned to Norway at roughly the same time, after accurately mapping some 100,000 square miles of new land.

2

"The North American continent reaches its greatest altitude in south central Alaska in the shape of a gigantic mountain."

— Edwin Swift Balch

FREDERICK A. COOK remarried on June 10, 1902, his thirty-seventh birthday. His bride was Marie Fidele Hunt, a warm-tempered brunette of French ancestry. She was the widow of a Philadelphia surgeon and the mother of four-year-old Ruth, whom Cook soon adopted. Since Marie was fairly well-to-do, Cook exchanged his horse and buggy for a car and became one of the first doctors to have his own X-ray machine. Meanwhile, his practice grew. A fellow physician observed that he had never known of a stronger or more sympathetic bond than that between Cook and his patients: "He was endowed with capacity and judgment of high order and . . . drew patients to him in great numbers and inspired a confidence . . . that neither time nor absence could destroy. . . . In return from long absences his patients not only returned but induced their friends . . . to seek his professional advice."[1] But now, for Cook, the daily routine of his profession was mildly frustrating. Once he began talking about Arctic exploration, he became oblivious of all else.

Marie Cook approved of her husband's exploring. But, she noted, Josephine Peary went to the Arctic with her husband; why couldn't Cook explore where she could be with him? It was something for him to think about. And he was also interested in the problem of reducing the weight of the equipment carried in the Arctic. In the Antarctic he and Amundsen had experimented with light-weight sledges and tents. Now he wanted to test his latest ideas in severe weather.

Six months after his marriage, Cook read a newspaper article about Mount McKinley in Alaska. It had been discovered only five years previously, and had never been climbed. Moreover, it was not simply a newly discovered mountain; it was a tremendous mountain, the highest on the North American continent, and Cook had a penchant for the gigantic.

One of his first moves, after deciding that he would attempt to attain Mount McKinley's summit, was to order a special tent from David T. Abercrombie, who ran a sporting goods store on lower Broadway in Manhattan. "When I first met Dr. Cook," Abercrombie would remember, "he came to my place and told me the kind of tent he wanted. . . . He wanted it made in the shape of an octagonal pyramid, unlike any tent I had ever made. Then he picked out some exceptionally light silk for it. I told him I thought it would not be strong enough, but he firmly declared that he knew better than I. It made me smile because I had been in the business for years and thought I knew pretty well the sort of material needed to withstand severe weather conditions. But there was no use arguing. . . . He would have it his way and he did. I made this tent and it served all right. . . . It doesn't weigh more than 3½ pounds and can be . . . put in a good-sized pocket."[2] Abercrombie regarded Cook as the most hard-headed and persistent man he had ever known, sound of judgment, most capable of carrying out his ideas. "He had his own ideas," Abercrombie said, "and I could not tell him a thing." Abercrombie did not mention that the silk tent, besides weighing only three and a half pounds, required no special poles. It was designed to be supported by the handles of ice axes.

By early May, 1903, the Cooks had closed their home at 670 Bushwick Avenue, then a fashionable address in Brooklyn, had placed Ruth with relatives, and were on their way to adventure. In Seattle they were joined by the rest of the party: Robert Dunn, who had made one trip on the Edmonton trail; Ralph Shainwald, who had explored in the Arctic and who became a lifelong friend of the Doctor; Walter Miller, a Seattle photographer; and Fred Printz, a horse-packer from Montana who had been employed on a government survey of part of the region about McKinley. Robert Dunn contributed $1,000 to the expedition, and Shainwald paid his own expenses and more, but everything else was financed by the Cooks out of their own funds, or with money advanced by *Harper's Monthly* for articles by the Doctor.

In Alaska the party disembarked at Tyonek, which was, in a straight line, 150 miles from the mountain. Marie Cook found Tyonek disappointing. It was a hamlet, simply a row of log huts plus some warehouses belonging to a trading company. The mosquitoes were bad, and those in the interior were said to be worse. She decided to limit her exploring, as her husband wrote, to "the more congenial coast in the vicinity of Valdez."

It was a wise move. Although much of the region the expedition would be invading had never been seen by white men, Alaskans who had tested it rated it some of the wildest country in the world. The mountain itself could only be reached on foot. Between it and the sea the trackless wilderness was characterized by underbrush, marshes, mosquitoes, and icy, glacier-fed streams that could only be crossed by fording or swimming. The annual rainfall was thirty to thirty-five inches, most of which came during the exploring season. The tree line ended at 2,000 feet, and for the next 2,000 feet and more the landscape was mostly rock. At 4,000 feet all vegetation stopped and the snow and glaciers began. The mountain itself was the tallest in a range that included twenty-one peaks over 10,000 feet high, all of them sub-Arctic mountains in an active earthquake zone.

On June 25, 1903, the Doctor's expedition to the summit of McKinley got under way: five men and fourteen pack horses. In the next fifty-four days he traversed the Alaska Range almost its entire length and entirely encircled the McKinley group. In rain that seemed almost perpetual, he traveled by foot, boat, and raft more than five hundred miles. On the mountain itself, along the southwest ridge, he climbed to 11,200 feet, then encountered impassable granite cliffs. With the sub-Arctic winter setting in, Cook was forced to leave the mountain. He returned to Tyonek on September 26, bringing with him a fair-sized geological and botanical collection. "Altogether," he wrote, "we had done all that determined human effort could in the short interval of an Alaskan summer."

Months after Cook had returned to Brooklyn, he became entrapped in the egoism of Robert Dunn, who wrote a series of magazine articles about the 1903 expedition, and afterward stretched the articles into a book. Dunn's book — *The Shameless Diary of an Explorer* — was inspired by Lincoln Steffens, who was familiar with explorers and was aware of the gap between their gossip and their books. "No book in that field," Steffens wrote in his autobiography, "had told all; they all left out the worst part of the wranglings and depressions which were an essential part of the truth about human nature in such tests." Dunn's task, unknown to Cook, was to go on the expedition, then reveal all. He did so, but from his own point of view entirely, and that was special.

Robert Dunn, out of Newport, Rhode Island, and Harvard College, was not independently wealthy. His voyages were financed by a rich aunt. At twenty-five, handsome and "fearless faced," he was not simply another exasperating but amusing young man. The problem was larger than that. Dunn was supremely sure of himself, as much so as the English aristocrats who were eventually satirized by Evelyn Waugh. Steffens had hired him as a reporter on the New York *Commercial-Advertiser*, but had soon recognized that Dunn was trouble.

Because Dunn had no respect for anybody, including his fellow reporters, Steffens' staff rebelled. "I did not want to discharge him," Steffens wrote. "I explained the situation and besought him to make up with the other reporters. 'You mean you want me to speak' — he looked around for an example, and seeing Cahan he continued — 'actually talk with Cahan?' 'Yes,' I said. 'All right, I will, just for you,' he said, and he walked up to Cahan and asked him, 'Say Cahan, why is it you East Side Jews never bathe?' No use. I had to fire Dunn."

Shameless itself turned out to be a ridiculously spiteful book which demonstrated that most of the expedition's wranglings and depressions were caused by its author. In it the Doctor was called the Professor. "The Professor was more than forty years old . . . of German descent, fair haired, large featured." This description Dunn enlarged years later in his autobiography, *World Alive:* "At forty, old to my twenty-five years, he still had a spark for exploring. But otherwise he was dumb, with a bovine face, straight pale hair and walrus mustache, milk blue eyes, a set smile and a slight lisp. There was a large-boned Mrs. Cook who called him 'Doctor.' "

Shameless was so bad that during the polar controversy the Peary Arctic Club, although it used everything else it could find, uttered not one slander based on Dunn's book. Its revelations included the interesting fact that during the climb to 11,200 feet, although everyone else had his own ice ax, Dunn had only a tent pole. Part of the descent was down a virtual ladder of ice. Halfway down the ladder Cook insisted on exchanging his ice ax for Dunn's tent pole.[3]

No other leader of an expedition has ever been placed in as stupid a situation as Dunn's book placed Cook. "One is thankful . . . that it is unique in the literature of travel," one McKinley veteran wrote of *Shameless.* Dunn's greatest failure was his inability to judge the expedition's total performance. In his *On Top of the World* Showell Styles wrote: "In 1903 Dr. Frederick A. Cook carried out a remarkable journey right around the mountain — a journey which has never been repeated." This statement was made in 1967.*

"The mountain climber and the arctic explorer," Cook wrote in *To the Top of the Continent,* ". . . run to kindred attainments. . . . In the general routine . . . both suffer a similar

* Of the 1903 expedition Bradford Washburn wrote: "The survival of the party may be largely attributed to the competence of Fred Printz and Robert Dunn" (*Mount McKinley and the Alaska Range in Literature*, Museum of Science, Boston, 1951). That Dunn was responsible for the brilliant record of the expedition, or any part of it, is just a small portion of the nonsense that has been presented as fact for the purpose of squeezing Cook into the identity established by the Peary Arctic Club. No climber who tried to ascend Mount McKinley with only a tent pole could be rated competent or responsible.

strain of hardships . . . followed by a similar movement of mental awakening, of spiritual aspirations, and of profound and peculiar philosophy. Thus the stream of a new hope . . . is started, and this stream seeks a groove down the path of life for ever after. It follows that he who ventures into the polar arena or the cloud battlefield of high mountains, will long to return again and again to the scene of his sufferings and inspiration."

In 1906 Cook returned to Alaska to attempt again to reach the summit of Mount McKinley. This time, accompanied by only one man, he made it.

The 1906 expedition included two other veterans of the 1903 party: Fred Printz, horse-packer, and Walter Miller, photographer. It also included Belmore Browne, artist and climber; Russell W. Porter, an artist-topographer who had made two trips to the Arctic; S. P. Beecher, cook; Herschel Clifford Parker, inventor and member of the faculty at Columbia University; and Edward N. Barrill, horse-packer, a buddy of Printz's from Montana. Marie Cook remained in Brooklyn with Ruth and the baby, Helene, who had been born in 1905.

After disembarking at Tyonek on May 28, the Doctor sent Barrill and Printz overland with the pack horses, then took the rest of the party up the Susitna River in the *Bolshoy*. This was a launch, constructed earlier to his specifications, that he had picked up in Seattle. Forty feet long and seven feet wide, it was specially designed for climbing swift rivers. It had a twenty-inch draft and a 25 h.p. motor, which gave it a speed of twelve miles per hour. Its screw revolved in a tunnel under the hill, which eliminated the problems caused by sand bars. He called it the *Bolshoy* because the word meant "big," and was the Russian-Indian name for Mount McKinley.

Going up the rivers the *Bolshoy* carried an extra passenger, Captain W. N. Armstrong, an Alaskan mining man. The Seward (Alaska) *Gateway* reported: "Away beyond the point where the river has been regarded as impassable for anything but an Indian canoe went the powerful launch of the Cook party. . . . Armstrong says it wiggled amazingly up rapids which foamed and dashed almost over it, through plunging torrents which would seem difficult for a trout to breast. 'Several times when we approached fierce rapids,' says Armstrong, 'I said to Dr. Cook, "You'll never go up there." "We'll try it anyway," he would say, and up we went.' "[4]

So the *Bolshoy* was everything Cook had hoped it would be; but for many days, after he had rendezvoused with the pack train, nothing else worked out satisfactorily. He had hoped to find, at the head of the Yenta River, a pass over the Alaska Range. He found three, none of which could be crossed. Russell Porter called the investigation of these passes, made on foot, "as strenuous work as I have ever been through."[5] Cook had also hoped to find a way up the mountain's southwest ridge, but he was stopped by impassable cliffs. The rain, meanwhile, was worse than in 1903. "Continuous cold drizzling rains," he wrote, "made the work . . . nearly impossible." But nothing really dismayed him. "He was always in good spirits," Porter wrote, "and ready for more than his share of the drudgery; resourceful and considerate of others." And in 1909 Waitman Wade, a traveler from Portland, Oregon, would remember: "I talked to him personally just before he made the attempt to ascend the west side of the mountain. He was very anxious to reach the summit. The fact that he exercised so much tact and diplomacy in cheering his men and guides on to that end made his eagerness to accomplish the goal very apparent."[6]

Meanwhile, although the party was still eighteen miles south of the mountain, they were already into July. Herschel Parker, who had decided that the effort of ascending McKinley during the rainy season was "a marine task," had to be back at Columbia by September; and Cook had to return to Tyonek to meet Henry Disston, the son of a saw manufacturer. Disston had pledged $5,000 to the expedition, in return for which Cook had agreed to organize a big-game hunt.* Cook and his party arrived in Tyonek on August 2. There he found a letter

* An unknown portion of this sum had been received by Cook. The costs of the 1903 and 1906 expeditions totaled $28,000. On the 1906 expedition Parker contributed $2,000, and it is probable that Browne and Porter paid their own way. Once again, *Harper's Monthly* gave Cook an advance on future articles.

from Disston canceling the hunt. He sent Porter out to map, and others to collect zoological specimens, then took the *Bolshoy* in for repairs at the machine shop of the Kaselif Salmon Cannery. Three years later Dr. A. C. Miller, surgeon at the cannery, still remembered his first sight of Cook.

"I could see at once," Miller declared in the New York *Herald* for October 5, 1909, "that here was a man whose nerves were in perfect control, the poise and dignity of the man and a certain air which showed a great reserve force impressed me. His hands were large and rough. . . . He did not talk much about himself." Dr. Miller added: "We in the Alaskan country know him to be a man of courage and spirit and of generosity too, for he gave all his slender store of medicine to treat the Indians." Dr. Miller recalled that prospectors had told him that Cook was "the toughest man who was ever in shoe leather in Alaska." He said Cook kept ahead of his guides, swam the icy mountain currents, slept in the snow, and showed an endurance that amazed men accustomed to the hardest kind of life.

After the *Bolshoy* had been repaired, Cook and Barrill loaded it with provisions, then ran it up the rivers and established a base camp near the foot of Ruth Glacier. With the climbing season almost over, Cook planned to cache supplies for the future, then explore the lower slopes of McKinley's northeast ridge. "We had just about determined," he wrote, "that the limit of our effort would be the north arete at 12,000 feet." From there he hoped to outline the glacier drainage and a future route up McKinley.

Cook and Barrill each carried about forty-five pounds of rations and equipment,* including sleeping bags made by

* The equipment carried by later expeditions was progressively heavier. In 1912 an eight-man expedition led by Belmore Browne and Herschel Parker carried some 600 pounds. In 1913 the four-man Stuck-Karstens party carried about 300 pounds. Although during the ascent someone reduced the weight by dropping a match into the baggage, this party still moved a minimum of 250 pounds each time they advanced camp. Shuttling back and forth, they climbed at least 60,000 feet. In 1932 the four man Lindley-Liek Expedition carried 1,200 pounds, plus 800 pounds of cosmic-ray equipment.

Marie Cook. These weighed five pounds each and had three layers: cravenette, camel's-hair blanketing, and duck skins covered with silk. Every layer was actually a robe, and could be used as a poncho.

They started out on September 8. By the end of the third day they were thirty-five miles up the glacier. A miner named Dokkin accompanied them to 6,000 feet, then turned back to the base cabin. On the third evening Cook and Barrill camped at 8,000 feet, from where the actual climb began. The next morning Cook got a side view of McKinley and "found that one height which . . . had looked impossible did not end on top of a knife-blade edge, as supposed, but had 25 to 50 feet of flat space on top."[7] They reached this spot, at about 12,000 feet, on the fourth evening and built an igloo. The next morning they saw ahead a smooth line of snow with a drop of about 4,000 feet on each side, and at 13,000 feet, a huge rock — 1,000 feet high — barring the line. Beyond was a steep arête leading into a glacier and a valley. They found a way around the great rock, then scratched for footing among ice blocks. Darkness overtook them as they were cutting steps in a sixty-degree incline. They dug a trench in the slope and spent the night. "We wrapped ourselves in a bundle with all our belongings," Cook wrote in *To the Top of the Continent*, ". . . then lashed the bundle to the axes, which were securely driven into the snow, and in this way held on for the night. The fine snow drifted down our necks and into the cracks. . . . But we did not dare to move for fear the snow would . . . crowd us out."

That night, as on the preceding night, they agreed to descend in the morning. When dawn came, however, they continued to climb and soon saw that the slopes above were easy and connected. At 16,300 feet Cook built another igloo. To reach the summit required two more days. The major problem was the rarity of the air. At 18,400 feet they camped in Abercrombie's silk tent. In the morning they could hardly move. They "jumped, kicked each other, and for half an hour tried to bring back the lost circulation."[8] At 10:00 A.M. on September 16 they reached the top of the North American continent, and with blood running from their ears and noses, attempted to absorb the thrilling view.

"Often I have been asked to describe my emotions as I stood there on the summit," the Doctor said later. ". . . When a man has fought the forces of nature long enough and hard enough to attain such exalted spots, his physical and nervous energies are so thoroughly exhausted that he is little more than a thinking automaton."[9]

They descended in four days. Cook gave Dokkin all of the provisions, enough for a year, then set out with Barrill in the *Bolshoy*. Near Susitna Station they met Fred Printz, to whom Barrill said: "I want to introduce you to the man who went to the top of Mount McKinley — Dr. Cook. Congratulate the Doctor."[10] At Susitna Station itself Russell Porter noticed a commotion and went down to the river. "There was the *Bolshoy*," he wrote, "with Dr. Cook at the stern and Barrill the packer just stepping ashore. 'Go back and congratulate the Doctor,' he said as I reached the boat. 'How so?' 'He got to the top.' "[11]

Weeks later Fred Printz informed the editor of his hometown newspaper that while Cook was still at the Station "five men were brought in who had been rescued by two men in a boat. They had stood on a big rock six days and six nights, only twelve inches of the rock being out of the water. Their boat had capsized on the rock . . . they were in terrible condition from the exposure and want. Their legs were badly swollen and beginning to rot and the flesh dropping off. Dr. Cook administered surgical aid."[12] And J. A. MacDonald, a trader at Susitna, wrote of this incident: "Although tired and in bad physical condition himself . . . he spent hours working over these men and did not give himself a thought until they were properly cared for."[13]

After returning to Tyonek, Cook sent everyone but Porter and Barrill out to Seattle. Porter remained to help him with the book he had already begun to write. Barrill's presence was required because of a lawsuit brought against Cook by a William Hughes, who charged that the expedition's horses had damaged his property. The trial occurred in Seward and the jury found for Hughes. On October 25, 1906, Cook paid the judgment in full: $600.00 plus costs of $15.80.[14]

Cook arrived in Seattle aboard the steamer *Saratoga*, checked into the Butler Hotel, and was in his room talking to a reporter when, to his astonishment, his daughter Ruth rushed in. Marie Cook had crossed the continent to greet him. On November 27, 1906, they returned to Brooklyn where he continued to work on the book, *To the Top of the Continent.* Before long, however, he was preoccupied with larger matters, and when the manuscript was delivered to the publishers by Marie, he was on the high seas headed for the North Pole.

Meanwhile, Edward Barrill and Fred Printz had returned to Montana and had informed the editor of their local paper that Cook and Barrill had reached the top of Mount McKinley.[15]

But from the moment when Cook reappeared in civilization and reported that he and Barrill had attained the summit, some Alaskans felt certain that he was a liar. It would be rude to charge them with jealousy, envy, or emotionalism. Their reasons were most rational. Mount McKinley was a tremendous and awesome mountain. Therefore, they imagined, its summit could only be attained by a man who had spent years on other mountains and was skilled in the techniques of climbing. But there was another reason for their believing what they believed, and in its way it too was rational.

"Why should otherwise respectable people be doubted," the geographer Edwin Swift Balch asked, "when they assert that they have been up some mountain?" He decided that most of the disbelief originated among those who lived in the neighborhood of the peaks. "It is a universal characteristic found in Switzerland, in Tyrol, in the Caucasus, at Mount Ararat, in the Himalayas, in the Andes, and now in Alaska — of the human beings inhabiting the plains and valleys near great peaks whose ascent they themselves have not made, to assert that others have not made the ascent."[16]

Among the doubting Alaskans was Hudson Stuck, Episcopal Archdeacon of the Yukon, and he had the simplest reason of all. "I would rather climb that mountain than discover the richest gold mine in Alaska," he wrote a friend. Moreover, the Archdeacon was very aware of the mountain's grandeur, and he demanded that its conqueror be an appropriate person. Somewhere in Alaska the Archdeacon had met the Doctor, and had identified him as "a prig" and "an ass." "It is going to take a better man than he," Stuck declared, "to reach the top of that mountain." Nor was the Archdeacon disappointed. When the "better man" officially appeared, his name turned out to be Stuck.

The Stuck-Karstens Expedition reached the summit of McKinley on June 7, 1913. Soon afterward, for reasons that will be explained presently, the exploring establishment accepted the sporting Episcopalian as the mountain's official conqueror. In his book about the climb, Stuck mentioned that in July 1912 Mount McKinley had been shaken by a tremendous earthquake that destroyed most of the northeast ridge, the route taken by Cook and himself. Having acknowledged the fact of the quake, Stuck wrote of Cook, ". . . it was quite impossible to follow his course from the description given in his book," and presented this as one portion of his proof that Cook was a liar.*

* This earthquake, itself the result of a tremendous volcanic explosion on Mount Katmai that shook the entire Alaska Range, had been recorded on a Washington, D.C., seismograph as "the most severe shock since the San Francisco quake of 1906" (Numa F. Vidal, "Who Climbed Mount McKinley?" *Saturday Evening Post*, February 18, 1950). Of the effects of this quake, as shown on the northeast ridge, Harry Karstens wrote while on the mountain in 1913: "Last year's shake has certainly ruined this ridge for good climbing. . . . There is no doubt in my mind that the shake up . . . has broken the snow slopes and left the ridge in the condition it is." (Entry of May 9, 1913, *The First Ascent of Mt. McKinley, Alaska 1913:* a verbatim copy of the Diary of Henry P. Karstens with preface and footnotes by Bradford Washburn, 1968. Privately printed.) And Grant Pearson, a member of the third party to reach the summit, wrote of the northeast ridge: "The earthquake had shaken that ridge to pieces from top to bottom. The sides and top were a chaos of huge rocks, snow and ice blocks that made every step a peril" (*My Life of High Adventure*, Englewood Cliffs, N.J., 1962, p. 136).

Mount McKinley is a double-peaked mountain whose peaks are about two miles apart. The south peak, which both Cook and the Stuck-Karstens party attained, is its true summit, three hundred feet higher than the north peak. But even if Cook's achievement is disregarded, Stuck's official "first" seems somewhat technical. When the Archdeacon and his party reached the summit of the south peak they looked across to the north peak and saw a bare wooden flagpole that had been implanted there in 1910. In that year two Alaskan miners, Billy Taylor and Pete Anderson, had not only climbed the north peak, but had dragged along with them, all the way, a fourteen-foot flagpole. At the top of the north peak, as Stuck wrote, Taylor and Anderson "firmly planted the flagstaff, which is still there."

The Taylor-Anderson expedition, known as the Sourdough Expedition, went up and down the mountain, from the 11,000-foot level, at an amazing pace. After a leisurely ascent to 11,000 feet, they climbed 9,000 feet up and 9,000 feet down, in, apparently, eighteen hours. "We made it all in one day, by God!" Billy Taylor recollected years later. "Just breaking day, a little after three, when we started, and I know it was dark — getting dusk — when we got back. I know it was an even eighteen hours."[17]

Although the climbing of Mount McKinley remains a splendid achievement, the mountain itself is now known to be by no means the monster that Stuck and others had anticipated. Stuck acknowledged this after his descent. With the exception of the northeast ridge, he reported, the mountain presented no "special mountaineering difficulties of a technical kind."[18]

Indeed, every known fact supports this. Between 1906 and 1941 ten men climbed to the summit. Of these, nine were, as one expedition leader described his own party, "without great experience in the techniques of climbing."[19] The tenth was Stuck, who had done some climbing in the Rockies. On McKinley he did well, but he was almost fifty years old and his companions outstripped him. Halfway up the mountain the direction of the ascent was taken over by Harry Karstens, aged thirty-two. Karstens was, certainly, a rugged Alaskan, but he was also a man who had never climbed a mountain in his life.*

By the end of the 1970 climbing season on McKinley, approximately 422 climbers had reached the summit. Of these, fourteen were women, six being members of an all-female expedition. But on McKinley, as elsewhere, those who climb up must also climb down. Over the years six men have been killed on the mountain, all of them during the descent.

Because the background of each of the 422 climbers is not known, it is not possible to identify the one climber most qualified to make the ascent; but Cook would certainly be a contender. The traveler who attempts great peaks must be, authorities say, "a good man on snow and ice, and should be at least moderately proficient on rocks."[20] Cook had spent more than eleven months in the Arctic; he had been icebound for thirteen months in the Antarctic. In both regions he had been very active and had become, by necessity, "a good man on snow and ice." In Europe in 1900 he visited the Alps and met Edward Whymper, the most famous mountaineer of his time, with whom he discussed mountain climbing. Whymper advised him: "Use your Arctic techniques."[21] And that Cook was skilled in such techniques is indicated by Robert Dunn. After observing Cook cut steps in an ice slope at approximately 10,000 feet on Mount McKinley, Dunn exclaimed: "God! I admire the way you take this slope." Later, in *Shameless*, Dunn recorded this statement, then added: "And by heaven . . . I still do."

But in spite of his brilliant record as an explorer in regions of ice and snow, the Doctor's modern critics continue to belittle him. In 1958 Bradford Washburn, director of the Boston Museum of Science, and the recognized authority on Mount McKinley, wrote that Cook's qualifications for climbing Mc-

* From the beginning the Stuck-Karstens Expedition had been under joint leadership. After the descent, however, the Archdeacon began to lecture and write about the climb. In the first newspaper articles, and in the original draft of his story for *Scribner's* magazine, the man who had called Cook "a prig" and "an ass" played up his own role, and played down Karstens's, to the point where Karstens's friends had to complain.

Kinley were "less than marginal for an exploit of this magnitude."*

To the Top of the Continent is not as detailed a report as a student of the McKinley problem would like it to be. The accounts of the later expeditions, however, are also not particularly satisfactory. "Examined comparatively with the other narratives," the geographer Balch wrote, "Cook's appears to be the best; both in its observations and its descriptions, it is the most satisfactory."[22]

Today the historical verdict, a creation of the Peary Arctic Club, is that the Doctor did not climb the mountain at all; that at the highest point he reached on McKinley, he was still at least fourteen miles in an air line from its summit.

That this verdict is false, and that Cook did attain the summit of McKinley, will be demonstrated here.

As Balch wrote: "It is the geographic evidence presented by later travelers which proves or disproves the geographic evidence presented by the first explorer in any region. The man who breaks into the unknown may say what he chooses and present such . . . observations as he sees fit. But if the next traveler corroborates the discoverer, instantly the first man's statements are immeasureably strengthened."[23]

In a satisfactory number of instances, as will be shown, the statements of those who followed Cook up the mountain do substantiate and thus strengthen his own observations, made four years before any other formal expedition got anywhere near the top of the mountain, and seven years before the summit was again attained.

Those who have, in recent years, denied Cook's achievement, have done so for reasons that they believe adequate. Nevertheless, they have recognized him as a disturbing man backed by disturbing facts. After he had descended in 1906 he

* "Doctor Cook and Mount McKinley," *American Alpine Journal*, 1958, p. 27. At the time that Washburn published this statement, only sixty-one climbers had reached the summit of the south peak. This includes the fifty-nine listed by the National Park Service, plus Cook and Barrill.

reported that the elevation at the summit was 20,390 feet.* In 1942 the elevation was officially determined, by Bradford Washburn, to be 20,320 feet. Official history's defenders, principally Washburn, have had to come up with some explanation of Cook's figure, because their man, Stuck, declared the elevation to be 20,700 feet. This meant that the man whom they maintained had not climbed the mountain was only 70 feet off, while their man, "history's" man, was 380 feet off. Washburn disposed of this problem by pointing out, not implausibly, that the earliest estimates of the height of the mountain were also remarkably close and provided precedents that Cook could have used as guides: "In 1898 Muldrow and Elridge had computed it to be 20,464 feet, and . . . Brooks reported a new height of 20,300 . . . made during the summer of 1902."

In other words, the Doctor's accomplishment was simply a lucky, guided guess.

But other problems, equally disturbing, remained to be explained. How could Cook — a man who, it would be alleged, never got closer than fourteen miles to the summit — report so accurately on the physical features of the high slopes of the mountain? He said that beyond 16,300 feet there was a great spread of surface, a broad vast snowfield. He said that a number of smaller ridges ran up to the mountain's two peaks. And he not only mentioned these features, he announced them first and described them correctly. And he also said that, except for the problem of the rarefied air, climbing conditions were comparatively easy, and again he was correct, seven years in advance of the next climber's report.

Of all of Cook's belittlers, only Washburn has made a valuable contribution to the solution of the McKinley problem. And

* Cook and Barrill carried two aneroid barometers specially marked for high climbing. The 20,390-foot figure was obtained from these instruments. Dokkin, at the base camp, also read a barometer while Cook and Barrill were climbing. During the expedition the mountain was also measured by triangulation. The New York *Herald* for October 15, 1909, quoted Cook as saying: 'When measured by triangulation the height indicated was 20,350 feet."

his contribution, which will be considered in time, simply reinforced the belief that official history was correct. Yet for Washburn, it would seem, there is something disturbing about Cook's accurate reports on the physical features of the upper slopes. In attacking the problem, Washburn has suggested that such features could be seen from two locations "30–35 miles northeast of McKinley,"[24] and that Cook did state that he studied the mountain from these locations. "It is my conviction," Washburn continued, "that the vast majority of Dr. Cook's narrative above 12,000 feet was conjured up from the memory of these two views."

Once again, the implication is that Cook only guessed, this time from a distance of 30–35 miles."

And so, as the present writer moves to demonstrate the falseness of the historical verdict, he must limit his presentation to observations for which no precedents existed that Cook could have used as guides. Nor can he include anything that Cook could possibly have observed from "30–35 miles" away. Indeed, he would be wise to withhold anything that Cook could have viewed with the naked or binoculared eye, unless it be virtually a phenomenon.

In 1906 very little was known about the effects of high altitudes on human beings. And what was known fell into no recognizable pattern. "The correspondence between the extent to which the atmospheric pressure is reduced," an Englishman wrote, "and the incidence of mountain sickness is but an irregular one."[25] Although Cook was a medical man, it seems that if he was "guessing," there was not much for him to use as a guideline in writing about the effects of the altitude on McKinley.

There was not much, but there was something. Dr. Filippo de Filippi's account of the Duke of Abruzzi's expedition to Mount St. Elias, the second highest mountain in Alaska, was published in England in 1900. That Cook was familiar with it seems probable, but the important fact is that Cook's experience on McKinley, as recorded in his book, was for the most

Frederick A. Cook as a young doctor, probably taken about 1892.

Robert E. Peary in his thirties.

The *Belgica* ice-locked in 1898. Cook used a ninety-minute exposure in moonlight to take this photo.

Crew of the *Belgica* chopping a channel through the ice.

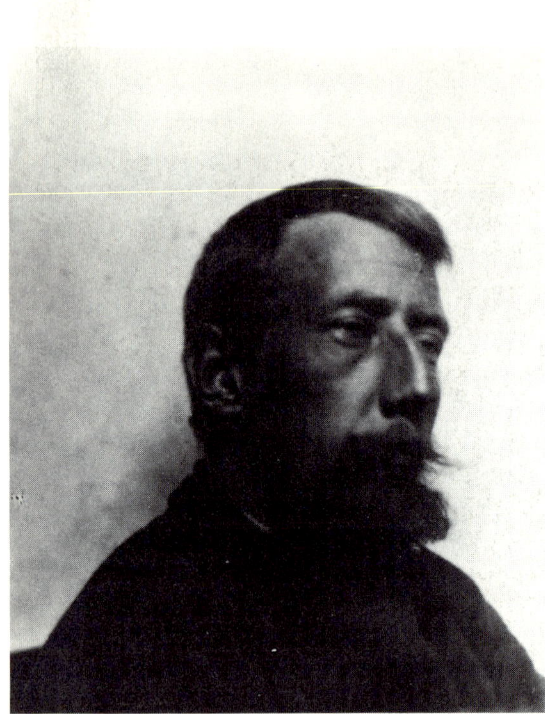

Roald Amundsen at age twenty-five. Cook took this photograph during the *Belgica* Expedition. Later he wrote the following caption:
"Roald Amundsen
First at the South Pole
First through the North West Passage
Master Seaman of a frozen world
Lost in an airplane
Seeking to rescue an enemy."

Cook at the close of the Antarctic winter.

Cook in Alaska.

Barrill in Alaska wearing camel's-hair section of sleeping bag as poncho.

Photogra

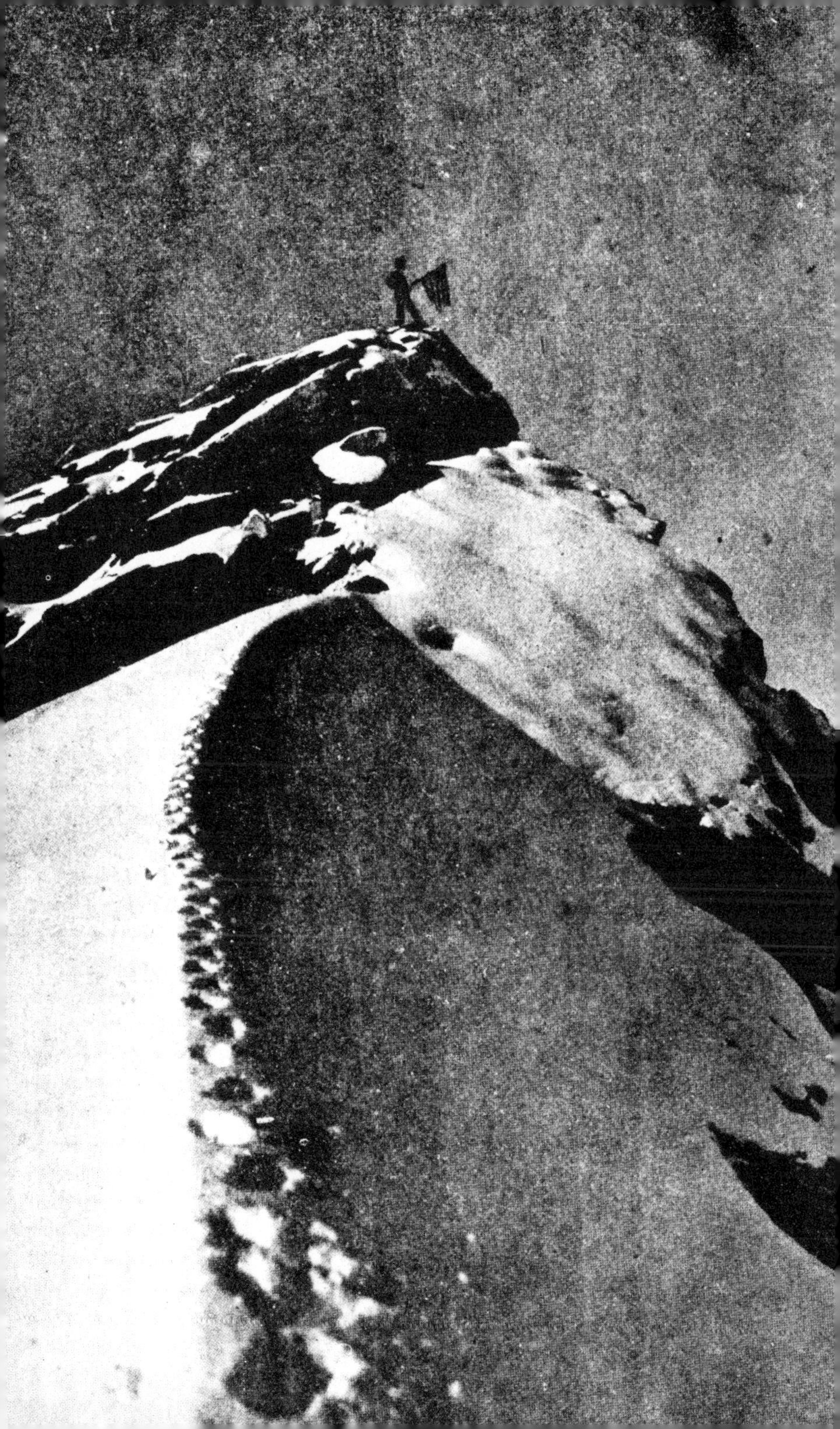

All attempts to obtain Bradford Washburn's permission for use of his photographs in this book (referred to in the text as Photograph 2 and Photograph 3) have been unsuccessful.

Photograph 2 can be found in the *American Alpine Journal*, 1958, opposite page 19. There it is identified as Plate 19 and is captioned, "True summit of Mount McKinley taken by Washburn from North Drift, July 19, 1942. Einar Nilsson and Robert H. Bates."

Photograph 3 can be found in the *American Alpine Journal*, 1943. It is opposite page 7 and is captioned, "The last hundred yards. Snow above 20,000 feet was packed so hard that crampons made little impression."

John R. Bradley aboard the *Bradley*.

Robert E. Peary, Arctic explorer.

(*Above*) Matthew Henson aboard the *Roosevelt.* (*Below*) The President says good-bye to the Commander aboard the *Roosevelt* just before it sails north.

"Svartevoeg—campi
500 miles from Pole.

"The igloo built, we
prepare for our daily
camp."

"Mending near the
North Pole."

Copy of note in Tube
Apr. 21, 1908 at the North Pole
Accompanied by the Eskimo boys
Ahwelah and Etukishook I reached at
noon to-day 90 N, a spot on the polar
sea 520 miles N. of Svartevoeg.
We were 35 days en route. Hope to
return to-morrow on a line slightly
west of the arrival route.
New land was discovered along
the 102 m. between 84 & 85. The
ice proved fairly good with few
open leads, hard snow and little
pressure trouble.
We are in good health and have
food for 40 days. This with the meat
of the dogs to be sacrificed will
keep us alive for 50 or 60 days.
This note is deposited with
a small Am. flag in a metallic
tube on the drifting ice.
Its return will be appreciated
to the International Bureau of
Polar Research at the
Royal observatory Uccle Belgium
Frederick A. Cook

Copy of the note Cook deposited in a brass tube at the North Pole.

“Toward Cape Sparbo in a canvas boat.”

“Homeward bound.”

Cook steps ashore in Copenhagen. The bearded man is W. T. Stead, Hearst's representative and dean of the assembled correspondents.

Cook passing through sea of faces in Copenhagen.

part entirely different from Filippi's, as reported in *Mt. St. Elias*. Dr. Filippi had much to say about the effects of mountain sickness on his party. Dr. Cook did not comment on mountain sickness, and he found the weather, above 18,000 feet, much more severe than Filippi found it. Dr. Filippi reported that above 16,000 feet his physical situation improved, and that "the temperature was very favorable, the cold not excessive (17.6° to 10° Fahr)."[26] Dr. Cook reported the exact opposite.

In writing of his physical sensations at his camp at 18,400 feet, Cook said in 1906: "The circulation was so depressed that it was impossible to dispel the sense of chilliness. Increased clothing or bed cover did not seem to make much difference. . . . Though the temperature was only 16° below, in its total effects it was colder than 60 below at sea level."[27]

Six years later Belmore Browne, writing of the Peary Arctic Club's second expedition to the mountain, would note virtually the same thing, and at a lower altitude: "Parker . . . wore at night a complete suit of double llama wool besides his mountain clothing, and yet he could not sleep for the cold, although Anthony Fiala, leader of the Ziegler Polar Expedition, slept comfortably in a duplicate of . . . Parker's bag, clad only in underclothing when the temperature was 70° below zero! This fact illustrates the comparative effect of cold between sea level and 15,000 feet close to the Arctic circle."[28]

Of the last night of the climb, Cook wrote: "Unable to sleep, we were only permitted to rest in a semi-reclining position with shoulders raised, in which attitude the heart was eased and breath came and went with less effect."[29]

And in 1913 Harry Karstens wrote in his diary concerning the last night of that ascent: "Everyone out of condition last night and no one slept. We tried from 7 to 10 but no go. So we sat around primus stove with quilts on our backs waiting for 4 o'clock."[30]

Cook's account indicated that he suffered extremely from the rarefied air on the upper slopes of McKinley, and that this was particularly true of the last few hundred feet before the summit. He wrote in 1906: "The last few hundred feet of the ascent so reduced our physical powers that we dropped onto the snow, completely exhausted, gasping for breath. We puffed and puffed, and after a while the sickening thump under the left rib became less noticeable. Breath came and went easier, and then the call to the top was uppermost."[31]

Archdeacon Stuck's experience, as he climbed the last few hundred feet, was similar. He wrote in 1914: "The familiar fits of panting took a more acute form; at such times everything would turn black before his [Stuck's] eyes and he would choke and gasp and seem unable to get breath at all. Yet a few minutes' rest restored him completely, to struggle on another twenty . . . paces and sink gasping upon the snow again. . . . It was curious to see every man's mouth open for breathing."[32]

None of the accounts of the summit are as detailed as one would like, and for a good reason. Filippi reported that at the summit of Mount St. Elias the climbers were "nearly all dull and apathetic."[33] The story of the climb could only be written by drawing on the combined memories of the whole party.

At the summit of Mount McKinley, Cook wrote later, "Our hands clasp, but not a word was uttered. We felt like shouting, but had not the breath to spare."[34] And Grant Pearson, a member of the Lindley-Liek Expedition of 1932, wrote of his party at the summit: "It was much too cold to yell."[35]

Of the view from the summit, Cook noted that he could see "narrow silvery bands marking the course of the Yukon and the Tanana."[36] Grant Pearson agreed: "To the north we caught the gleam of the Yukon winding through its broad, flat tundra."[37]

Stuck was at the summit on a hazy day. Consequently, he did not see the Yukon. He did agree with Cook, however, about the dark tone of the sky overhead. Of this Balch wrote: "A remarkable proof of the success of Cook and the success of Stuck are their observations about the sky at the top. Cook, at ten o'clock in the morning, writes that 'the sky was as black as that of midnight' and later of 'a curious low dark sky' and 'the neutral gray blue of space.' Stuck writes, 'We first noticed the darkening tint of the sky in the Grand Basin, and it deepened as we rose. It was a deep, rich, lustrous transparent blue, but intensely blue.' Here is one of those details which a man does not invent."[38] Cook's sun goggles were smoke-colored, Balch added; and Stuck's were amber.

Cook, in 1907, wrote that he left a record of the ascent in a nook slightly below the summit: "A record of our conquest was, with a small flag, pressed into a metallic tube and left in a protected nook a short distance below the summit."[39] Grant Pearson reported virtually the same thing: "I watched them cache the tube in some bare rocks 500 feet below the summit."[40]*

Speaking of the ascent after he had returned to New York, Cook said he and Barrill had intended to remain at the summit for two hours but "stayed only twenty minutes."[41] Grant Pearson reported: "In spite of the biting cold we stayed up there on top of the world for thirty minutes."[42]

Those early climbers who followed Cook up the mountain agreed with him about 16,000 feet, supported him above 18,000 feet, agreed with him at 20,000 feet, and agreed with him at the summit, the altitude of which he reported with superior accuracy. The commonly accepted historical verdict is that Cook's account of his ascent is fiction. No other explanation of the parallels between the accounts of Cook and those who followed him has ever been offered, and that explanation is utterly impossible.

Did or did not Dr. Frederick A. Cook attain the summit of Mount McKinley?

He did.

But on October 4, 1909, Edward N. Barrill signed an affidavit in which he testified that he and the Doctor had not climbed the mountain, and that at the nearest point to the summit that they reached, they were still fourteen miles from the top of the mountain.

* So far as this writer has been able to determine, none of the records left at the summit by the pioneer parties has ever been recovered.

That the polar controversy had begun shortly before was not a coincidence; nor was it a coincidence that Barrill's testimony was delivered in the office of a representative of the Peary Arctic Club. The fact was, Cook was forty-one years old in 1906 and he did have an Achilles heel — photography. The photograph that he had presented to the world as a picture of the summit of Mount McKinley was a photograph of a peak only 8,000 feet high, and Barrill knew it.

"Dr. Cook stated at this time and place," Barrill swore, "that the same condition existed there as did exist at the top of . . . McKinley. . . . Dr. Cook and I went to the top of this point together, and he said, we will go back down and get a picture of this. . . . The Doctor took the American flag out of one of the bags and told me to hold it there on the end of the ice ax, which I did. The Doctor . . . then took the picture."[43]

For the pioneer climbers, sadly equipped by present standards, the weather at the summit of McKinley was frightful. It ruined Archdeacon Stuck's photography, causing him to make as many as three exposures on the same film. "Our hands were by this time so numb," Stuck wrote, "as to make it almost impossible to operate the camera. . . . Our top of the mountain photography was a great disappointment."[44] The Lindley-Liek Expedition reached the summit in 1932. Of the situation there Lindley wrote: "The cold was very intense and it was impossible to keep the mittens off for more than a few seconds. The result was that with our three cameras . . . we bungled everything and have nothing to show."[45]

In fact the summit of McKinley was not successfully photographed until 1942. The photographer was Bradford Washburn. In 1947, leading a party that included his wife, Washburn again reached the summit of McKinley. In 1951 he made his third ascent, this time by an exceptionally difficult route. In 1956 he returned to McKinley to photograph the details of the peak — known by McKinley buffs as the "fake peak" — that Barrill swore Cook photographed. Its location had been known since 1909, Barrill having supplied a map with his affidavit. For Washburn, Cook's photograph was "probably the most controversial picture in the entire history of exploration. Dr. Cook supported it throughout his life as representing the true top of Mount McKinley, and all of his proponents have insisted likewise."[46] Years earlier, the Peary Arctic Club had zestfully promoted the concept "False in One, False in All," and Washburn, with his camera, was out to reaffirm, if not by proof then by inference, the accuracy of the historical verdict: that Cook was a fraud.*

At the scene Washburn found that the "fake peak" was rapidly disintegrating. Nevertheless, enough of its profile — roughly twenty percent — remained solid. Washburn secured a series of photographs that virtually duplicated portions of the profile presented in Cook's photograph. Today there seems to be no reason to deny that Washburn's photographs demonstrate what he contends they do: that Cook did photograph the "fake peak" and present it as a picture of McKinley.

Bradford Washburn's aggressive photographs contain the most serious evidence ever produced against Cook, for they do not come in the form of one of the Peary Arctic Club's affidavits which, as shall be shown, were purchased. Anyone who admires Cook and regards him as a far better man than his belittlers can imagine, and who is confident that the more pressure that is put on Cook the better he will appear, must meet Washburn's challenge; must answer the question, Why did Cook present a photograph of the "fake peak" and allow the public to believe it was looking at a picture of the top of the North American continent?

What follows is speculation.

It seems obvious that Cook had large ambitions. He was far more ambitious than Stuck, for example, who only wanted to climb McKinley. For Cook the ultimate prize was the North Pole. "There is nothing I would rather do," he said of the Pole in 1907. "It is the ambition of my life."[47]

* Washburn's report was published in the *American Alpine Journal* in 1958. In the next issue of that annual Francis Farquhar wrote: "The claim of Dr. Frederick A. Cook that he reached the summit of McKinley in 1906 has been exhaustively examined and completely proved to have no foundation in fact whatsoever."

Of polar explorers Vilhjalmur Stefansson has written: "Few of them have been scientists, and polar exploration has never been a science. It has rather been something between an art and a sport."[48] This statement surely applies to Cook and Peary. Despite their medical and engineering backgrounds, they were not scientists but sportsmen, hunters of the North Pole. After Cook had attained the Pole and had returned to civilization he said: "I did not do this thing for anything but sport, and because I take a real interest in the problem."[49] Their adventures are most properly located within the realm of sport, and within the larger realm of show business.

A fundamental fact of exploration is that it costs money, usually a great deal of money. To raise the sum needed to get to his goal has always been the explorer's fundamental problem. Because of the conditions in the society in which they lived, Cook and Peary had no alternative but to dramatize themselves before the public. In civilization they were actors — entertainers, lecturers, educators — in the great world of show business.

In those days exploration, like other fields of human endeavor, contained its full share of humbug. The public's imagination was regularly tickled by gentlemen who desired to attain the Pole via balloon or dirigible. Explorers as reputable as Roald Amundsen were agreeable to announcing that they had signed a contract with Carl Hagenback, a circus owner, for twenty polar bears, all of them to be three years old, which the explorer would endeavor to make draw his sledges when he went to the South Pole.

Although the Peary Arctic Club contributed most of the money required for its man's later expeditions, it did not pay for everything. A sizable portion Peary raised himself through lectures. Most of these were arranged by the National Geographic Society. There was a time, however, when Peary, less famous, was represented by a Major Pond. Cook was also a member of Pond's team of lecturers.

It is probable that on McKinley Cook was thinking ahead to the Pole, knew that an expedition to it would be expensive, and assumed he would have to finance it himself by lecturing. If so, he must have considered that he would have to show his future audiences something specific and dramatic. It seems probable that his luck with photographs at the summit was no better than Stuck's or Lindley's, and that during the descent he stopped to take extra photographs as insurance against all possibilities. When his summit photographs proved valueless he, a sportsman rather than a scientist, probably decided to use his insurance picture. Although it was a foolish action, it can not be regarded as the sort of deed that is described as "a grave fraud on the American people."

Perhaps he reasoned that a picture of a mountain is only a picture. Just as a picture of a lovely woman is only a picture, by no means the real thing, so he may have believed that extreme accuracy was unnecessary.

In those days some editors would have agreed with him. They would have included the editor of the New York *Globe*, which was owned by General Thomas Hubbard, the president of the Peary Arctic Club. On September 3, 1909, one day after Cook had announced his attainment of the Pole, the *Globe* published a photograph of a man in Arctic clothing standing beside a cairn of rocks and holding an American flag. "Dr. Cook and the flag he planted at the Pole," the *Globe* announced. "That is a duplicate of the picture he took after he had actually planted the flag at the North Pole . . . and the picture shows the American flag standing there now unless the Arctic winds have overturned it." At the time the point was to give the viewer an idea of what a scene or object looked like. The compulsion for photographic exactness was not strong.*

* Magazine editors were also cavalier about photos. As Helene Cook Vetter has pointed out in an unpublished defense of Cook, two captions in his article in *Harper's Monthly*, May 1907, were radically changed by the editors of his McKinley book. Bradford Washburn states that at least six photos in that book were miscaptioned and presented as showing heights greater than they actually were. None of this can be blamed on Cook who, except in the political sense, was an extremely sensible man who surely understood that McKinley would eventually be climbed by others. In his North Pole book Cook wrote of his McKinley book: "This book, being printed at a time when I was unable to see the proofs, contained some mistakes."

Yet it seems impossible that Cook did not foresee that as the years went on other climbers, better equipped, would also ascend to the summit of McKinley, and that one day a climber would return with a clear photograph of the summit. He must have understood that whatever photograph he presented to the public would have to show, historically, a scene very similar to the scene about the summit.

It is time to consider three photographs.

Photograph 1: Cook's photograph, which he presented as the scene at the top of the continent. It is in the tradition of summit photos. The angles of the peak rise sharply to the tip and Edward Barrill is posed at the very top, approximately one hundred yards from the camera. The peak itself, beneath Barrill's feet, is bare rock, the snow ending about twenty feet below the tip. In the center of the photograph is a trail of footsteps in the snow along the crest of a ridge that falls off sharply to the left and right. The photograph does not present the scene on the top of the summit. Rather, it shows the summit viewed dramatically from some one hundred yards below. It contains a sense of climax.

Photograph 2: Bradford Washburn's original photograph at the summit of McKinley, taken in 1942. The scene presented is entirely different from that shown in Cook's photo. Although Washburn's picture shows two men holding a flag, the picture does not contain a feeling of climax. A close examination of this photograph, however, suggests that it might have been possible to take a much more dramatic shot.

Photograph 3: An additional photograph, also taken by Bradford Washburn in 1942, of the summit of Mount McKinley. It was first published in the 1943 *American Alpine Journal*, and appeared opposite p. 7. Like Photograph 1, it is in the tradition of summit photos. The tip of Mount McKinley is viewed dramatically from one hundred yards below, and the photo contains a sense of climax. The caption in the *Journal* read: "The last hundred yards. Snow above 20,000 feet was packed so hard that cramptions made little impression."

So far as the present writer knows, the existence of Photograph 3, and the resemblances between the scene presented in it and the scene presented in Photograph 1, have not been noted previously. Despite the fact that the tip of the peak in Cook's photo is bare rock, while the tip of the peak in Photograph 3 is covered by snow, the two scenes have much in common. In both photographs the angles running up to the tip of the peak are extremely similar, as is the snow-covered crest of the ridge running up the lower center of both photographs. The present writer regards Photograph 3 as the key to the solution of the Mount McKinley problem. He believes that Cook chose the "fake peak" to photograph because its tip resembled the tip of McKinley. The similarities between Photograph 3 and Photograph 1 are evidence that Cook's memory of the scene as he struggled up the last hundred yards was very keen. Except for the absence of snow at the tip, the scene that he presented to the public as a picture of the tip of McKinley did look remarkably like the actual tip as photographed by Washburn. Cook's use of the "fake peak" as McKinley's "stand-in," therefore, is understandable.

It was not a grave fraud, yet it was misrepresentation, it was cutting a corner, and from the moment he first employed his photograph in magazines and lectures, Cook was wide open to attack. He had made that one small, miserably slight slip that, in large affairs, is sometimes fatal. Edward Barrill knew the truth, but he also knew about the misrepresentation. For his knowledge he was purchased by the Peary Arctic Club, and afterwards made an imposing contribution to the ruin of that American adventurer who is, as will be seen, the equal of any of the legendary heroes of tragedy and mythology.

3

BY THE TIME he returned from his disastrous four-year expedition, Robert E. Peary had been in the business of Arctic exploration for sixteen years, some seven of which he had spent in the Arctic itself. There he had been transformed from an eager novice into a "maimed old man," as he called himself, whose mind was closed to everything but the North Pole. Back in civilization he went to Philadelphia for an operation on his feet. His surgeon cut into the stubs of his toes, drew the tissues forward, and built cushions for the stumps. Afterward, he was able to walk with less difficulty.

Before long he was restless. "The lure of the North. It is a strange and powerful thing," he wrote in *Nearest to the Pole*. "More than once I have come back from the great frozen spaces . . . telling myself that I had made my last journey thither. . . . It was never many months before the old restless feeling came over me. . . . I began to long for the great white desolation."

He then returned to the problem of the Pole. Even with his feet in terrible condition, he had gone out a hundred miles on the pack ice. He continued to be convinced that the Pole could be reached, and so informed the Peary Arctic Club. But he would have to have better equipment. He required a ship powerful enough to push its way through the ice and deposit his expedition at a base far north of those he had used previously. Such a ship, he estimated, would cost $100,000.

The club's founder, Morris K. Jesup, agreed to give

$25,000 providing Peary raised a like sum himself. To obtain the balance the club invited financial contributions from the respectable. Its dignified pamphlet stated in part:

> The attainment of the Pole means present and enduring fame for this country.
>
> It means the sign of man's physical conquest of the earth.
>
> It means an impetus to further geographical work by this country in other important fields.
>
> It means an object lesson in the spirit of emulation, of high ideas, of persistence and determination; and a spur and a stimulus to every boy and young man with an atom of ambition and intelligence, throughout the length and breadth of the land, and to their children after them. A stimulus far beyond that of text books or precepts, and the value of which cannot be gauged by dollars and cents.
>
> It means that we pluck and hold forever the last of the great world prizes for which strong and adventurous nations have struggled.
>
> A PRIZE NEVER TO BE RE-WON, NEVER TO BE SURPASSED.[1]

The pamphlet also included a statement by President Theodore Roosevelt: "No better — and I may add, no more characteristically American — work could be done than Peary's efforts to go to the Pole." Later the President gave permission for the new ship to be named for himself.

The *Roosevelt* was built not to sail the seas but to fight the ice. Its stubby design — 184 feet long, 35½ feet at the beam — permitted swift maneuvering in the ice-jammed seas. Its wooden hull was braced with steel beams. Its egg-shaped sides could rise easily when squeezed by ice. Every previous Arctic boat had been a sailing ship with an auxiliary motor, but the *Roosevelt* was a steamship with auxiliary sails. The engineering details of its propeller, shaft, and rudder were ingenious, as were the powerful deck appliances for warping the ship out of dangerous positions in the ice. Its cabins were steam-heated and lighted by electricity. It was built to go north as an American ship, a symbol of American mechanical ability.

With Roosevelt's backing, leave was no problem for Peary.

The Navy granted him three years, and after he had passed the required tests, promoted him to the rank of commander. But the money question remained vexing. James C. Colgate, banker, gave $12,000; and Thomas H. Hubbard, lawyer, donated $10,000. Nevertheless, the ship was not released by its builders until they had received a $50,000 check from George Crocker, banker and director of the Southern Pacific Railway. Meanwhile, provisions were required. The world of show business now came to Peary's aid: the Hippodrome raised $25,000; a South African Buffalo Bill show, $10,000. Finally Peary had more money than he needed.

The *Roosevelt* sailed from New York on July 16, 1905. As it dropped down the Hudson, Peary "stood amidships, bowing to the plaudits that came from all sides of the river," the newspapers reported. Out in New York Bay "volley after volley of salutes roared from forts and clubs as the ship passed."

"I am going now in God's name," Peary said, "and with the help of God I hope to accomplish the end in view."

But he did not. Although the *Roosevelt* succeeded in placing him at Cape Sheridan, 60 miles north of Conger and 435 miles from the Pole, he was forced to turn back at latitude 87°6′N, after breaking the record for the Farthest North by 32 miles.

He returned to New York in 1906 and announced that he would go north again in 1907. Then the delays began. The *Roosevelt* would have to go into dry dock; its hull needed replating and new boilers were required. Moreover, Morris K. Jesup had died and no one had taken his place. The Commander was fifty-two years old when, almost a year behind schedule, his final expedition sailed on July 6, 1908. Years earlier he had declared: "The more dramatic your expeditions are, the more incompetent you are." But the situation was different now. Man's effort to reach the Pole had developed international overtones and the Commander was pleasantly aware that he was sailing north as his country's official candidate for the office of discoverer of the North Pole.

Indeed the whole nation, or at least its leaders, was in a conquering mood. At the most recent Republican National

Convention, Chauncey Depew, a spokesman for big business, had declared:

> The American people now produce $2,000,000,000 worth more than they can consume, and we have met the emergency and . . . we have our market in Cuba . . . in Puerto Rico . . . in Hawaii . . . in the Philippines, and we stand in the presence of 800,000,000 of people, with the Pacific as an American lake, and the American artisans producing better and cheaper goods than any other country in the world. . . . Let production go on . . . let the factories do their best, let labor be employed at the highest wages, because the world is ours, and we have conquered it by Republican principles.[2]

And so thousands of patriotic citizens lined the banks of the Hudson as, once again, the *Roosevelt* departed. Before it left American waters, it was inspected by the President. As Roosevelt was leaving, Peary said:

"Mr. President, I shall put into this effort everything there is in me — physical, mental, and moral."

Roosevelt replied: "I believe in you, Peary, and I believe in your success — if it is within the possibility of man."

But in addition to being aware of his own status, Peary already knew that Cook was in the Arctic and had sent word that he would attempt the Pole. He had learned of this through a letter that Cook wrote to Herbert L. Bridgman, whom Cook then regarded as a friend. "I have hit upon a new way to the North Pole and will stay and try it," Cook wrote. "By way of Buchanan Bay and Ellesmere Land and northward through Nansen Strait over the Polar Sea seems to me a very good route. There will be game to the 82nd degree, and there are natives and dogs for the task, so here is for the Pole."

The note astonished Bridgman. He immediately telephoned Bob Bartlett, now skipper of the *Roosevelt*. Years later Bartlett wrote: "Imagine my consternation, after a hard summer's work on the *Roosevelt* added to her failure to leave, when I was called to the phone by Dr. Bridgman, who said:

'Did you know that . . . Dr. Cook has been left north to go to the Pole?'

'What?' I yelled.

'Exactly that,' said Mr. Bridgman.

'But how on earth can he make it without equipment or ship?'

'He can't,' said Mr. Bridgman with finality, and hung up."[3]

At the time, Peary did not give Cook's venture much credence. He was convinced that his "American Route to the Pole," via Smith's Sound, was the only possible route to the Pole. That there might be an alternative he was incapable of realizing.

A few days before sailing, Peary had received a visitor: the explorer Vilhjalmur Stefansson, just in from Alaska where he had heard several natives declare that Cook had not climbed Mount McKinley. In New York the rumor seemed a small thing. Peary brushed it off, declaring: "Cook is an honorable man."[4] Soon afterward, however, he qualified this attitude. Did honorable men trespass? Did honorable men invade another's domain? Because the New York *Times* had purchased the rights to his story of his expedition, he deposited with that newspaper a letter, which it eventually published:

"I beg to note that Doctor Cook has located himself in Etah, which has been my rendezvous and depot for years; that he has about him my Eskimos and dogs assembled at Etah with the expectation of meeting me . . . that he is appropriating for his own use the services of the Eskimos whom I have trained in methods of protracted, serious sledge work and is utilizing their intimate knowledge of the routes and game resources of the land to the North, which they have gained under my lead and guidance. . . . I wish to say that I regard Dr. Cook's action in going north 'sub rosa' . . . for the admitted purpose of forestalling me as one of which no man possessing a sense of honor would be guilty."[5]

Something about Fred Cook, some romantic or uncommon streak, denied the normal and attracted the irregular. His expedition to the Pole was financed, not by a gang of respectable tycoons, but by a professional gambler. The Doctor departed for the Pole not "standing amidships, bowing to the plaudits," and not on a ship named for the President of the United States; but quietly, and on a white and gold schooner named for that gambler, the *John R. Bradley*.

Together with his brother, Colonel Edward T. Bradley, whose horses would eventually win four Kentucky Derbies, John Roger Bradley owned what was probably the world's most exclusive gambling establishment, the Beach Club, usually known as "Bradley's," in Palm Beach. Membership, easily revoked by the Bradleys, was one of the badges that distinguished certain rich men from others. And so, although it was stated at the beginning of this book that Cook was not supported by any club of any sort, that statement is not exact. Most of the costs of his expedition were paid out of the profits of the Beach Club, a sporting establishment founded to relieve, if not the members of the Peary Arctic Club, then their plutocratic peers, of as much money as possible.

Bradley's wealth did not impress Peary, who was not profiting from it. He once wrote President Roosevelt: "Known in certain circles as 'Gambler Jim.' I have heard he was formerly a card sharp on the Mississippi River until driven out, and it is a matter of fact that he runs a gambling hell at Palm Beach, where both men and women gamble."[6]

In repose, Bradley looked like a well-groomed and prosperous broker; but he was also a nervous, watchful man. "Bradley was talking in his nervous, rapid way," a reporter would note; "gesticulating, twisting in his chair. . . . His eyes are round, alert, watchful; his face resolute, somewhat hard."[7] He was ambitious to become the champion big-game hunter of America. "Give me a horse, a gun, and a dog," he once said, "and you can keep a hundred north poles." He and Cook had been introduced by David T. Abercrombie, and had known each other for over six years. Bradley rated Cook a very good man, and once observed of him: "He impressed me as a seasoned and resourceful explorer, full of courage, the self-confidence that is born of knowledge, and a circumspection that is born of caution and calculation. Dr. Cook is no dreamer."[8]

Cook's journey to the North Pole began on a day in March, 1907, when Bradley proposed an Arctic hunting expedition and asked him to command. Cook accepted immediately, then went to Gloucester, Massachusetts, where from funds provided by Bradley he purchased a 111-ton fishing schooner with a clipper bow. He added three inches of white oak above and below the water line, sheathed the bow and stern with steel, had the ship rigged for the Arctic, installed a 75 h.p. engine, and brought the interior up to yachting standards.

Originally, the plan was for Bradley to shoot walrus and polar bear, while Cook photographed the Eskimos. Things soon changed. "Dr. Cook and I were lunching one day," Bradley wrote, "and he said to me, 'Why not try for the Pole?' I replied, 'Not I. Would you like to try for it?' He said, 'There is nothing I would rather do. It is the ambition of my life.' He thought it would cost only about $8,000 to $10,000 more to furnish the equipment for this purpose.* Finally I said: 'We'll fit this expedition for the Pole and say nothing about it.' . . . We figured it this way: in case we . . . found the natives not well or the dogs scarce or any other conditions unfavorable, we could call it a hunting trip and quietly return home again."

Except in the minds of Peary and his friends, there was nothing improper about another explorer attempting the Pole and using North Greenland as his base. For years every Arctic explorer had cherished the hope of being the first to reach the Pole. "Why did I desire so ardently to reach the Pole?" Cook wrote. "The attainment of the Pole meant at the time simply the accomplishing of a splendid, unprecedented feat — a feat of brain and muscle in which I should, if successful, signally surpass other men."[9]

* Bradley's total expenses were what he described as "considerably less than $50,000." The journey to the Pole was, as Cook wrote, "but an extension of this yachting cruise." The $8,000 to $10,000 figure is the only one available to gauge the cost of the journey to the Pole itself. Part, and possibly all, of this sum was contributed by the Cooks. The explorer Anthony Fiala said: "I know he spent every cent he and his wife had. The sum John R. Bradley put up was far short of paying the expenses of his trip" (Brooklyn *Standard-Union*, September 8, 1909).

In New York, Bradley advertised for a steward and hired Rudolph Franke, a husky, twenty-nine-year-old German. Two years later Franke, whose English was only fair, talked with newsmen who reported Franke's memory of his first meeting with Cook at Gloucester: "He was busy overhauling the supplies and his alert manner and his understanding of every detail, the way that he had even then mapped everything out, even to the smallest thing, impressed me."[10] For both men it was the beginning of a lifelong friendship.

The *John R. Bradley* sailed from Gloucester July 3, 1907. Cook wrote in his notebook: "After a last dinner at the Surfside at 7: PM we embarked on the Bradley and soon after pushed out of Gloucester — out on the easy swell of a quiet sun. The night was clear and beautiful, and at last we are enroute for the far north for big game and adventure."[11] When they reached Etah, an Eskimo settlement consisting of four tents and an island-protected harbor, conditions were favorable.

Bradley wrote:

"Dr. Cook and I were getting breakfast one morning when he said:

" 'I'm going to stay.'

" 'All right,' I replied; 'You're past twenty-one years of age. Think it over before you finally decide!' "

The Doctor informed the crew of his intentions and asked for one volunteer. Everyone stepped forward. He then chose Rudolph Franke. Afterwards, the supplies were unloaded at Annoatok, 32 miles north of Etah and 700 miles from the Pole, and on August 27 the *John R. Bradley* sailed south. Cook wrote in his notebook: "We lost very little time in putting up shelter after watching the yacht slowly settling under the storm-swept sea, and giving way for a time to thoughts of home and the end of warm comforts we set to work building our hut. . . . Before the Bradley was out of sight the four walls of our house were complete."

Two years later Bradley reminisced about the days at Etah and Annoatok: "Here is a little incident to show Cook's patience and how he plays along at a thing and won't give up. It is just that characteristic that won him the victory. We struck off from the ship one day in a motor boat and went to North Star Bay to get walrus for the dogs. After getting 18 or 19, we started back, and although the sun was up, it was cold. Just then the engine broke down. Well, we were in a plight. I did not even try to do anything, but curled up in some skins and smoked. We had plenty to eat, and there was no danger. The boat was too big to move with oars. Our men stuck the anchor in a small iceberg and kept us free of the ice with long poles. . . . Well, Cook worked steadily trying to start the spark in that engine for twelve solid hours. I kept saying — Oh, let the old thing alone. It won't go. But he never stopped, and kept turning that wheel until one would think he would go mad. He took it partly to pieces and did everything imaginable, but an occasional toot-toot was all he could get out of it. Finally some dories . . . towed us in. That was one o'clock at night. Cook . . . went to work again for another hour, and at last I heard the cheerful toot-toot, and it was all right again. You know, Cook is just that sort of man. He never complains, never swears, don't care whether his shoes are tied or not, but he just keeps plodding along."[12]

Cook's solution to what he sometimes called the "polar problem" differed from Peary's in four important ways.

First, he believed in a small party. "A numerous party divides itself into cliques," he wrote, "which are always opposed to each other, to the leader, and to the best interests of the problem on hand."[13] From the edge of the polar sea to the Pole, his party consisted of himself and two Eskimos.

Next, as on McKinley, Cook traveled light. His sledges weighed fifty-five pounds; Peary's weighed ninety pounds. Cook's sledges were made by himself and Franke at Annoatok. He had brought with him, aboard the *Bradley*, one composite sledge designed by himself and his brother Theodore. He had also brought north enough second-growth seasoned white hickory to make ten more sledges. The wood came from Theodore's farm in Sullivan County, New York. The sledges were each twelve feet long and two and a half feet wide. Their construction employed struts, crossbars, and posts, all of which were designed for interchangeability. The runners were shod with lignum vitae, which lessened the friction. Lashings were of rawhide. Judging from photographs, Cook's sledges were beautifully crafted. Peary's sledges were made by Henson and, like Mexican cart wheels, were built out of solid planks.

Third, Cook took along a collapsible boat. "The slats, spreaders, and floor pieces were utilized as parts of the sledges," he wrote. "The canvas cover served as a floor cloth for our sleeping bags. Thus the boat did useful service for a hundred days and never seemed cumbersome. . . . Without it we could never have returned." Peary had no boat.

Finally, Cook's route to the Pole was entirely different from Peary's. "I aimed to reach the top of the globe," he said, "in the angle between Alaska and Greenland, a promising route which had not been tried." He had profited from Otto Sverdrup. "When his *New Land* was published," Cook said, "I saw a new route to the Pole, but I told no one."[14] Sverdrup had described a region that contained plenty of fresh game, and had provided information about the condition of the ice. "The new route," Cook wrote, "seemed to promise . . . immunity from the highly disturbing effects of certain North Greenland currents." By this he meant that the ice might be quieter, smoother, slower drifting, and easier to travel on.

Many months after he had attained the Pole, Cook met Sverdrup in Copenhagen. They were soon joined by a reporter to whom Cook introduced Sverdrup by saying: "This is the man to whom I owe my success in life." Sverdrup responded: "What you have done is great, beautiful. I tell you so from the bottom of my heart."

Cook then explained, the reporter wrote, that "Sverdrup had spent years in the difficult and unglorious task of mapping the Polar regions. It was by following the indications on the maps of Sverdrup that he was able to find his way so rapidly to the North Pole."

Sverdrup then told the reporter: "I believe Cook arrived at the Pole because he did not cling to the old route usually followed — that Peary is now following. The rapid currents of this route, which carry off the ice, may be said to make it impossible to reach the Pole. Dr. Cook had the good sense to follow his own ideas in the matter of route. He took the only good one on account of the slow displacement of glaciers north of Nansen Sound, and he had the delicacy to say that I revealed the route to him. This is true. I am the first to publish a survey."[15]*

On February 19, 1908, with his equipment proved and his men and dogs conditioned by training marches of up to five hundred miles, Cook left Annoatok on the first stage of his journey to the Pole. With him he took nine Eskimos, eleven sledges, and 103 dogs. His immediate goal was the region where Sverdrup had reported that fresh game was plentiful. After a few anxious days Sverdrup's information proved accurate; and so, until the edge of the polar sea was reached, Cook's party had the enormous advantage of eating fresh meat daily.

Meanwhile, the Arctic night was just beginning to lift, and the Arctic cold was at its fearsome worst. It was so cold that when Cook tried to write in his diary, the pencil hardly left a mark. After four hundred miles of forced progress over snow and over ice, battling the most furious storms of the season, he reached the great cliff called Svartevoeg at the northernmost point of Heiberg Island. There, for the first time, he saw in the far distance the jagged, mountainous heaps of polar ice. He reduced his party to a pair of twenty-year-old Eskimos — Etukishook and Ahwelah — two sledges, and twenty-six dogs, the other Eskimos returning to Annoatok. On March 18, 1908, some three and a half months before Peary sailed from New York, he started north over the ice.

At Svartevoeg he had given the returning Eskimos a letter to Franke: "While I expect to get back to you by the end of

* On September 29, 1909, in Brussels, the Duc d'Orleans, then embarking on his third expedition to the Arctic, observed: "When one has read Sverdrup's book Dr. Cook's route seems rational and logical" (New York *Herald*, September 30, 1909).

May, still I wish you to be ready to go to Acponie, the island off North Star, where the whalers' steamers come, by the fifth of June; and if I am not back, go home with the whalers. I think however we will be back. Gather all the blue fox skins you can. These must be our money on the return trip."[16]

Early in June Franke and some Eskimos started for North Star Bay with his and Cook's property: five boxes, one trunk, one bundle of ivory tusks. Halfway there Franke injured his leg and turned back. To make room for himself on the sledge, he had to cache the property. Back at Annoatok his leg improved and he again started out, this time in a dory. Once again his leg went bad, but he continued on, and after finding the bay empty of ships, turned back toward Annoatok. When he reached Etah he saw the *Roosevelt* and its supply ship *Erik* at anchor.

Soon after the *Roosevelt* arrived off Etah, the Commander notified the President that all was well with the expedition. There was only one difficulty, he explained: it was hard to get Eskimos and dogs "owing to Cook's presence."[17] Today it is known that at Etah "Cook's presence" was very much on Peary's mind. The evidence includes the tantalizing letters of Ross Marvin, a member of the expedition.

"Dr. Cook seems to be the whole topic of conversation here," Marvin wrote his friend L. C. Bement, "but whatever I will tell you I wish you would consider . . . confidential. He . . . left a cache at Cape Hubbard and found plenty of muskoxen and bear this side of there. In fact he seems to have had better luck than we thought for. . . . I would not dare write this about Dr. Cook if I did not feel sure that you will keep it to yourself."[18] A few days later Marvin again wrote to Bement: "I feel that I must drop you a few lines of importance for fear I may not get another chance. It is just this, Lou, the Dr. Cook affair has become a hard nut to crack. I am writing Peary's confidential letters . . . and so my lips must be closed. So you can see how I stand. I know more about it than anyone else, but I can say less. . . . I hope you will understand the position I am in. I would like to tell YOU all, but I owe a duty to Com. Peary."*

When Franke arrived at Etah his leg was still a problem and he had not seen a white man in seven months. He dragged himself aboard the *Roosevelt* and found the steward preparing breakfast. He asked for coffee and food, but was refused, so he struggled back to shore and slept with the Eskimos. Bob Bartlett soon sought him out and apologized, then brought him back to the ship and listened to his story. Franke not only had a bad leg, he also had scurvy, and he desperately wanted to go home. "Please, Mr. Peary," he wrote, "let me now go home with your other vessel. For the whole life I will be thankful to you. For the kindness I thank you very much and if I can be of any use to you, it will be a great pleasure to me to do what I can do. I remain, gentleman, respectfully yours, Rudolph Franke. P.S. Excuse my bad English. I am German."

Peary had no objection to Franke returning on his supply ship *Erik*, but he was disturbed by the problem of Cook's supplies. What would happen, Peary could wonder, if the Eskimos got into these provisions? He was accustomed to trading a tin cup and saucer for a team of dogs, and could not afford to have the Eskimos lose their incentive to hire out as sledge drivers to the Pole. After deciding to take over Cook's supplies, Peary landed Boatswain Dennis Murphy and Cabin Boy Billy Pritchard to live in Cook's house and guard the provisions. He also ordered a sign placed beside the door of the house. According to Franke it read: "This house belongs to Dr. Frederick A. Cook, but Dr. Cook is long ago dead and there is no use to search for him. Therefore, I, Commander Robert E. Peary, install my boatswain in this deserted house."

* Ross Marvin died during the expedition. The original version of his death, the one reported by the Eskimos, was that he fell through thin ice and drowned. This report was accepted by Peary. In 1911 Cook noted that Marvin's death had never been satisfactorily explained. In 1928 one of the Eskimos who had accompanied Marvin confessed to missionaries that he had gotten into an argument with Marvin and shot him. The Eskimo was not tried, mainly because the authorities could not decide who had jurisdiction.

Another bothersome situation then developed. Franke not only wanted to go home on Peary's ship; he expected to take with him, on Peary's ship, not only his own personal property, but also Cook's. And Cook's property, as it turned out, was valuable. It included some ivory and a trunk of blue fox skins that Franke valued at $10,000.

Although Cook had once been, for Peary, "an honorable man," he was now an utterly dishonorable invader who had entered Peary's domain "for the admitted purpose" — had Cook not said he would try for the Pole? — "of forestalling me." Accordingly, as the Commander advised the Peary Arctic Club, "I told Franke I would not take furs or other materials away from here for anybody; that I would send for all this stuff, except the furs and horns, and he could take them home with him." As for the furs and horns, Peary explained, "he could turn them over to me or leave them where they were. He did the former."

Franke's account is less laconic. After Bartlett had retrieved the property, the Commander "ordered me to open Cook's trunk," Franke wrote, "which I was obliged to do. He wanted to keep Dr. Cook's letter to me, but after several demands gave it back to me. I had to hand over the furs, just as the enemy has to hand over their arms to the victorious party. Some of the furs were wet and mildewed but of excellent quality and nearly 200 in number."[19]

But Peary was not merciless. Since the destination of the supply ship was St. John's, Newfoundland, he gave Franke fifty dollars to pay for his expenses from there to New York.

Traditionally, Peary's admirers have viewed Franke with serene rationalism, an attitude that persisted through 1960, when Peary's most recent biographer wrote of Franke: "On numerous occasions he charged Peary with taking furs and ivory in return for the passage home. This argument became somewhat weaker, however, when one asked why Franke should not have paid for his transportation. Few expeditions are likely to provide free food and passage for strangers."[20]

Peary would have agreed. There are indications that he was

never satisfied with the size of his profit at Etah. A newspaper reported: "The Commander also wished to send to Mr. Bradley an additional bill for the services of three men, referred to as Eskimos, whom he had assigned to guard Cook's house, presumably night and day. The Peary Arctic Club considered the matter and finally decided that it would be well not to forward the claim for this interesting indemnity on the ground that Dr. Cook had not asked Commander Peary to guard his stores."[21]

But otherwise the club was faithful to its man, who advised that the blue fox furs were practically worthless — "wet, mildewed and rotting" — and that the ivory horns had virtually no value — "broken from knocking about."[22] So informed, the club decided that the stranded Franke had sailed south at no cost to anyone but themselves. They billed John R. Bradley $100 for Franke's passage. The statement was itemized, for "sending Franke home for 'humanity's sake.' "[23]

Whether Bradley paid this bill is unknown, but at least one portion of the Franke affair was settled in a way that must have pleased the Commander. Marie Cook sent the club a fifty-dollar check to cover the money he had given Franke, and that, surely, was comforting. She, at least, was honorable.

It is possible to regard Cook and, more so, Peary, as Melville regarded Ahab: "All my means are sane, my motive and my object mad." Yet Cook was a man of his times, and representative of its spirit, which was that of conquest. He was determined "to assert the supremacy of living man . . . to prove that the living brain and palpitating muscle of a finite though conscious creature could vanquish a hostile nature which creates to kill."[24] But Cook was also a man of all time, a superb example of what J. R. L. Anderson has called the "Ulysses factor." "Other animals have a sense of adventure and certainly enjoy hunting," Anderson has written, "but deliberate risk-taking in pursuit of a goal of no apparent value is not the habit of any animal other than man. In man the factor can be an urge as compelling as sex."[25] The factor is especially noticeable, Anderson has stated, "in communities either dominant or about to become dominant."

When Cook and his tiny party of two other human beings and twenty-six animals left all land behind them and began working their way across the icy skin of the sea, he was embarking on the most tremendous of private American adventures. For it he had done his homework and, as much as any man can when challenging the unknown, he knew what he was doing.

One characteristic of his journey was isolation. It was isolation to a fabulous degree. He was working his way, and it was enormously hard work, into a region in which no life existed. There were no human beings, no animals, no birds; nothing but ice, sky, mirages, noise — the booms and crashes of the floes as they ground into each other, then split — and water from which evaporation arose like smoke from a volcano. "This lack of life," he wrote, "over the great reaches of space was intensely depressing."

Into this territory he and his Eskimos hauled from civilization 805 pounds of beef pemmican, 130 pounds of walrus pemmican, and 50 pounds of musk ox tenderloin, plus additional provisions. His equipment also included a sextant made by Hurleman of France, a glass artificial horizon, a pocket compass, a liquid compass, three chronometers, a pedometer, and a watch from Tiffany's.

In the beginning he found the land-shelf ice fairly good for travel. Then the smoother, glacierlike ice gave way to smaller floes separated by crushed ice and difficult pressure ridges — the polar pack. Ice such as this has been compared to the chaos of a concrete road broken up partly by impact and partly by explosives, magnified ten times. "If this abominable mess 'stayed put' it would be bad enough, but it doesn't," Guy R. L. Potter has written. "This ice . . . is floating, and under the influence of winds, tides, and ocean currents, is in constant motion. Here the wind is driving the ice together with the result that great pressure ridges up to 25 feet high are formed, or the pack indulges in its favorite pastime of 'rafting' — piling one huge cake of ice on top of another. A change of wind, and the ridges impeding your progress magically disappear — to be replaced by 'leads' of open water which at best mean delay (when every hour may mean the difference between success and failure) and at worst, disaster."[26] As Cook had imagined, the surface improved as he went farther and farther north, and from about the 88th parallel, ice conditions were comparatively good.

The straight-line distance between Svartevoeg and the Pole was some 520 miles. He covered it in thirty-five days. His greatest distance in one day was 29 miles, and on some days storms prevented him from traveling at all. His daily average was 15 miles. During the trek he paused seven times to locate his exact position by sextant. Each time he took readings for both latitude and longitude. The chain of observations began at latitude 82°23′N, longitude 95°14′, about 460 miles from the Pole. He kept ahead of the sledges, and for hour-by-hour and day-by-day travel he navigated by compass.

He traveled through weather almost impossible to imagine. It was not so much the cold, it was the cold plus the wind. Since his time, wind-chill tables have been developed which show that at minus 40 degrees Fahrenheit and 40 knots of wind, exposed human flesh freezes in about a minute and a half. Cook, properly dressed, survived such conditions. "The wind . . . struck us at a painful angle and brought tears. Our moistened lashes quickly froze together as we winked, and when we rubbed them and drew apart the lids the icicles broke the tender skin. Our breath froze in our faces. Often we had to pause, uncover our hands, and apply the warm palms to the face before it was possible to see."

Each night he and Etukishook and Ahwelah slept in an igloo. Each morning they would drink two cups of tea apiece, and eat a biscuit, a chip of frozen meat, and a chunk of pemmican. Then they would creep out of their sleeping bags, push their shivering legs into the bearskin cylinders they used as trousers, work their way into frozen boots, and climb into fur coats. Then someone would kick out the front of the igloo and they would emerge and dance about to stimulate the heart action.

In his letter to Franke, written at Svartevoeg, Cook had

said: "For the present we have seen nothing of Crocker Land." He was referring to new land that Peary said he had sighted from the top of Svartevoeg in 1906, and named for George Crocker, the banker. On the twelfth day out from Svartevoeg, however, Cook observed what he believed to be new land: "On March 30 the horizon was partly cleared . . . and over the western mist was discovered a new land. The observations gave our position latitude 84 deg 47 min; longitude 96 deg 36 min. The urgent need of rapid advance did not permit a detour to explore the coast." He called it Bradley Land. During the controversy, with the Peary Arctic Club "proving" that he never got within five hundred miles of the Pole, his supporters argued that if Bradley Land existed, it would refute the club's "proof." But Bradley Land went unobserved by later explorers and, along with Peary's Crocker Land, was declared nonexistent. Today, aerial photography has provided a plausible explanation of the "new land" phenomenon: ice islands. "Tabular masses of ice . . . are known to drift in the area of the Arctic Ocean between Alaska and the North Pole in a slow clockwise motion," John Euller wrote in 1964. Euller pointed out that neither Cook nor Peary could strengthen their claims by falsely reporting the discovery of land. "Were both men liars? A more plausible explanation is that both had sighted an ice island, probably the same one. . . . The 150-mile distance between the two sightings does not contradict the observed drift of present-day islands."[27]*

Cook also reported that between the 87th and 88th parallels he traveled for two days over old ice without pressure lines or hummocks, and that he was inclined to believe this was ice on low or submerged land.

As he pushed on, conditions became more and more enervating. The dogs' tails, ears, and noses drooped and the Eskimos

* Between eighty-five and one hundred of these islands are known to exist today. The first known identification of an ice island was made by Captain C. W. Thomas (USCG), aboard the *Eastwind* while escorting the captured German naval transport *Externestiene* through the northeast Greenland ice pack on October 16, 1944.

also felt dispirited. "When perspiration oozed from our pores, as we forced forward, step by step," he wrote, "it froze in the garments and the warmer portions of our bodies were ringed with snow. Daily, unremittingly, this was our agony." Through it all he was possessed by what he called "the northward craze," but Etukishook and Ahwelah were only along for a knife and a gun apiece and because they trusted him. At a point one hundred miles from the Pole, they refused to go on. He encouraged them and as he did so his own spirits rose. Soon they were moving again.

As they drew closer and closer to the Pole along the 97th meridian, Cook's mind was filled with pride. "In this land I was master. I was sole invader. I strode forward with undaunted glory in my soul."

On April 21, 1908, Frederick A. Cook and his Eskimos became the first human beings to attain the northern extremity of the planet Earth. Of the scene there he wrote: "The desolation . . . was such that it was almost palpable. . . . What a cheerless spot this was, to have aroused the ambition of man for so many years."

Every six hours from noon on the twenty-first to midnight on the twenty-second he took observations of the sun, which was about twelve degrees above the horizon, and fixed his position with what he regarded as "reasonable certainty." Of the difficulties of taking observations he later wrote with admirable candidness: "The chronometers have been shooting the shoots of the pack for weeks . . . therefore, time, that very important factor upon which all astronomical data rest, is at best only a rough guess. For this reason . . . the determination of longitude when nearing the Pole becomes difficult and unreliable." Concerning latitude he continued: "The fingers are cold; the instrument must be handled with mittens; the cold is such that at best a shiver runs up the spine, the eye blinks with snow glitter and frost. The arms, hands, and legs become stiff from cold and from inaction."

Just before they turned south, Cook enclosed a short note and a small American flag in a metal tube which he buried in the snow. As they moved out his spirits were low. "I could get no sensation of novelty as we pitched our last belongings on the sleds. . . . A sense of the utter uselessness of this thing, of the empty reward of my endurance, followed my exhilaration. I had grasped my *Ignus Fatuus*. It is a misfortune for any man when his *Ignus Fatuus* fails to elude him."

When Peary informed President Roosevelt that he was having trouble obtaining Eskimos and dogs "owing to Cook's presence," he was prevaricating. Except for the two Eskimos and twenty-six dogs with Cook, the rest of the natives and their animals were back at Etah before the *Roosevelt* left New York. When Peary's expedition sailed north from Etah it was a fully equipped Peary-type expedition that included forty-nine Eskimos and 246 dogs.

By September 5, 1908, Captain Bob Bartlett had sailed, maneuvered, and rammed the *Roosevelt* through the ice to Cape Sheridan, five hundred miles from the Pole. From there the supplies were hauled to Cape Columbia, one hundred miles further north, where the expedition dug itself in for the long Arctic night.

On Peary's early expeditions the entire party had traveled as one unit, but for his 1906 expedition he had devised what he regarded as a "traveling machine," a shuttle system of supporting parties, each of which, before returning to land, would break trail and haul supplies progressively farther north, with Peary and his party bringing up the rear. The advantage of the system was that when the time came for the final dash to the Pole, Peary and his division would be in a good position on the ice, and in superior shape physically. This method, which he described as the "Peary system," failed in 1906, when the ice split and open water separated the divisions for long periods; but in 1909 nature was cooperative.

The first division of Peary's final assault on the Pole departed on February 28, 1909, and one day later the whole expedition — seven explorers, eighteen Eskimos, and 123 dogs — was on the ice proceeding north along the 70th meridian. Every five days or so, one of the supporting parties turned back toward land. A month later the last of these parties, led by Bob Bartlett, turned back. Just before he did so, Bartlett wrote out a certificate: "Arctic Ocean, April 1, '09. I have today personally determined our latitude to be by sextant observation 87°47′49″N. I return from here in command of the fourth supporting party. I leave Commander Peary with . . . men and dogs . . . in good condition, the going fair, the weather good. At the same average as our last eight marches, Commander Peary should reach the Pole in eight days. Robert S. Bartlett, Master, S.S. Roosevelt."*

Bartlett later gave out that he was a very disappointed man when Peary, as per plan, ordered him to turn back, just 132 miles from the Pole; "It was a bitter disappointment. . . . He said I must go, so I had to do it." But in 1910 Matt Henson, who continued north with Peary, contradicted Bartlett. "Captain Bartlett was glad to turn back when he did. He frankly told me several times that he had little expectation of ever returning alive."[28] Aside from Peary, Bartlett was the only explorer present who knew how to use a sextant; the only man who could have verified Peary's observations at the Pole. Accordingly, Peary was criticized later for sending Bartlett back. The Commander responded: "The Pole was something to which I had devoted my whole life. I did not feel that under these circumstances I was called upon to divide with a man who, no matter how able and deserving he might be, was a young man and had put in only a few years of that kind of work, and who had, frankly, as I believed, not the right to it that I had."

After Bartlett and his party had turned back, Peary was left with four Eskimos, five sledges, forty dogs, and one other

* It is possible to regard Bartlett's certificate as unreliable. Many months later, when Peary appeared before a subcommittee of the House Naval Affairs Committee, Congressman Roberts examined Bartlett's certificate and noted that it appeared that three separate pencils had been used in writing it. In addition, Bartlett made a mathematical error in figuring his position, which he should have stated as 87°41′4″, a matter of six miles.

American, the man he formally described as "my negro body servant," Matthew Henson.

"I can't get along without Henson," Peary once acknowledged.[29] Otherwise, he was sparse in his comments about the black explorer, confining himself to statements such as: "Henson, with his years of Arctic experience, was almost as skillful at this work as an Eskimo. He could handle dogs and sleds. He was part of the 'traveling machine.' " The most generous statement about Henson was made by Donald B. MacMillan, a member of the 1908 expedition: "Henson, the colored man, went to the Pole with Peary because he was a better man than any of his white assistants."[30]

In photographs Matt Henson, who was ten years younger than Peary, appears as a genial, handsome black man who, into his forties, remained almost as superbly conditioned as a sprinter or an astronaut. "He is two or three inches shorter than Peary," a reporter wrote, "but with the same deep chest development. Light for a negro, his nose is pronouncedly Roman verging on the Semitic. . . . The expression of the lower part of his face is heavy and phlegmatic."[31]

During the years that Henson had spent as a most unusual body servant, an unsurprising situation had developed between employer and employee. Henson no longer regarded himself as simply Peary's servant, and was attempting to establish a more dignified identity. Except for Peary, Henson had spent more time in the Arctic than any other American, so that there was a definite logic in his feeling that he deserved to be regarded as the explorer that, beyond all doubt, he was. If Peary did attain the Pole, it was only because Matthew Henson, for fifty dollars a month and all the pemmican he could eat, broke his trail and took him there.

Although Peary would say of Henson, "He is as subject to my will as the fingers of my hand," the Commander's diary indicates that over the years Henson had become bad about calling Peary "Sir," bad about showing Peary respect in small things, and bad about paying attention when Peary was talking to him. This puzzled Peary, who on at least one occasion talked to Henson about his attitude and concluded by saying, in effect: "Now, is there anything which, if different, would make things pleasanter for you?"[32]

But if Peary was puzzled about Henson, Henson was also puzzled about Peary: "He was never understandable."[33] Despite their twenty-two-year acquaintance, the two explorers who were assaulting nature could not comprehend each other.

And so, in 1909, when two Americans attained what they identified as the North Pole, one was a man with white skin and one was a man with black skin, and the relations between them, at the Pole, were not much different than what relations between the whites and the blacks are, today, in civilization.

Although one result of the expedition was a bulky, three-hundred-page book, *The North Pole*, which Peary signed, the story it told was so evasively undramatic that an English geographer remarked: "Tennyson turned the rough Arthurian knights into polished Victorian gentlemen. In like manner, Peary presents a desperate encounter with the fiercest forces of nature as a drawing room or Sunday School story. In all his previous dealings with the Polar pack he had come off not only second best, but very badly, whereas his last trip is of little more interest than a railroad journey."[34]

Yet any expedition toward a goal as exotic as the North Pole is inherently dramatic, and Peary's 1909 journey contained its full share of extraordinary situations. Of the seven explorers who started across the ice, one was murdered, a rare event in Arctic exploration; while the relations between the two Americans who went to the Pole became so bad that on their way south to land — across that great stretch of ice — they exchanged hardly one word, and the only language heard was Eskimo.

Early in the polar controversy the two-toed, fifty-three-year-old Commander declared that he had walked every step of the way to the North Pole. "I want to say right now that there was no riding on these marches. Each man works right alongside the sledges or his dogs, as the case may be, and when conditions are such that he can place his hand on the back of the vehicle he considers that he is getting a great treat."[35] But Henson remembered it otherwise: "He rode on a sledge most of the way and back. Practically we carried him to the Pole and back. He probably did not walk more than two miles a day."[36]

At any rate, after Bartlett had turned back, and as Peary and Henson and the Eskimos continued north, the condition of the ice improved; "the going was better than ever," Peary wrote. If Henson's statements can be relied on, then as Peary approached the Pole his mind, like Cook's, became more and more excited. Although the Commander's thoughts continued to be characteristic, they also became increasingly peculiar. He had disposed of Bartlett, with whom he did not feel called upon to share the prize. Now, according to a statement written by Henson months later, Peary was scheming to exclude black Henson and attain the mystic prize in white solitude.

On the fifth day after Bartlett had turned back, one of the Eskimos came to Henson. "He said that it was mean that Peary had quietly planned with him and one other Eskimo boy to leave me in camp the following morning and go off to the Pole by himself. . . . It stunned me at first, because Commander Peary had spoken nothing of it to me. My first impulse was to protest, but on second thought I decided to wait. In fact, I believed that the full distance had already been covered. One can tell to within a mile or so how far he walks on the northern ice, and I reckoned that we were even now at the very Pole."[37]* Henson believed that because Peary was riding on a sledge, he could not accurately judge the distance traveled.

The next morning Peary and two Eskimos set out with instruments, leaving Henson in camp repairing a sledge. "In about an hour," Henson reported, "the Commander returned. His face was long and serious. He would not speak to me."

" 'Well, Mr. Peary,' I spoke up cheerfully enough, 'we are now at the North Pole, are we not?'

* Wally Herbert, leader of the British Trans-Arctic Expedition of 1968–1969, wrote in *Across the Top of the World* (London, 1969): "Usually the guesses were quite good . . . seldom that our guesses were more than a mile from the mean."

" 'I do not suppose that we can swear that we are exactly at the Pole' was his evasive answer.

" 'Well, I have kept track of the distance and we have made exceptional time,' I replied, 'and I have the feeling that we have now just about covered the 132 miles since Captain Bartlett turned back. If we have traveled in the right direction we are now at the Pole. If we have not traveled in the right direction then it is your fault.'

"Commander Peary made no reply, but going off by himself made three separate observations. . . . At the conclusion of his tests he ordered out the American flag, selected a hillock of ice, and gave the word to erect the Stars and Strips thereon. I did so, then I led a cheer for Old Glory."

Henson concluded: "Having fooled himself in the matter of distance, and by an oversight permitted me to be with him at the North Pole, he was a bitterly disappointed man."[38]

Historically, not every explorer has followed what, in this instance, can be thought of as an unusual aspect of the Peary system. Of Roald Amundsen one commentator observed: "Amundsen equipped each of his companions with a sextant and compass; and when at the South Pole, he placed each of these companions in such a position that all and any of them might claim in history, and with truth, an equal participation."[39]

But for the Commander things were different. It was to have been, for him alone, a mystic experience: "MINE . . . to be credited to me, and associated with my name, generations after I had ceased to be."*

Of the situation described by Henson, Peary made no mention. He did, however, like the Hensonless Cook, express a definite sense of disappointment at the Pole. "The Pole at last," he wrote in his diary. "The prize of three centuries. Mine at last! I cannot bring myself to realize it. It all seems so simple and commonplace."

* In a sense, Cook was also motivated by this desire. Although possession itself did not mean as much to him as it did to Peary, he definitely had the desire to excel, and to have his excellence, his name, recognized historically.

That he was at the Pole, Peary was certain. In *The North Pole* he wrote, "I had taken in all thirteen single or six and a half double altitudes of the sun [which was seven degrees or less above the horizon], at two different stations, in three directions, at four different times. In traversing the ice . . . I had passed over or very near the point where north and south and east and west blend into one."

He then tore a strip off the American flag that he had carried on all his expeditions. He placed the strip in a glass jar along with a note — "have formally taken possession of the entire region, and adjacent, for and in the name of the President of the United States" — and, like Cook, deposited the jar in the ice.

After thirty-three hours about the Pole Peary gave the word for the return. "From the time we were at the Pole," Henson wrote, "Commander Peary scarcely spoke to me. Probably he did not speak to me four times on the whole return journey to the ship. . . . He would arise in the morning and slip away on the homeward trail without rapping on the ice for me, as was the established custom."

On the journey south, Peary reported, weather conditions were excellent and the trail was mostly firm. One of the signs that enabled the party to keep on the trail itself was the urine stains that the forty dogs had left on the way up, a fact that Peary did not record. Double marches were made on many of the days going south, and the daily mileage was extraordinary. After sixteen days Peary and his party passed the glacial fringe and arrived at Ellesmere's terra firma. "When the last sledge came to the almost vertical edge of the fringe, I thought my Eskimos had gone crazy," Peary wrote. "They yelled and danced until they fell." One Eskimo exclaimed: "The devil is asleep or having trouble with his wife, or we should never have come back so easily."

It is commonly believed, by travelers, that getting there is the hardest part, and that the return somehow seems shorter. Cook found things otherwise. He had spent two months journeying from Annoatok to the Pole. He would spend twelve additional months getting from the Pole to Annoatok. During these twelve months he and his tiny party would not see, until the last moment, one other human being. "We were alone, all alone," he would write. ". . . This loneliness was so oppressive that tears came more easily than conversation."

Going south from the Pole he chose to travel by a more westerly route. The movement of the pack made backtracking impossible, and he was curious about what he might discover along a new trail. Believing that the set of the ice was easterly, he proceeded south along the 100th meridian and was surprised to find that he was being carried to the west.* He changed course but was soon attacked by fog so dense and persistent that for periods of up to twenty days he had no idea where he was. When he was able to use his sextant, he discovered that he was 120 miles south of Svartevoeg. Between himself and the mainland lay fifty miles of crushed ice. Although he had his collapsible boat, the sharp edges of the still-forming young ice would have slashed the canvas like a knife. His last entry in his field notes was: "We have been carried adrift far to the south and west, and examination of ice eastward proves that all is small ice and open water. Heiberg Island is impossible to us. What is our fate? Food and fuel is about exhausted, though we still have ten bony dogs. Upon these and our little pemmican we can possibly survive for twenty days. In the meantime we must go somewhere. To the south is our only hope."

Finally he and the Eskimos reached a small island. In all this time the only evidence of life that they had seen was one bird, the sight of which had made them cry. Now, on the island, they saw a bear, which they shot and ate raw. "The advantages of a fire," Cook wrote, "were not considered." Later they killed a gull. "It was divided without the tedious process

* This he reported in 1909. Recently, scientists have verified that, in the region through which he traveled, the ice does drift west. In 1964 John Euller wrote: "Cook could not have invented or anticipated this drift; the error caused by it lends great credibility to his account of his journey" (*Arctic*, December, 1964, p. 44).

of cooking." They traveled on and were able to shoot bear, seal, and caribou. Eventually, the ammunition exhausted, they began to starve. "To me the end was now near," he wrote years later in *Return from the Pole*. ". . . Our lips were blue with that grey blueness which bespeaks the failing blood supply and the weakened heart action." Finally, using a looped line, they captured some gulls and life improved.

"To me it seemed," he wrote, "that death must be looked for in the background of every picture of life and must therefore be rated as a guiding force to extract the best out of existence before the sorrows of the end. But above all, that resigned expectancy of death in which I had lived with profit for days now offered a new dominion of life, a reawakening, a regeneration almost in the nature of a resurrection."

Despite the perils, he and the Eskimos knew moments of tremendous exuberance. After a hare had been killed with a slingshot and had been put in a pot to cook they "with gloating eyes, watched it simmer. I was thrilled with the joy of sheer living. . . . This was a breakfast for a king."

Eventually they reached North Devon Island. From there open water made sledge travel impossible. Now the collapsible boat proved itself. Cook put one sledge and the few remaining supplies into the boat and set out for Annoatok, some eight hundred miles away.

"Grim and suffering with hunger, we clung madly to life," he wrote in *Return from the Pole*. "Passing a glacier which rose hundreds of feet out of the green sea, we encountered heavy waves that rolled furiously from the distant ocean. Huge bergs rose and fell against the far-away horizon. . . . The waves dashed against the emerald walls of the smooth icy Gibraltar with a thunderous noise. We rose and fell in the frail canvas boat, butting the waves, our hearts each time sinking. . . . The indifferent stage of starvation was at hand when we pulled into a nameless bay, carried the boat on to a grassy bench, and packed ourselves into it for a sleep that might be our last.

"We were awakened by the glad sound of . . . walrus

calls. Through the glasses, we located a group far off shore, on the middle pack. . . . Quickly we dropped the boat into the water . . . and pushed from the famine shores with teeth set for red meat.

"The day was beautiful, and the sun from the west poured out . . . golden light. Only an occasional ripple disturbed the glassy blue through which the boat crept.

". . . The animals were on a low pan . . . where we hoped to land and creep up behind hummocks. The splash of our paddles was lost in the noise of the grinding ice and the bellowing of walrus calls.

"So excited were the Eskimos that they could hardly pull an oar. . . . The boat finally shot upon the ice, and we scattered among the ice blocks for favorable positions. Everything was in our favor. We did not for a moment entertain a thought of failure, although in reality, with the implements at hand, our project was tantamount to attacking an elephant with pocket knives.

"We came together behind an unusually high icy spire only a few hundred yards from the herd. Ten huge animals were lazily stretched out in the warm sun. A few lively babies tormented their sleeping mothers. There was a splendid line of hummocks, behind which we could advance under cover. With a firm grip on harpoon and line, we started.

"Suddenly Etukishook shouted, 'Nannook!' (bear). We halted. Our instruments were no match for a bear. But we were too hungry to retreat. The bear paid no attention to us. His nose was set for something more to his liking. Slowly but deliberately he crept up to the snoring herd while we watched with a mad, envious anger welling up within us. Our position was helpless. His long neck reached out, the glistening fangs closed, and a young walrus struggled in the air. All of the creatures awoke, but too late to give battle. With dismay and rage, the walruses sank into the water, and the bear slunk off to a safe distance, where he sat down to a comfortable meal. We were not of sufficient importance to interest either the bear or the disturbed herd of giants.

"Our limbs were limp when we returned to the boat."

The next day they harpooned a walrus, then feasted and slept. When they awoke they found that the bears had pawed apart every cache of stones in which they had stored meat. There was nothing they could do except sail on.

Although in the end the boat saved their lives, nature continued to be aggressive. At times walruses pierced the canvas cover with their tusks. Then Cook and the Eskimos would paddle madly to an iceberg, pull out the boat, and repair the rip with leather cut from boots. Then they would be off again. Once they rode an iceberg for many miles, but then a great current rushed in and they found themselves, on the berg, being carried back beyond where they had climbed aboard.

Such incidents, plus storms, prevented them from making much progress towards Annoatok. With the polar night coming on, Etukishook and Ahwelah discovered a cave, a sort of underground den, at Cape Sparbo on the shores of Jones Sound. Cook decided to winter there.

"We were hard-looking men at this time," he wrote in *My Attainment of the Pole*. ". . . Dressed in rags, with ugly brown faces, seamed with wind-fissures, we had reached, in our appearance, the limit of degradation. At the Pole I had been thin, but now my skin was contracted over bones offering only angular eminences as a bodily outline. The Eskimos were as thin as myself. My face was as black as theirs. They had risen to higher mental levels, and I had descended to lower animal depths. The long strain, the hard experiences, had made us equals. We were, however, still in good health and were capable of considerable hard work."

On the edge of starvation, with the Arctic winter coming on and armed with nothing but pocket knives and their native cunning, they made bows and arrows, lances and harpoons, using hickory off the sledge for shafts and tipping them with points of whale bone. There is something exhilarating about Cook's account of how, under Stone Age conditions, he and the Eskimos battled the musk ox and obtained the supply of meat that enabled them to survive in the underground den during one hundred days and nights of Arctic darkness.

"The opening of the fight with stones," he wrote in *My*

Attainment, "was now a regular feature which we never abandoned in our later development of the art, but the manner in which we delivered the stones depended upon the effect which we wished to produce. If we wished the musk ox to retreat, we would make a combined rush, hurling the stones at the herd. If we wished them to remain in position and discourage their attack, we advanced slowly and threw stones desultorily. . . . If we wanted to encourage attacks, one man advanced and delivered a large rock as best he could at the head. This was cheap ammunition and it was very effective.

"In this case the game was in a good position for us and we advanced accordingly. They allowed us to take positions within about fifteen feet, but no nearer. The lances were repeatedly tried without effect, and after a while two of these were broken.

"Having tried bow and arrow, stones, the lance and harpoon, we now tried another weapon. We threw the lasso — but not successfully, owing to the bushy hair about the head and the roundness of the hump on the neck. Then we tried to entangle their feet with slip loops just as we had trapped gulls. This also failed. We next extended the loop idea to the horns. The bull's habit of rushing at things hurled at him caused us to think of this plan.

"A large slip loop was now made in the center of the line, and the two natives took up positions on opposite sides of the animal. They threw the rope, with its loop, on the ground in front of the animal, while I encouraged an attack from the front. As the head was slightly elevated the loop was raised and the bull put his horns in it, one after the other. The rope was now rapidly fastened to stones and the bull tightened the loop by his efforts to advance or retreat. With every opportunity the slack was taken up, until no play was allowed the animal. During this struggle all the other oxen retreated except one female, and she was inoffensive. A few stones at close range drove her off. Then we had the bull where we could reach him with the lance at arm's length and plunge it into his vitals. He soon fell over, the first victim of our new art of musk ox capture."

On November 3, 1908, the sun went down. It did not reappear until February 11, 1909. Inside the den Dr. Frederick A. Cook, of 670 Bushwick Avenue, Brooklyn, New York, found himself leading the life of a Stone Age man. Because they had no protection from the bears, which had not yet gone into hibernation and were attracted by the smell of the meat stored inside the den, they rarely stepped outside. "We were therefore doomed to hibernate in our underground den for at least a hundred nights. . . . We could not have been more thoroughly isolated if we had been transported to the surface of the moon."

The Eskimos passed the time singing and sewing. Having no thread, they unraveled their stockings, then used the yarn to sew skins together for clothes. Cook spent the time writing up field notes. He used a stone for a writing desk and lay prone while he wrote. The light came from burning fat. He estimated that he wrote 150,000 words.

Months later, when New York reporters were questioning his story, he showed one section of the notes he had written in the cave. The *Herald* reported:

"The chirography was almost microscopic, and often hundreds of words were crowded together like a multitude of pigmies taking their morning walk on paper. The scarcity of pages had compelled . . . an economy which caused him to rival the ingenuity of those patient souls who write the Decalogue on the back of a penny postage stamp.

" 'That's enough for me,' said one hard-headed Thomas who had leaned over the record. 'No man alive would sit up nights doing this sort of thing for fun.' "[40]

Inside the den, before the sun reappeared, Cook and the Eskimos — strangers hiding in a house — heard sounds that announced that the Arctic world was reawakening. The rats were the first to reappear. Then came the wolves and foxes. Finally they heard noises that told them that the bears were coming out of hibernation.

The reappearance of the first bear was described in a charming passage in *My Attainment of the Pole.* At the time, Cook was through with conquest, and was one with nature.

"In our new and philosophical turn of mind," he wrote, "we thought better of bruin. In our greatest distress during the previous summer he had kept us alive. In our future adventures he might perform a similar mission. After all he had no sporting proclivities; he did not hunt or trouble us for the mere fun of our discomfort. . . . His aim in life was the very serious business of getting food. Could we blame him? Had we not a similar necessity?

"A survey of our caches proved that we were still rich in the coin of the land. There remained meat and blubber for our needs, with considerable to spare for empty stomachs. So, to feed the bear, meat was piled up in heaps for his delight.

"The new aroma rose into the bleaching night air. We peeped with eager eyes through our port to spot results. The next day at eleven footsteps were heard. The noise indicated caution and shyness instead of the bold quick step we knew so well. There was room for only one eye and one man at a time at the peep-hole, and so we took turns. Soon the bear was sighted, proceeding with the utmost caution behind some rocks and banks. The blue of the snows, with yellow light, dyed his fur an ugly green. He was thin and gaunt and ghostly. There was the stealth and the cunning of the fox in his movements. But he could not get his breakfast, the first after a fast of weeks, without coming squarely into our view.

"The den was buried under the winter snows and did not disturb the creature, but the size of the pile of meat did disturb its curiosity. When within twenty-five yards, a few sudden leaps were made, and the ponderous claws came down on a walrus shoulder. His teeth began to grind like a stone cutter. For an hour the bear stood there and displayed itself to good advantage. Our hatred of the creature entirely vanished. . . . With a clearing horizon and a wider circle of friendship our den now seemed a cheerful home. Our spirits awakened as the gloom of the night was quickly lost."

A few days after the sun had reappeared, they started for

Annoatok, three hundred miles away. Thirty miles from their goal they were once again starving. Dragging behind them their half-stripped sledge, they struggled on, keeping themselves alive by chewing parts of their boots and leather lashings. On April 15, 1909, they pulled themselves to the top of an ice hummock and saw Annoatok in the distance. There, miraculously, the Eskimos glimpsed them and hurried out on sledges.

With them came one American, Harry Whitney, who had come north on Peary's supply ship *Erik* and had received Peary's permission to remain and hunt big game.

"My Eskimos discovered one day," Whitney wrote, "three moving figures slowly making their way towards Annoatok over the tumbled ice of Smith Sound. We could scarcely be certain at first that they were men, but presently our dogs were harnessed to sledges and we were dashing away to meet them. The few miles that intervened were quickly traversed, and what was my astonishment to find one of the travelers to be a white man, and what my further astonishment when he introduced himself as Dr. Frederick A. Cook." Whitney described Cook as "the dirtiest white man I ever saw. . . . His hair was long, reaching to his shoulders."

Whitney also testified: "His two companions dropped on the sledges of the other Eskimos, but Dr. Cook declared he would rather walk."[41]

This is magnificence. After a fabulous journey, and in a starving condition, Cook was still on his own two feet and was attempting to make it all the way. But the certainty of survival was psychologically overpowering. "His strength," Whitney added, "did not last much longer and he rode back."

When they reached Annoatok, Cook, knowing himself to be in a starving condition, requested Whitney to feed him just a little at a time. If he should insist on more, Whitney was to tie him up.

The great fourteen-month journey was over; the titanic Arctic trek, four thousand miles, had ended; and Cook had prevailed.* He was home in the box hut that had been built by himself and Franke, and he was surrounded by the supplies that had been deposited by the *Bradley*. Cook had defeated nature, but now, almost immediately, he was faced by a new opponent whom he was less qualified to oppose — man.

Boatswain Denis Murphy, Peary's man at Annoatok, must have been a brute: "a gangling, raw-boned Newfoundler," the New York *World* reported, "a man of volcanic temperament with an arm of steel."[42] Murphy being illiterate, Cabin Boy Billy Pritchard's job was to read Peary's orders aloud once a week. Such duty was harder than it might seem. The *World* eventually discovered that Harry Whitney had "won the animus of the boatswain by interfering when Murphy bossed the little cabin boy with a club and cuffed the lad until he wailed for mercy."

This creature was not on the scene when the starving Cook arrived. When he did appear he could not imagine "that his chief desired any courtesies extended to Dr. Cook, no matter how famished he was," the *World* noted. "On one occasion when appealing to . . . Murphy . . . to extend the courtesies of the camp to the wasted and half famished explorer, Harry Whitney was threatened by an ax by Murphy and had to threaten Murphy in turn with a shotgun before the firey boatswain's temper cooled. . . . Pritchard, it seems, was on Whitney's side of the quarrel and seized a gun." Murphy temporarily retreated to Etah. All of this Cook toned down when, eventually, he was quizzed by reporters: "There was a dispute between myself and Murphy, who delivered to me the written instructions he had received from Mr. Peary. . . . These instructions showed that he was making a trading station of my depot, the contents of which had been used for trading for furs and skins."[43]

With Murphy temporarily absent, Whitney worked for

* The four thousand figure is Cook's own estimate. Those who deny that he attained the Pole will only allow him 1,640 nautical miles, a figure that does not include any allowance for deviation.

"half a day with hot water and brush removing the dirt that had accumulated on the explorer. . . . It was when he removed the fur clothes that Dr. Cook's terrible condition was seen, as his arms and legs were nothing but skin and bones."[44]*

Harry Whitney was the first person to know that the Doctor had attained the North Pole. On or about April 15, in the box house at Annoatok, and possibly while Whitney was scrubbing away at the dirt, Cook announced his achievement. "Uttering this for the first time in English," he wrote later in *My Attainment*, "it came to me that I was saying a remarkable thing. Yet Mr. Whitney showed no great surprise, and his quiet congratulations confirmed what was on my mind — that I had accomplished no extraordinary or unbelievable thing; for me the polar experience was not the least remarkable considered with our later adventures."

Cook then asked Whitney to tell no one that he had attained the Pole. He wanted to make that announcement himself. He suggested that Whitney merely say that Peary's Farthest North had been beaten. Whitney agreed, and kept his word.†

Cabin Boy Billy Pritchard was in the box house when Cook informed Whitney about the Pole, and was either immediately present or overheard the conversation. Exactly what happened

* Of his reaction to his improved situation Cook wrote: "The most notable change in the personality was a strange foreign feeling. . . . We had become exotic. This . . . was to be a more or less permanent quality . . . native to Nowhere" (*Return from the Pole*, New York, 1952).

† Harry Whitney, sometimes confused with Harry Payne Whitney, became an important figure in the polar controversy, during which he was referred to as "a one-man reception committee for returning discoverers of the North Pole." He was born December 1, 1873, in New Haven, Connecticut, and was the son of Stephen Whitney, a member of an old New England family, and Margaret Johnson Whitney, whose father was a sugar importer in New York City. He attended the public schools of New Haven and St. Paul's School on Long Island. Instead of going to college he sailed for Australia aboard a schooner. Later he owned ranches in Arizona and Montana, and was in the copper business. He eventually settled in Kennett Square, Pennsylvania. He died in 1936.

is not known, but the Doctor did ask the cabin boy to say nothing. Pritchard agreed, and like Whitney, kept his word.

Occasionally, Murphy reappeared. He was told nothing. "Murphy asked me abruptly, 'Have you been beyond 87°?' " Cook said later, "but I was determined not to let Mr. Peary know of my movements, and replied evasively that I had been much further north."*

Aboard the *Roosevelt* the Commander was even more cautious about his own tremendous news.

On April 24, 1909, at Cape Sheridan, Bob Bartlett happened to be on deck when the Eskimos shouted that Peary was coming. As Bartlett recalled it later, he ran out onto the ice and with outstretched hand exclaimed: "I congratulate you, sir, on the discovery of the Pole!" Peary, amused by Bartlett's excitement, laughed and replied: "How did you guess?"

Two other members of the expedition, George Borup and Donald MacMillan, soon understood that Peary had succeeded. They were out in the field establishing depots along the coast when they received a message from Peary: "Arrived on board yesterday. Northern trip entirely satisfactory." This could mean only one thing.

Otherwise, it appears that those associated with Peary's "traveling machine" did not know positively that their work had contributed to a successful and memorable deed. Months later Whitney told reporters: "During the time I was on the *Roosevelt* I was not told by Commander Peary that he had succeeded in reaching the Pole, nor did anyone on the *Roosevelt* tell me. There was, however, some talk among the crew . . . that he must have reached the Pole because he returned so soon, and with plenty of provisions."

In this strange situation Henson's position was most bizarre.

* When the *Roosevelt*, coming south, arrived at Annoatok, Whitney informed Peary of the trouble he had had with Murphy. The New York *World* for October 2, 1909, reported: "Peary did not manifest any interest in the subject. As a matter of fact Peary became cold and forbidding as a Greenland ice cap the moment Cook's name was mentioned."

"From the time of my arrival at the *Roosevelt*, for nearly three weeks," he declared, ". . . I would catch a fleeting glimpse of Commander Peary, but not once in all that time did he speak one word to me."

After the *Roosevelt* had arrived off Annoatok, the situation, it would seem, became comical. With Whitney and Pritchard keeping their word to Cook, no one was telling anybody anything.

4

After resting for only two or three days, Cook prepared to travel to civilization. He intended to sledge south to Upernavik, the capital of Greenland's northernmost province, then catch a boat to Denmark or Canada. The sledge journey to Upernavik was, by itself, a tremendous undertaking. It was long, nearly seven hundred miles by the route he planned to take; and it was dangerous. In 1895, for example, when Peary was thinking of making the same journey, Josephine Peary, who would not have her husband risk his life unnecessarily, raised $10,000 to send a ship north.

Harry Whitney tried to talk Cook out of it. Whitney explained that his family would be sending a ship to pick him up in August. He invited Cook to wait and sail south with him. But the Doctor had no intentions of lingering. Moreover, by northern standards he was now wealthy. Marie Cook had sent some supplies — knives, hatchets, utensils, and delicacies such as butter — north on the Canadian ship *Arctic*. Cook bartered with the Eskimos and soon owned a sledge and dogs.

Before leaving for Upernavik he made a decision, itself entirely rational, which would eventually cause him grief. He divided his papers into two parts. One part he carried with him; the other he left with Whitney. "It is a long and difficult journey to Upernavik," Whitney would explain later. "I was expecting a vessel . . . and therefore Dr. Cook placed in my charge his instruments and such of his personal belongings as might be injured or lost in sledge transportation."[1] The manuscript written in the underground den contained the results of the sextant observations taken during the trip to the Pole. This Cook took with him. But the original work sheets, from which the results had been obtained, he packed into boxes, which he left with Whitney. He also left with Whitney his instruments, and at Whitney's request, a small American flag that he had carried throughout his trek. Should he lose his life going south, Cook explained later, the work sheets would be evidence of his having attained the Pole. "I had to travel over high land in two places," he informed reporters, "with glaciers and difficult places to negotiate. The ice was extremely rough and there was a good deal of water to be expected that would have subjected the instruments to a risk which was entirely unnecessary."[2]

Sometime during the third week in April, only a few days after he had staggered into Annoatok, Cook started for Upernavik. With him he took one reluctant Eskimo, reluctant not because he feared the dangers of the journey but because "*Peari annutu*" (Peary will be mad). On May 21 Cook arrived in Upernavik where, since it was early, he spent several hours walking around the settlement, itself simply a collection of huts for three hundred Eskimos, plus some frame houses for the officials. Finally he knocked on the door of Governor H. Kraul. The Governor himself opened the door and saw, as Cook wrote: "I was a hard-looking visitor. I wore an old sealskin coat, worn bearskin trousers, stockings of hareskin showing above torn seal boots. I was reasonably dirty. My face was haggard and bronzed, my hair was uncut, long and straggling."

The Governor said: "Have you any lice on you?"

The Doctor said no, was then welcomed, and spent the next few weeks as the Governor's guest.

The *Godthaab*, a Danish blubber boat, arrived in June carrying Jens Daugaard-Jensen, inspector for North Greenland, his staff, and a few Danish scientists and reporters. They heard Cook's story with extreme skepticism. Knud Rasmussen was also on the *Godthaab*.* He said of Cook at this time: "He looked upon possible skeptics with dignified and proud superiority." When the *Godthaab* sailed north to call at the Eskimo settlements, the Danes heard, with Rasmussen doing the interpreting, that Etukishook and Ahwelah had been to the Big Nail. By the time the ship returned to Upernavik, the Danes' skepticism had vanished.

Meanwhile the Doctor was anxiously awaiting the arrival of another Danish government ship, the *Hans Egede*, which would carry him to Copenhagen. Greenlanders writing to friends in Denmark described him as being very nervous, very anxious to return to civilization, because he had heard a report that Peary had reached the Pole and he wanted to make his own announcement first. On August 9, 1909, he sailed aboard the *Hans Egede*. The Greenlanders reported that his nervousness disappeared the moment he boarded the steamer. Going south the ship paused at Engesminde and picked up the members of the Stolberg-De Quervain Expedition, sponsored by the Geographic Society of Berlin. The German explorers were delighted to meet Cook and later told reporters that at a point about the Sermittlet Fjord on North Greenland they had been told, by an Eskimo in a kayak, that "one Dr. Cook" had discovered the "Great Nail."[3]

It was at Neurke, a tiny Eskimo settlement, that the Commander learned that Cook was not only alive, but was making

* Rasmussen was the son of a Danish missionary and a part-Eskimo mother. After being educated in Denmark, he returned to Greenland to study the Eskimos, whose language he spoke fluently. The Danes regarded him as an expert on the Eskimos. Cook, who knew him as Kudu the Dane, had met him at North Star Bay and had invited him aboard the *Bradley*. "He was dressed in old greasy furs," Cook recalled, "and from him there came the stench of train oil. . . . I said to Bradley: 'We must invite Rasmussen to dinner.' Bradley said: 'No, for God sakes no! I will get seasick from the odor.' To find a way out of the difficulty I asked the Captain to take Rasmussen to his mess." At the time Rasmussen thought Cook "was something like a secretary to the American hunter. He did not speak a word about his plans." Some months later Rasmussen saw Cook at Etah. "He was at that time outgoing," Rasmussen wrote, "and I had the opportunity to ascertain that a more sensibly equipped expedition could not possibly be thought of."

utterly ridiculous claims, such as: "he told the white men at Etah that he had been a long way North." Peary did not say that he himself had burst out laughing when he heard of the statement. He limited himself to observing that the Eskimos "laughed at Dr. Cook's story." Henson, however, was not so scrupulous. He reported that he and the other members of Peary's expedition considered "the story . . . so ridiculous and absurd that we simply laughed at it." After the collective laugh, Henson added, "we dropped the matter."

But by August 17, when the *Roosevelt* arrived at Etah, Peary was taking the situation seriously, for he understood that he had the task of obtaining the evidence that would prove to the world the ridiculousness of his rival's story. He interviewed Whitney, who reported the minimum: Cook had been "a long ways north." Afterward, silent but menacing, Peary sat in a corner of his cabin in the *Roosevelt* while other members of the expedition cross-examined Etukishook and Ahwelah. There was apparently, in something as rigorous as an extended cross-examination, a communication problem, with Henson being the only cross-examiner who had any ability to speak Eskimo. "We couldn't talk Eskimo," Bob Bartlett said years later. "Peary never really pretended he could talk Eskimo. I know he says in his book that it is easy to pick up the language. It was easy to pick up enough words to get along. But we never talked more than a jargon — just a rough grouping of nouns and verbs and adjectives without any attempt at grammar."[4] The cross-examination, it appears, bewildered Etukishook and Ahwelah. When it was over they went to Whitney and asked him, he reported, "what Peary's men were trying to get them to say. Peary's men had shown the Eskimos maps and papers, but the Eskimos declared that they did not understand these papers."[5]

At any rate, the results of the cross-examination pleased the Commander. When he returned to America he announced that Cook's Eskimos had told him many things, all of which added up to what he believed to be satisfactory evidence that Cook had not even gone out of sight of land. That some might think that his version of what the Eskimos said his rival did was prejudiced, and that he should do whatever he could to protect himself from such charges, does not seem to have occurred to Peary. Harry Whitney, the only American present who was not officially connected with Peary, was not invited to the interrogation.

Months earlier, at Etah, Commander Robert E. Peary had, through no fault of his own, been forced to deal with a problem — Rudolph Franke. Now, and once again at Etah, and once again through no fault of his own, he was forced to deal with another problem — Harry Whitney. The ship that Whitney expected had not arrived, and thinking that it might have been wrecked, he wanted to go home on the *Roosevelt.*

Yes, Peary decided, Whitney could come home on the *Roosevelt*, but — he could not bring Cook's property with him. This Peary forbade. Nevertheless, Whitney packed Cook's instruments, papers, and flag in his own luggage and carried it aboard the *Roosevelt.* Just before sailing, however, Peary called Whitney to his cabin. "When I said I did not want anything belonging to Dr. Cook aboard this ship," Peary declared, "I meant that I did not want a single thing he had. Now I am not going to say anything more about this. I am going to take you on your word as a gentleman not to take a thing belonging to Dr. Cook aboard this ship."

Whitney was now faced with the same dismal situation that had defeated Franke. He could yield to Peary's demands, or he could spend, potentially, a second winter in the Arctic. With the assistance of Bob Bartlett, he placed Cook's property in a cache near the shore and sailed with Peary.

Bartlett later denied that he had any hand in this matter. "Perhaps someone helped him with the box, but I wasn't the one who did it."[6] Henson remembered it otherwise: "Bartlett saw all the things as he helped Mr. Whitney bury them at Etah."[7]

Three days out from Etah, the *Roosevelt* met the schooner *Jeanie*, which the Whitney family had sent north. Whitney transferred to it immediately. At the time he had no reason to think that doubt would pollute Cook's claim to the Pole. He made no attempt, therefore, to go back to Etah to retrieve Cook's property. After the polar controversy had exploded, the New York *Herald* quoted Whitney as explaining: "*Jeanie* is the smallest boat to cruise north of the Arctic Circle in many years. She depended almost entirely on her sails for motive power, for at the time I joined her the auxiliary motor did not work in a way that was satisfactory, and it finally gave out entirely. . . . There was no engineer on board who understood the engine, and there was the possibility that we would get caught in the heavy ice with a ship not fit to navigate in."

On August 26, 1909, the *Roosevelt* stopped at Cape York. There the Commander found a letter left for him by the captain of an American whaling ship. From it he learned, officially, that Cook was claiming the Pole, that he was now in Upernavik, and that he was bound for Copenhagen. The *Roosevelt* set out for Indian Harbor, Labrador, the nearest communications outlet. It was fifteen hundred miles away.

Aboard the *Hans Egede*, bound for Copenhagen, Frederick A. Cook's identity as the conqueror of the North Pole was no longer based on his own say-so. He was cheerfully accepted as such by the Danish party, whose leader, Daugaard-Jensen, had notified the government of Denmark:

> DR. COOK REACHED THE NORTH POLE APRIL 21, 1908. ARRIVED MAY 1909 AT UPERNAVIK FROM CAPE YORK. THE CAPE YORKERS CONFIRM TO KNUD RASMUSSEN THE VOYAGE OF COOK.

Cook himself, at forty-four, had not completely recovered from his trek, but his weight was back to normal, 175 pounds, and he was satisfied about himself and he was happy. He was dressed in the only clothes he owned: a gray jacket and brown trousers, neither of which had been pressed in two years; a visored sailor's cap, and Eskimo boots. His blond hair was very shaggy, his mustache untrimmed.

At Lerwick in the Shetland Islands the ship paused, a boat was put over the side, and a mate rowed him to shore so that he could send two cables. This was Daugaard-Jensen's idea. The Danish official thought that the world should be aware of Cook's deed, at least in its bare details, before Cook arrived in Copenhagen. The first cable was to Marie:

> SUCCESSFUL. WELL. ADDRESS COPENHAGEN.

The second was to the New York *Herald*. He had had no previous contact with that paper but he knew that its publisher, James Gordon Bennett, was interested in explorers. He also knew that he himself possessed only forty dollars, and that his story was worth money. He advised the *Herald* that he was leaving a two-thousand-word exclusive dispatch with the Danish consul at Lerwick, and that he was asking $3,000 for it. Bennett was delighted, and so, on the morning of September 2, 1909, the civilized world finally learned that Cook had attained the North Pole. This news the *Herald* announced in a huge headline, which spread across all columns of its front page:

> THE NORTH POLE IS DISCOVERED BY DR. FREDERICK A. COOK WHO CABLES TO THE HERALD AN EXCLUSIVE ACCOUNT OF HOW HE SET THE AMERICAN FLAG ON THE WORLD'S TOP.

His dispatch entirely filled the rest of page 1, on which his name, and Bradley's, were the only names mentioned. On the following day the *Herald*'s full-page headline read:

> MARVELOUS DETAIL OF DR. COOK'S EXPEDITION TO THE POLE DESCRIBED IN FULL BY JOHN R. BRADLEY, WHO BACKED HIM.

And on the day after that, the headline read, once again full page:

> "I CAN PROVE I REACHED THE POLE" SAYS DR. COOK AS HIS STEAMSHIP NEARS THE PORT OF COPENHAGEN.

On the morning of September 4, 1909, a sparkling day, the *Hans Egede*, with all flags flying and the conqueror of the Pole aboard, steamed into the harbor of Copenhagen. For hundreds of years Denmark had been sending men into the Arctic, and thousands of Danes now lined the waterfront to greet the man who had won the north's greatest prize. The force of their reception dazed him. "Like a bolt from the blue," Cook wrote in *My Attainment of the Pole*, "there burst upon me the clamour of Copenhagen's ovation. . . . Like a darting army of water bugs innumerable craft of all kind were leaping towards us on the sun-lit water. People shouted, it seemed, in every tongue. Wave after wave of cheering rolled over the water. . . . All about, balancing on unsteady craft, their heads hooded in black, were the omnipresent picture operators at work. All this passed as a moving picture itself, I standing there dazed, simply dazed."

As the ship slowed, the welcoming committee came aboard and Cook, standing at the head of the ladder, was congratulated by the King of Denmark's eldest son, the tall, silk-hatted Crown Prince Christian; by the King's brother, Prince Waldemar; and by the American Minister, Maurice Egan. Then he followed them down the ladder into a launch. Again the cheers rolled over the water, and as he stepped ashore, his cap raised in gratitude, a woman rushed forward with a bouquet of roses. Then the crowd reached out to touch him and he lost the roses, lost his cuff links, even lost his coat buttons. Minister Egan, Commander Hovgaard, master of the King's yacht, and one policeman formed a ring about him. They were joined by W. A. Stead, Hearst's principal representative in Europe. For three days now the world had known that the Doctor had won the Pole, but had learned little else about him. Stead went to work immediately. As Cook and his bodyguards attempted to work their way through the surging crowd, Stead seized him around the waist from the rear and was soon able to report: "In the scrimmage I learned first that Cook is an inch below my own height, which is 5 feet 9½ inches, and that I could talk into his ear without stooping; second, from the grip around his waist I learned that he is well set-up, not spare but solid, with no superfluous flesh. . . . He is self-composed and took placidly the enthusiasm of the crowd. . . . These things I sensed as I held him in a bear-like hug, while we slowly plowed our way toward the carriage."

After they had reached the carriages and the parade had proceeded a short distance, they were halted by the pressure of the crowd. Cook and the others squeezed their way through the gate of the Meteorological Institute. It had an iron fence around it, and so, for the first time since landing, he had a chance to draw a deep breath. Meanwhile the crowd was becoming impatient. Then the Crown Prince arrived and said:

"Doctor, you must speak to them and let them see you."

"But I speak no Danish. They couldn't understand me, even if I had something to say, which I have not."

"Speak anything in any language. They probably will not know the difference anyway."[8]

Accordingly, from the balcony of an upper window of the Institute, he addressed a sea of excited faces. He had no memory of what he said, but the applause was tremendous.

Meanwhile, Minister Egan had arranged to have his own carriage brought up to the front door of the Institute, and a taxi to the rear entrance. Accompanied only by Commander Hovgaard, the Doctor slipped out the back way and, while one photographer caught him beaming with relief, easily reached the taxi and rode to the Phoenix Hotel. In his suite, bedecked with flowers and stacks of telegrams, he found that the Danes, who had taken his measurements while he was still at sea, had provided a complete wardrobe. A barber and a manicurist soon appeared. He forgot to tip the manicurist, a memory that would linger for months. He was delighted when, most unexpectedly, his old trailmate from the first McKinley expedition, Ralph Shainwald, entered his suite. Shainwald, who was touring Europe, took charge of his valeting.

He then went to the American Legation. "The gentleman who appeared faultlessly attired for luncheon," Minister Egan noted, "was a far different person from the Robinson Crusoe figure of the morning. There was no rest, however. . . . Admirers . . . filled the courtyard, lined the stairs, and even flowed into the drawing room. He was quite willing to answer questions."

He was then driven to the palace, where he had a two-hour interview with the elderly King.

Nine hours earlier, while Stead was still hugging him from the rear, Cook had agreed to a press conference, but had requested that it be put off until the following day. This, of course, was impossible. When he returned to his hotel from the palace a growling squad of reporters confronted him. They were led by Stead, who had prepared a list of questions entitled, "When Is a Discoverer Not a Discoverer?" to which answers were demanded. There then took place, in a deserted banquet hall, an hour-long interview, which produced, as one reporter phrased it, "the first hunk of raw meat thrown to a ravening world."

At the table in the banquet hall Cook sat for a moment with his face bowed in his hands so that he could get a grip on himself. Then Stead, gray, bearded, and alert, stood up. H. M. Lyon's description of what he called the "Great Interview" was published in *Collier's* magazine, and is worth repeating:

"Two things the press of the world would like to have Doctor Cook express an opinion about, deposed Stead. Not that he . . . or any of the rest of the press of the world had the slightest doubts of Doctor Cook's et cetera, et cetera; but inasmuch as the whole affair was up in the air, would he, Doctor Cook, say that he really thought, so far as he was able to judge, in his own mind, and deep down in his own heart, and all that sort of thing, that he had discovered the North Pole?

" 'I think so,' replied Doctor Cook, blushing like a schoolboy.

" 'You have set your foot "right on it," ' interpolated Stead.

" 'Oh, I couldn't say that. I got to where there wasn't any longitude.'

"A terrific nodding of reporters' heads. He had got to where there wasn't any longitude. Pencils bristled.

" 'Well, Doctor Cook — now, mind you, these are not my personal sentiments' (slapping Cook heartily on shoulder) —

'I am a Cookite myself from the top of my head to the soles of my feet — but the world, we can readily foresee, is going to be divided into Cookites and anti-Cookites. For the benefit of us Cookites, then, will you say, first, that your records are authentic, and, second, that you consider yourself a competent man to take down records?'

"Cook admitted that he had that sort of an opinion of himself. He had carried certain instruments, such as a sextant, a chronometer, and a barometer, and he affirmed that he knew how to use these instruments.

" 'But you did not set your foot,' returned Stead, 'upon the exact point of the Pole.'

" 'I doubt if anybody could do that. I got within the circle, I think. I went around it for two days making observations.

" 'What does it look like?' interrupted a mild-voiced person.

" 'Ice,' testified the explorer.

" 'Ah, yes, ice,' repeated the mild person.

"Stead came back to his point. 'If you did not set foot on the Pole, Doctor, you at least got within gunshot of it. I say, from where you stood you could have fired a bullet over the exact point.'

" 'Yes, I should say so.'

"A Dane in the background was displaying convulsions. His larynx was trying to adjust . . . to emit some English. 'What — did — you — say — about — a — gun?'

" 'He could have shot a gun across the Pole,' announced Stead.

"Every reporter in the room wrote that down.

" 'Now some details as to your journey up there, Doctor; your dash to the Pole.'

" 'It was simply that — a dash. We did not try to carry all the heavy instruments. . . . Therefore, there is nothing so very scientific about the achievement. . . .

" 'You say "we" traveled,' continued Stead. 'Do you mean — '

" 'Myself and the two Eskimos.' Then the explorer made appropriate Eskimo noises. It transpired that he was naming the Eskimos. A voice asked him to spell the names. Cook looked rather bored and started in on the alphabet. It took about two minutes for each name, the going being rather heavy. Mr. Stead detonated each letter as it fell from the explorer's lips.

" 'You can get these two men to testify that you have been to the Pole?' was the next question.

" 'Yes. That is, they know where they went. They have no knowledge of . . . latitude and longitude. . . . They can testify in a general way to the number of days' travel they made from a certain point of departure. . . .

"Then Cook very patiently explained to the circle of rather glittering eyes that he had no reasons for trying to hoodwink the world as to his achievement.

" 'It would take a colossal cheek,' remarked Stead, frankly — but that they would have to take his word for it that he had been where he said he had been until his records could be examined by a proper board. 'I am in this work for the love of the work, gentlemen,' he said with a tired, patient smile. 'I am not in it for money. And I have brought back just exactly the sort of records and proofs that every Arctic explorer brings back.'

"The press of the world was beginning to warm up to the discoverer. Previously they had had their doubts. The press of the world also began to show signs of wanting to ask silly questions. Such as: Did the explorer like to eat fox? . . .

"Had he planted the Stars and Stripes at the Pole? Well, he had set up a flag and taken a photograph of it. But afterward he had taken this flag down. . . . Whitney now has this. There was now a little flag, in a metal cylinder, reposing somewhere in the drift.

" 'Stars and Stripes?' insisted Stead.

" 'Yes,' admitted Cook. 'Stars and Stripes.' Just what was in Mr. Stead's mind at the time is occult. . . .

"Would he please spell the Eskimos' names again? He did so, Stead accompanying. . . .

"A puckery-lipped, thin little man sidled up and said: 'One moment, Doctor Cook. Just one moment.'

" 'What is it?' he asked.

" 'I want to know, are you a Christian?'

" 'I'm afraid I can't answer that question without being misunderstood. Just say in a general way that I am, but that I don't belong to any particular church.'

" 'One moment, Doctor. Will you deliver an address — '

" 'Do you want to sell your book? At any price?'

" 'Will you sign a contract for the lecture platform?'

"But the explorer had fled. The Great Interview was over."[9]

Afterward the United Press correspondent wrote:

"Calm and imperturbable though wincing under the cruelty of the thrusts . . . Dr. Cook modestly met every inquiry with a directness and frankness that quickly won all of his hearers."[10]

The representative of the London *Times* wrote:

"He entirely satisfied me as to his good faith. The sincere manner in which he answered awkward questions produced in all present a profound impression."[11]

And Stead wrote:

"Some believed in Dr. Cook at first; all believe in him now."

But Stead's "all" was not quite accurate. From the start, Philip Gibbs, a young and enterprising English journalist who would eventually be knighted, was convinced that Cook was out to bluff the world. Gibbs had been one in a group of reporters in a motor boat who had shouted questions to Cook when he was still aboard the *Hans Egede*. "They came along in a motor boat," Cook said later. "I talked to them for five minutes — all went back and wrote pages of polar stuff."[12] Of this encounter Gibbs wrote: "Dr. Cook, the hero, was hiding in his cabin. He . . . came out . . . with a livid look, almost green. I never saw guilt and fear more clearly written on any human face. He could barely pull himself together when the Crown Prince of Denmark boarded his ship." Of Gibbs' charges Cook observed: "Since all the other reporters got from . . . this same interview and all decried Gibbs' reports publicly — I paid little further attention to him." As Cook indicated, details such as those reported by Gibbs were noticed by no other reporter, and Gibbs was taken off the story.

Later that evening the Doctor met with officials of the Royal Danish Geographic Society. They questioned him about his astronomical observations. The result was that the society decided to award him its Gold Medal.

Such was the manner in which he spent his first day in civilization.

At some time during the following day he was visited by officials and scientists of the University of Copenhagen. Afterward their leader, Rector Torp, announced that they had "put an exhaustive series of mathematical questions to Dr. Cook, based particularly on those of his contentions on which doubt had been cast. Dr. Cook answered them all to our full satisfaction. He showed no nervousness or excitement at any time."[13]

Being so completely certain of his own position, and believing that his property was safe with Harry Whitney, Cook then volunteered to submit to the University of Copenhagen his field calculations and instruments. He would do so, he said, as soon as he had obtained them from Whitney. This proposal Rector Torp accepted on behalf of the university.

Meanwhile, his mail was huge and he was besieged by invitations. The New York *Herald* reported:

"A correspondent saw him in his apartments at the Hotel Phoenix, which were gaily bedecked with flowers and flags. The explorer was in the hands of a barber. He was trying to talk and read a telegram at the same time. Outside the door a German count and the president of a geographical society waited for an audience. Many ladies had comfortably ensconced themselves in the halls and about the stairway.

"A secretary from the American legation jumped constantly to answer phone calls, and in the intervals attempted to cope with a mail bigger than that of presidential candidates. In the meantime a string of messages came popping in with cards. 'Are you getting tired of this?' the correspondent inquired.

" 'No man can honestly say that he was tired of such attention after so short an experience,' Dr. Cook replied, scanning a note from the German Minister, 'but I do feel that I am getting more attention than my share. Now what shall I do about this?'

he asked, picking up an invitation . . . to address the Berlin Colonial Society. 'I would like to do that, of course, but I want to get back to America.'

" 'I suspect that there are a few people who would like to see you.'

" 'I know of three,' said Dr. Cook, smiling."[14]

He was thinking of his wife and daughters.

Two years later, in *My Attainment of the Pole*, he would write: "I supposed that the newspapers would announce my return, and that there would be a three-days' breath of attention, and that that would be all." And as his third day in civilization was drawing to a close, such was the way things appeared. The story was dying and the reporters were leaving Copenhagen. That night a Danish publisher gave a banquet for those correspondents who remained. It was planned as an evening of eating, drinking, and speeches, and the Doctor was the guest of honor. But soon after the first speaker had begun, a messenger slipped into the banquet room and handed the host an envelope. He opened it, read it, and was surprised. He then passed it on to Stead, who after reading it, rose, held out his hand for silence, and read aloud: "In a wire from Indian Harbor, Labrador, dated September 6, 1909, Peary says: 'Stars and Stripes nailed to Pole.' "

Cook is the best witness of what happened next.

"The tension was tremendous in that banquet hall," he wrote, "as the newspaper men grasped the significance of the message. A running fire of argument broke out around the table."[15] Many of the reporters branded the cable a hoax, mainly because of the flamboyant language. But Cook thought it did sound like Peary. When asked to comment he stood up and said: "I am proud that a fellow American has reached the Pole. As Rear Admiral Schley said at Santiago, 'There is glory enough for us all.' He is a brave man and I am confident that if the reports are true his observations will confirm mine and set at rest all doubts." Afterward, an attempt was made to go through with the banquet, but it failed. "The guests, their super-developed news sense atingle," he wrote, " . . . slipped away singly at first, finally en masse, to typewriters and telegraph stations."

So ended his third day in civilization.

A day or so earlier, prodded by Minister Egan, Cook had cabled the President, now William Howard Taft, the information that he, an American citizen, had reached the North Pole. The President had responded with congratulations.

Back at the cable station at Indian Harbor, the politically aware Commander needed no man to suggest how he should spread his news. One of Peary's minor talents was an ability to get everyone into the act. At the Pole he had unfurled not only the Stars and Stripes, but the flags of the Daughters of the American Revolution, the Navy League, the Red Cross, and his college fraternity, Delta Kappa Epsilon. Now he announced his achievement in cables to the President, the Department of State, the Navy, the Governor of Newfoundland, his publishers, and Kane Lodge, No. 454, F. and A.M., of Brooklyn. To Herbert Bridgman he cabled:

> WIRE ALL PRINCIPAL HOME AND FOREIGN GEOGRAPHICAL SOCIETIES OF ALL NATIONS, INCLUDING JAPAN, BRAZIL, ETC., THAT THE NORTH POLE WAS REACHED APRIL SIXTH BY PEARY ARCTIC CLUB'S EXPEDITION UNDER COMMANDER PEARY.

With this out of the way, he notified the Associated Press on September 7:

> COOK'S STORY SHOULD NOT BE TAKEN TOO SERIOUSLY. THE TWO ESKIMOS WHO ACCOMPANIED HIM SAY HE WENT NO DISTANCE NORTH AND NOT OUT OF SIGHT OF LAND. OTHER MEMBERS OF THE TRIBE CORROBORATE THEIR STORY.

So began the tremendous North Pole controversy.

Three days later Peary cabled the New York *Herald:*

> DO NOT IMAGINE HERALD LIKELY TO BE IMPOSED UPON BY COOK STORY, BUT FOR YOUR

> INFORMATION COOK HAS SIMPLY HANDED THE PUBLIC A GOLD BRICK. HE'S NOT BEEN AT THE POLE APRIL 21, OR ANY OTHER TIME. THE ABOVE STATEMENT IS MADE ADVISEDLY AND AT THE PROPER TIME WILL BE BACKED BY PROOF.

The newspaper-reading public was astounded. At the end of over three hundred years of endeavor, the North Pole — for earth-bound man "the last great geographic prize" — had been claimed not by just one but by two explorers. And, astonishingly enough, inside a period of five days. And now one of the explorers was calling his rival a liar and a fraud, and saying he could prove it. The *Nation* called the situation "an unparalleled scientific sensation which may continue for years to come."

No member of Peary's expedition recorded their impressions of the Commander as the *Roosevelt* sailed south from Etah. But a Captain Blanford, who dined aboard the ship at Battle Harbor, a little town at the southeastern point of Labrador, reported: "Peary was in a terrible rage against Cook for what he called his brazen effrontery in concocting such a story. Peary said Cook's story should be classed with Munchausen. Just as soon as he reached civilization he would tell a story which would puncture Cook's bubble and astound the world."

Meanwhile, in New York, Herbert L. Bridgman and other members of the Peary Arctic Club were dismayed by their man's fierceness. "Bridgman was frantic . . . because he could not reach Peary, but Peary's wires were coming through," Cook eventually learned and informed a friend. "Finally Bridgman went to the Herald and over their system got messages through to Peary asking him to close his attacks . . . and give no details about his work. Then followed messages to meet somewhere for a conference before anything else was to be given out."[16]

Although Cook could supply no date, the contact was definitely made before September 16, when, while the *Roosevelt* was still at Battle Harbor, thirty-two newsmen arrived aboard the Canadian cable-layer *Tyrian.* Among them, representing the New York *World*, was a splendid reporter named Barton W. Currie.

"Three whaleboat loads of reporters and photographers swept down upon the *Roosevelt*," Currie wrote, "like so many boarding parties of pirates, swarming over the sides by ladders and ropes or anything handy. . . . Peary was in his cabin. . . . As he stepped out onto the broad afterdeck he faced the muzzles of a dozen cameras, and what might have appeared to him as the onslaught of an eager band come to strip him of his secrets. . . . As Peary . . . squared his broad shoulders against the mizzenmast . . . the eyes of all the boarding journalists were suddenly drawn to the American flag that fluttered above. This seemed to have an electrical effect . . . and before a word was spoken to Peary three rousing cheers were sent up to him. He bowed to this and smiled from ear to ear, showing . . . his big strong teeth, that are almost wolfish. . . . He looked a good deal like a dramatized miner, in his square-cut blue flannel shirt, rough black trousers and huge brimmed sombrero. His sandy mustache bristled out on both sides like two rough brushes twisted to a point. There was a two-day's growth upon his cheeks. But his skin was clear as a woman's and remarkably smooth for a man of his years. Every inch of him, every ounce of him was as hard as Bessemer steel."

Peary's first words were: "Gentlemen, I thank you for coming to see me. It is an honor and I want to meet every one of you." He then passed around the circle shaking hands. Next, he asked to be excused long enough to read some letters that had been brought to him, and said he would soon grant an interview. It took place an hour or so later, in a large twine loft over a trading store. The loft was barren of chairs and contained only one small bench, some casks, and heaps of cod nets and trawling traps. Peary arrived with Captains Dickson of the *Tyrian* and Bartlett of the *Roosevelt.* He settled himself on a pile of nets and the reporters perched wherever they could, or squatted on the floor.

"The sunlight that streamed into the low windows of the loft," Currie wrote, "was as brilliant as the concentrated rays of a spotlight, cutting out vivid patterns on the floor and giving a peculiar stagey effect. . . . Peary's big, sandy head, his ever-pulsating muscles and constantly working nostrils stood out in a shaft of this vivid sunlight with cameo sharpness. A Labrador gale, uncanny in the brilliant sunlight, whistled and groaned and snarled with wolfish howls at the eaves. The scene was one that cut itself indelibly into the mind.

"Commander Peary puffed out his chest with a deep inhale of breath as he squared off for the first question."

He was asked if he had found any evidence of Cook at the Pole.

" 'There was not the slightest indication of Cook or anyone else.'

"This was said with a vehemence that approached a snarl.

" 'Is it possible,' broke in another of the interviewers, 'that Cook might have been there and you not have found any evidence of him?'

" 'Yes,' said Peary with another snap of the jaws, then checked himself suddenly and put out his hand. 'Wait a minute, I said yes, but let me put it this way. Without reference to Cook, I will say that there are hundreds of routes outside of mine, any one of which could have been taken by a *reputable* explorer with a *well-equipped** expedition and have left no traces which I would have noticed.'

"As Peary settled back with a grim smile this question was suddenly sprung:

" 'Is it possible to fake observations of the Pole so as to deceive scientists?'

"Peary stood up and while the muscles of his face worked convulsively, snapped back:

" 'In the opinion of Admiral Sir George Nares of the British Navy, Admiral Melville of the United States Navy, and myself, it would have been possible for a skillful man to fake observations of the Pole, even to the extent of deceiving scientists.'

* Emphasis added.

"Just as another question was being put Commander Peary broke in with a nervous gesture and said:

" 'Now we are getting on this question of Cook, and I want to tell you where I stand so that you won't ask me any more questions of this kind: with respect to Dr. Cook and his claims, I repeat what I have said that Dr. Cook has not been at the Pole. I shall pay no attention to any fake stories or side issues. . . . The issue is: has Cook been at the Pole? Now I do not propose to answer that any further or to produce my proof until there is a properly authorized statement by Dr. Cook before a reliable, disinterested party. I do not propose to make any reply to what statements or stories friends or adherents of Dr. Cook may issue.'

". . . Commander Peary, when questioned . . . concerning his observations, said he was not prepared to discuss them beyond a certain point. . . . 'I am not at liberty to say just what I observed when I made sure I was at the Pole.'

"Peary indulged in a peculiar smile at this point. That he would not go beyond a certain mysterious line was palpable in his attitude. Without waiting for another question he went on:

" 'I don't want to appear to refuse to answer questions, but, gentlemen, you must understand that under the peculiar circumstances which now exist . . . I do not feel that I can consistently give information as to what I observed as to conditions at the Pole. I propose to hold back these facts until other statements as to conditions at the Pole have been submitted. . . .'

"This question was put to Commander Peary:

" '. . . In your dash to the Pole you say that above the 89th parallel you made one march of forty miles in twelve hours. Is this not exceptionally fast traveling for the Arctic?'

"Commander Peary threw back his head and expanded his chest. Then, with his usual click of the teeth, as if biting off the subject forever, he responded:

" 'The speed from the 89th parallel to the Pole was not fast for me, but would have been very fast for any other expedition.' "[17]

And so, while giving no information about himself, he was demanding that Cook produce plenty. He was, in fact, playing his hand with exceptional caginess. And it was a curious hand. That there had been no formal announcement, aboard the *Roosevelt*, that he had reached the Pole, was a small matter. But that the voyage south was not swift was interesting. The Doctor had charged south to Upernavik, and had the jitters until he sailed for Denmark. But Peary, before informing the world of his accomplishments, had lingered along the route.

He had, indeed, his secrets. His official position has always been that he did not learn that Cook was claiming the Pole until he arrived at Cape York, but Barton W. Currie would soon write of Peary at Sydney, Nova Scotia:

"His interviewers put to Peary again the question . . . 'When did you first hear that Dr. Cook claimed to have discovered the North Pole? Was it when you got the letter from Captain Walker of the whaler Morning at Cape York?'

" 'I heard while in Etah that —' His jaws snapped together like a bear trap and he flung himself back in the chair so that it creaked and rocked. Winking his eyelids and working his jaws for a moment, he said more softly than he had yet spoken:

" 'I do not wish to say any more yet. Let us waive that.' "

Robert E. Peary was a man who had trouble remembering what he had said previously, and he had come close to letting something slip.

Currie continued:

"Matt Henson threw some light on the mystery. . . . It was at Etah, Henson said, that the Commander first heard of Cook's . . . dash. . . . The *Roosevelt* got to Etah on August 13,* nine days before the letter from the whaling skipper was received."[18]

Why did Peary conceal such items? Why was he so slow

* In *Hampton's* magazine for September, 1910, Peary said the *Roosevelt* arrived at Etah on August 17. Its timetable was given as: July 18, sailed south from winter quarters; August 17, arrived Etah; August 26, left Cape York; September 5, arrived Indian Harbor; September 21, arrived Sydney, Nova Scotia.

about spreading his huge news? No one will ever know what was on the mind of this dramatic man as he lingered, but it is possible to point to a very substantial advantage that he gained by doing so. It was that, as shall be shown, before sending the New York *Times* his original story on what he personally had seen about the Pole, he was able to read what Cook had reported about conditions at that same spot.

It was a curious hand.

In Copenhagen the reaction to Peary's vehemence was immediate and informed. The *National Tidende* observed that Knud Rasmussen's support of Cook was based on reliable evidence, and that Peary was too much a party to the case for his word on what the Eskimos told him to be accepted unconditionally: "Those who remember how Peary behaved when . . . he saw Sverdrup as his competitor will be certain that Peary would be an uncompromising enemy of anybody having the audacity to rival him in a run for the Pole."

Sverdrup himself declared that Peary would never admit that the Pole had been reached before he got there. He described Peary as the most jealous of men, certain that he had a lease on the Pole: "He is sure to be a keen, sharp adversary and is not afraid of using any means."

And Dr. Frederick A. Cook said: "To Mr. Peary, the explorer, I am still willing to tip my hat. But Mr. Peary's unfounded accusations have disclosed another side of his character." About this time he proposed that the Danish government send a ship at his expense to get Etukishook and Ahwelah. The authorities replied that it was too late in the season.[19]

But otherwise the Danes were splendid. Twelve hundred persons attended the ceremony when the university made him a Doctor of Philosophy. When he stood up to speak he could not say a word for the first five minutes because of the continuous applause. His last public appearance was before the Royal Danish Geographic Society. By this time he was very tired. "At the conclusion of my address," he wrote years later, "I stepped down from the platform ignorant that a decoration was to be conferred upon me. . . . Prince Christian passed me, mounting the rostrum, as I stepped down. He murmured something that I did not understand. Then as I remained standing below him . . . he began a speech of presentation of a Gold Medal. . . . My blunder embarrassed him so he floundered sadly in his address and I fidgeted in complete discomfiture through the ceremony. I never knew whether I received the medal from the floor or stepped back up to the level of the presentor."[20]

In addition to his medal and his honorary degree, he acquired in Copenhagen what he needed most of all, a secretary. "By the time I left Copenhagen, as I figured later," he wrote in *My Attainment of the Pole*, "offers for book and magazine material had aggregated just one and one-half million dollars. . . . During the first few days I had absolutely no system for caring for this correspondence, hundreds of important cablegrams remained unopened, and huge offers of money were ignored. It was only after Minister Egan sent Walter Lonsdale, in response to my request for a competent secretary, that some intelligible information was gleaned from the mass of correspondence."

Walter Lonsdale, a member of Egan's personal staff, remained with Cook for three months but was unable to control the Doctor's enthusiasm for ignoring money. Although *Hampton's* magazine offered to meet any price he asked for magazine rights to his story, and Hearst offered to double anyone else's bid for newspaper and magazine rights, he simply sold his story to James Gordon Bennett for $25,000. The magazine *Town Topics* estimated that this story alone was worth $100,000. "Mr. Bennett offered me $5,000 additional for the European rights," Cook wrote. ". . . To this offer I made no reply, giving Mr. Bennett the sole news rights of the story for the entire world." The *Matin* of Paris offered him $50,000 for the rights to the French translation of the story that would appear in the *Herald*. This figure included the fee for a lecture in Paris. Only after he had sailed did he realize that he could have gone to Paris and given the lecture, then sailed to New York by a fast boat.

Those who knew how he was handling his business affairs considered the situation pitiful. Stead described him as "a naive, inexperienced child who sorely needed someone to . . . tell him what he ought to do in his own interests."

But he was trying to do the larger things correctly, and he considered that the larger things included courtesy. Yes, he wanted to get home, but he also wanted to show his gratitude to Denmark. He chose, therefore, to return to America on the *Oscar II*. It was a ten-day boat, but it flew the flag of Denmark.

He was returning to a land in which, at the time, he had a multitude of supporters and not too many critics. Peary's accusations had not been admired by the public. A Captain Frank A. Houghton, identified in the *Herald* as the builder of the *Roosevelt*, declared: "I know Commander Peary quite well. His latest manifesto, to the effect that Dr. Cook . . . shall now produce his proofs that he has been to the Pole, before his accuser will produce his to the contrary, is really refreshing. . . . The attitude of Dr. Cook is straightforward and manly throughout." The editor of *Current Literature* wrote: "There was no lack of criticism for Peary's reflections on him as premature and inspired by envy."

But at the same time, many publications were sniping at the Doctor. Selling the *Herald* the exclusive rights to his story had been a mistake. His position would have been better if he had given his dispatch to all the wire services, who would have distributed his news to virtually every daily paper in the country. In the extremely competitive journalistic war that soon developed, those newspapers who were not able to purchase syndication rights to the story did not hesitate to treat him aggressively. "Slighted journalists," the worldly *Town Topics* noted, "have raised and encouraged envious scientists to formulate doubts as to the accuracy of Cook's statements."

In New York, immediately after Cook's original dispatch had been published, the Peary Arctic Club hacked at two of his statements. The first was that his average daily mileage was fifteen geographical miles per day going north to the Pole. Such speed, the club and its friends maintained, was impossible. Cyrus C. Adams of the American Geographic Society wrote: "Four miles per day is considered a fair average over polar ice, although Cagni made seven miles." Then Peary's initial account of his expedition broke in the New York *Times* and the world learned that the Commander claimed an average of twenty-five miles per day. The club, accordingly, abandoned that line of belittlement. And the club had also scoffed at Cook's witnesses — two Eskimos. The club was confident that its own man's certifiers would be respectable and reassuring. Bridgman said: "I believe two white men were with Peary at the Pole to collaborate his observations." But when the club learned that it was just black Henson, that line of belittlement was also abandoned.

And so, initially, other arguments were used against Cook. His ability to use a sextant was challenged. The supply of food that he took with him was "proved" inadequate. Marie Cook told the United Press: "My faith has never wavered and I am glad my judgment of my husband's ability has been vindicated." Even so, reports circulated that the domestic life of the Cooks was unhappy, and that there would be a separation. This was formally denied by Dr. R. T. Davidson, speaking for Marie Cook.

The New York *Times* had paid Peary $4,000 in advance for the story of his expedition, but it treated Cook fairly at first. In the days immediately following his announcement typical one-column headlines in that paper read:

SCIENTISTS ACCEPT DR. COOK'S EXPLOIT

EXPLORERS PRAISE COOK'S BRAVERY

QUESTIONERS LIKE MANNER OF DR. COOK

AMERICAN SCIENTISTS BELIEVE IN COOK

But after Peary's announcement, the *Times* changed its tune:

COOK'S POSITION WORRIES FRENCH

EUROPE IS AGAINST COOK:
LAUGHS AT SUGGESTION OF A CONTROVERSY WITH PEARY

WASHINGTON AWAITS PROOFS
PEARY'S MESSAGE STRENGTHENS DOUBT IN COOK'S STORY

NO PROOF THAT COOK SCALED MT. MCKINLEY

The *Nation* declared: " 'Controversy' is altogether too dignified a term to describe the miserable war of words that now rages about the Pole. The situation is deplorable. The most dramatic achievement in the scientific annals of the age is being written down in Billingsgate."

That the expeditions to the Pole were scientifically important was a widespread misunderstanding. One man who knew that they were sporting achievements only was John R. Bradley. He told a reporter:

"You must understand just what this expedition was. It was not scientific in aim. . . . He started out simply to make a dash for the Pole. He made it. He won. . . . Think of the trip back. That means more to me than finding the Pole. What an exploit it was. What a man to do it! Why, it ought to put life into every boy in America."

"You think the exploit typically American?"

"I certainly do. It was original, ingenious, daring. Do you remember when our horses won at the English races and made a hero out of Tod Sloan? Well, do you know what did the trick? It was light shoes. English horses wore heavy shoes, had worn them for years, and the owners never thought of changing. That's the English way. The American way is to try new tricks, so we shod our horses light and won. Ever climb Pike's peak . . . or run a race, or take a long trail? Then you know what one ounce means at the end of it. Dr. Cook applied this principle to his trip. Of course there were other factors that helped him win. He had the advantage of others' experience and used it. That's natural. If you started to build a steamship today you wouldn't go back to Fulton's model, would you? Then he had the right route, knew how to live like an Eskimo, had good dogs, sleds, men, a wonderful constitution, a physician's knowledge, and luck — all these things helped wonderfully; but after all, what is the chief difference between Dr. Cook's expedition and every other effort to reach the Pole? Why, he went light. He had aluminum shoes on, you might say . . . it was a dash to the Pole . . . and he won."

Bradley also said, of Cook's journey: "I call it a good sporting performance — the greatest ever."[21]

Dr. Frederick A. Cook sailed for America on September 9, 1909. The Danes gave him a tremendous send-off. The people broke through the police barriers, women threw flowers, the ships in the harbor made a great display, and a Danish admiral informed him: "Green-eyed envy and jealousy are doing their envenomed work, but we in Denmark believe in you absolutely."

In his cabin he said to Lonsdale: "Ten days of peace and quiet. Ten days, and I'll be home."

II

Nature (Human) Versus Cook

5

CAPTAIN BRADLEY OSBORN was an American soldier of fortune. "I am an Admiral, sir," he informed one reporter. "I was an Admiral in the Mexican navy after the Civil War. I have been a Commander in the navies of Argentina and Venezuela. The latter country decorated me with the Order of Busto del Liberador. I was the only newspaper man at the fall of Fort Sumter. . . . I was Farragut's signal officer at New Orleans. I was with Dupont at Port Royal. I helped man the old St. Mary at Honolulu . . . when her commander called for volunteers to fight the two French men-of-war at that harbor. I happened to be there after a whaling voyage. I had been on several whaling voyages and in the Arctic and Antarctic fur trade."

Now, in his eighty-first year, Osbon was a familiar figure on the streets of New York, where he regularly appeared in a bottle-green frock coat. Still peppery and involved, he was secretary of the Arctic Club of America. This organization, totally unconnected with the Peary Arctic Club, had been founded by the survivors of Cook's ill-fated *Miranda* expedition of 1894, and its members, led by Osbon, had made the arrangements for that event of which the New York *Herald* would report: "He who first stood upon the apex of the world, was welcomed home yesterday amid a demonstration of popular confidence and enthusiasm without a parallel in the history of this city."

The excitement began early in the morning on September 21, 1909.

"I was up with the rising of the sun," Cook wrote. "We arrived at Quarantine soon after seven. About us on the waves danced a dozen tugs with reporters."

One of the tugs was the *Gilkenson*, which carried Marie and the children, plus his brothers and John R. Bradley. As the tug approached, the *Oscar II* prepared to lower a gangplank. Soon William Cook was rushing up the gangplank while the Doctor, dressed in frock coat and silk hat, was rushing down. They shook hands warmly, then descended to the *Gilkenson*. Meanwhile, fifty reporters and photographers had boarded the liner and a few had slipped down to the tug and were present when Cook greeted his wife. "Mrs. Cook appeared pale and nervous when she emerged from her cabin, and she apparently did not relish the battery of photographers she had to face. She and her husband embraced silently and both seemed too much affected to say anything for several moments."

Finally Cook asked: "Where are the children?"

Ten-year-old Ruth was the first to appear. He took her in his arms and kissed her. Then came Helene, a wistful youngster of four. "Hurrah for my father and the Pole!" she cried as she rushed into his arms.

After the tug had cut away from the *Oscar II*, the reporters still aboard the liner hired launches and soon swarmed over the sides of the *Gilkenson*. Bradley rushed Cook into a cabin, but he came out repeatedly to pose for the photographers. Both the reporters and his brothers noticed that he was tired — "Bronzed and happy, though very tired" — and his brothers took turns begging the photographers to allow him a few moments with his wife. "He is worn out," William Cook declared, "and if this thing goes on he will break down."

The *Gilkenson* brought him to the *Grand Republic*, a white side-wheeler that normally carried excursionists. Now she was graced with bunting in the flags of all nations and was carrying five hundred admirers of Frederick A. Cook, none of whom gave a damn for Peary's accusations, and all of whom carried

American flags and behaved like characters in an animated cartoon. "When the tug neared the forward port gangway," a reporter noted, "there was a wild rush of those on board to this point. The old vessel was sadly listed to one side by this rush."

The wilder part of the day began as soon as he transferred to the *Grand Republic*. Since the Peary Arctic Club had managed to have the Mayor of New York refuse to allow a public reception in Manhattan, it was to Brooklyn, his home for almost forty years, that Cook was returning in triumph.* Bird S. Coler, president of the Borough of Brooklyn, was aboard the *Grand Republic*, and immediately attempted to deliver his official speech of welcome. The crowd, however, had already encircled the hero, who was swept across the freight deck and up into the salon. Someplace along the line a pretty girl gave him a garland of roses and made a little speech that began, "You, hero of the Northland." Cook blushed and said "Thank you."

In the salon Captain Osbon, fearing that he would not get a chance to speak for the Arctic Club of America, elbowed his way through the throng and reached Cook's side, then shouted: "The Arctic Club should have a chance here! This is the Arctic Club's boat! I've got to say something and I'm going to say it."

John R. Bradley exclaimed in turn: "Captain! Captain!"

Osbon observed Bradley over his glasses, failed to recognize him, and shouted back:

"You leave me alone. I guess I know my business. I'm supposed to be running this excursion."

"But I'm Bradley!"

* At the time Brooklyn was what the Brooklyn *Eagle* called a "hotbed of exploration." George Washington DeLong, who had tried for the Pole in 1870, had lived there. So did Anthony Fiala, who had twice been to the Arctic. Herschel Parker lived at 21 Fort Green Place; Herbert L. Bridgman lived at 604 Carlton Avenue; August Loose, who will enter the story later, lived at 437 Thirteenth St.; Peary, when on duty at the Brooklyn Navy Yard, had his quarters on Flushing Avenue. Cook's home was at the corner of Bushwick and Myrtle. It was still standing in 1971, but the neighborhood had decayed.

"I don't care. I've got something to say and I'm going to say it."

Bradley shrugged and the elderly Osbon turned to Cook and said simply:

"Well, Dr. Cook. Welcome. How are you?"

The anticlimax amused the crowd, and Bird S. Coler again attempted to deliver his speech, but the people were reaching out for Cook and appeared to be about to overwhelm him. Osbon shouted:

"For decency's sake. Will you be Americans for once and behave yourselves! All of you go up to the hurricane deck. Give the Doctor some room to breathe in. There'll be plenty of opportunity later for all to shake the Doctor's hand."

By this time six soldiers from the Forty-seventh Regiment had formed a ring around Cook and were able to move him out of the salon and onto the hurricane deck. Bird S. Coler resolutely followed.

A dozen or so representatives of the Explorers Club of New York, bedecked in ice-colored ribbons, were standing in a hollow circle near the roof of the salon. The crowd rushed up the gangway and overwhelmed this formation. Meanwhile, the reporters and photographers had climbed up into the rigging. Someone shouted "Put the Doctor on the roof!" and he was unceremoniously boosted onto it. A handshaking line then formed along the deck. Since the roof of the salon was about three feet above the deck, he had to lean over to grasp the hands of his well-wishers.

At all times, the noise was intense. The whistles of the *Grand Republic* and its escorting vessels were blasting away, a band was playing, and from the rigging the photographers were shouting:

"Oh Doctor! This way, Doctor. Take your hat off, Doctor! Dr. Cook, please look up. Oh you Doctor! Give the photographers a chance!"

As for the Doctor, "Throughout the ordeal, for ordeal it was," one reporter wrote, "the Doctor remained perfectly cool and collected. He wore 'the smile that will not come off.' "

Then the moment came when Bird S. Coler again began his

official speech of welcome. But as he spoke the whistles began to wail, so that when Cook replied it was to words that no one heard.

Ten thousand people were waiting at the dock. Coler escorted him ashore and into the lead automobile of a parade that included three hundred cars. It started up South Fifth Street and ended at the Bushwick Club, where the handshaking continued until his hand went lame. At the banquet that night, handshaking was prohibited. But not entirely. Cook did shake hands with eighty-seven-year-old F. I. Heidenberg, who, scarcely able to walk, managed to make his way into the clubhouse. With tears streaming down his face, Heidenberg declared:

"Oh yes, the great man will shake hands with such an old Knickerbocker as me. Why my grandfather was born in old New York. I'm New York through and through. You must let me shake his hand."

The Doctor grasped Mr. Heidenberg's hand and shook it warmly.

During the evening reporters asked him about Harry Whitney. He replied: "I have the greatest faith in Harry Whitney." He declared that he was certain that he could establish absolutely his claim to the Pole.

The festivities continued until eleven. Then, after being serenaded by five hundred members of the United Singers of Brooklyn, he and his wife escaped to Manhattan where she had reserved a suite at the Waldorf-Astoria.*

On September 20, 1909, at Sydney, Nova Scotia, three thousand people moved toward the waterfront to hail the arrival of Robert E. Peary. The schools were closed, business

* The account in the Brooklyn *Eagle* has been used as the fundamental report on the day, but material has been borrowed from the stories in the *Times*, *World*, *American*, and *Herald*. A slight liberty may have been taken with Bird S. Coler, whose movements aboard the *Grand Republic* were variously reported. In some papers the *Grand Republic* was referred to as the *Grand Union*. After Cook, John R. Bradley was the most prominent man of the day. In his speech Cook referred to him as "the man who paid the bills."

was suspended, the Prime Minister was on hand, the American and British flags were flying, the ships in the harbor were dressed, and out in the Atlantic Josephine Peary, aboard a yacht, was waiting for her husband. When he failed to appear Josephine was distressed and the people on shore returned to their homes "in no gentle frame of mind," a reporter wrote, "over what is called the Peary style of delay."

The delay was caused by Cabin Boy Billy Pritchard.

At Battle Harbor a few days earlier, according to Barton W. Currie of the *World*, Pritchard had sworn "that Dr. Cook had not mentioned the North Pole. . . . Boatswain Denis Murphy . . . backed this statement up. They were grimly sullen about it, too, bearing themselves as men who had been badgered for weeks over that single issue of fact."

But in the meantime the Doctor, then still aboard the *Oscar II*, had told the Associated Press correspondent of the situation between himself, Whitney, and Pritchard, and had said that he was releasing them from their pledges. This news was relayed to the Associated Press in New York, then cabled to Battle Harbor and passed on to Peary. En route to Sydney, after being informed of the contents of the Associated Press wire, the cabin boy acknowledged the true situation. Peary's reaction was to head for the nearest cable station — St. Mary's Island, seventy miles out from Sydney — and spend the next day communicating with New York.

After the Commander, twenty-four hours late, had appeared in Sydney and the appropriate ceremonies were over, he was interviewed by Barton W. Currie, who wrote: "When told by this writer that Dr. Cook had received a tremendous welcome in New York, Peary snapped his great jaws and glared fiercely from under his bushy eyebrows."

Earlier Peary had said that he would waive all comment on Cook, but — "almost in the same breath" — he added that he was not going to wait for the authority of science; he was going to end the controversy with a sudden discharge of artillery.

" 'What I have to say,' said Peary with an inflection that was almost a snarl, 'will not be long delayed, you may rest assured on that score.' "[1]

He then read out a formal statement, or as Currie wrote, "declared with that wolfish grimness that translates the tremendous vigor of the man": "Acting on the advice of General Hubbard [president of the Peary Arctic Club] and . . . Bridgman . . . I prefer not to accept any invitations or ovations until the present controversy has been settled by competent authorities."

It is probable that, at Sydney, the Commander took the opportunity to read the first newspaper he had seen in months, the Sydney *Daily Post*, published on the morning of his arrival, September 21, 1909. If so, he had the chance to read:

"While the world-wide excitement is growing warm over the stories of Cook and Peary, it is not generally known that there are three men living quietly in Cape Breton who were twice in the Arctic with Cook and once with Peary. A staff correspondent of the *Post* has spent two days with these men. . . .

" 'Do you think Cook reached the Pole?' was the first interrogation which naturally came to our lips.

" 'If Dr. Cook says he reached the Pole there is not a shadow of doubt about it,' was the prompt reply.

"The following is the story corroborated by each one of the men who were Cook's companions away up on the Greenland coast.

"Dr. Cook is a splendid character. He is a gentleman clean through; brave, generous to a fault, always thinking of the comfort of others and never for one moment sparing himself. Never for one moment did he ever lose his temper; no circumstance, however trying, ever seemed to ruffle his genial spirit. He was an Arctic enthusiast, and studied everything. . . . Dr. Cook gave his professional services to the natives at every point. He healed their wounds, pulled their teeth, and dealt out drugs with a free hand without thought of reward or recompense. . . . Why should Cook not reach the Pole? He was physically as fit as any man who ever went north; he knew Arctic conditions as thoroughly as Peary or any other man; he had dogs, Eskimos, game, plenty of supplies, and more than that, he had the pluck of a man to make the dash. If Peary's story of the northern ice is true, there can be no doubt of Cook's story. . . .'

" 'Which of the two do you consider the more competent man?'

" 'In a way they are not comparable. Both are equal to anything that can be done by man on polar ice. Both have pluck, endurance and the stamina to resist the awful depression of northern solitudes. Of the two men, possibly Peary would be less affected by depression incident to the northern night. But in disposition and temperament the two men are entirely dissimilar. Cook is genial and open-hearted under all conditions. We never once saw him ruffled or in a fit of the blues. He is always the same, affable, genial and untiring. Peary is more reserved and carries the habit of discipline and conquest with him. . . . In his own mind he owned . . . the natives, the dogs, the game; the whole horizon was his and all for his own glory.' "

When Peary, from Sydney, left by train for his home on Eagle Island, fifteen miles up the shore from Portland, Maine, the Canadian towns along the line were not responsive to his passage; but when he crossed the border into Maine the celebrating began.

"The little village of Vanceboro is the northernmost American village," Barton W. Currie wrote. ". . . There is a bridge spanning a mill creek which marks the border between British and American soil and on the tracks across this bridge a dozen torpedoes were planted to warn of Peary's approach. There are 550 people in Vanceboro and 549 . . . were gathered at the station platform waiting for the discharge of the torpedoes. . . .

"At the first report men, women and children cut loose with cannon, firecrackers, revolvers, bells and horns. But the prettiest tribute of all was paid by the school children of the township, who were marshalled in a solid mass on the station platform, waving flags and singing national anthems.

"As the train stopped and the rumble of its wheels ceased the shrill voices of the children burst into the strains of 'America.'

They sang every verse of that stirring song. When at last it was still enough to be heard all Peary could stammer out was 'I thank you. Again I thank you' and his face twitched and his eyes blinked with an emotion you would not expect in a man of his supposedly rugged sort."[2]

At Bangor he received a loving cup, but the atmosphere was cool: "Scant applause and cold official formality," Currie noted. His home town of Portland made up for this. Here the now familiar scene began once more: "Fifty thousand people lined the streets and yelled themselves hoarse," Currie reported, "as the carriage containing the explorer . . ."

That night, before the banquet at the Falmouth Hotel, the management had to turn out the lights in order to clear the corridors.

After Fred and Marie Cook had escaped to the Waldorf-Astoria, he received from her some unanticipated news. He was virtually bankrupt. She and their children had existed for months on nothing but loans from friends and relatives. This situation did not become public until two months later when his lawyer told reporters: "While he was away the Knickerbocker Trust Co. failed and all the money Mrs. Cook had deposited there was gone. The mortgage on their home in Brooklyn had been foreclosed and the Cook family was in straits. Dr. Cook set out at once, as soon as the money began coming in from the lectures, to straighten out the debts that existed. It was not long before he settled up all he owed."[3]

And so, throughout the sixty-some days between his return to America — "he who first stood upon the apex of the world" — and his flight, incognito, to Europe — "the greatest imposter the world has ever known" — Cook's affairs were controlled by two facts. He was tired, noticeably tired when he arrived. And in order to earn a large sum of money quickly, he was forced to accept an exhausting lecture schedule — more ordeals.

The excitement, accordingly, continued. "From that day until I left New York," he wrote in *My Attainment*, "my life was a kaleidoscopic whirl of excitement. . . . Each day thereafter, from morning until night there was a continuous rush of excitement; at no time, until I fled from it, did I get more than four hours sleep a night — disturbed sleep at that. . . . In sixty days . . . not less than two hundred lectures, dinners, and receptions, not to mention the unremitting train of press interviews."

During this period, presumably after paying off all debts, he made approximately $80,000. "Most of his expenditures, however, were badly advised," his lawyer said, "and I doubt that he had as much as $50,000 when he went away."[4]

Very little is known about Walter Lonsdale, who served as Cook's secretary through four hyperactive months. What information exists suggests that he may have been, in the Shakespearian sense, comical. Although he was surely of some assistance to the Doctor, his value as an adviser is dubious. Only one thing is certain: the anonymous reporter from the Brooklyn *Eagle* disliked him. Concerning a mass interview that Cook gave the day after he had arrived, the man from the *Eagle* wrote: "The Brooklyn explorer, humble as ever, looking as commonplace as any of the thousands of everyday people found in the streets every day, let the reporters probe him at will for half an hour. Secretary Lonsdale . . . did what he could to protect him from too severe an ordeal. Despite the fact that Lonsdale was formerly a secretary to the American legation in Copenhagen, he is extremely English, and he irritated the scribes just a bit, for one reason or another."[5]

On the following day the man from the *Eagle* reported:

"Walter Lonsdale, his imported English secretary, who brought over from London six trunks of clothes, kept a number of people waiting for an appointment with Dr. Cook, sitting around for an hour and a half while he consumed his breakfast. He then took a constitutional for ten minutes, and on his return sent for the folks who were waiting and told them he was awfully sorry, don't you know, but they would have to wait a little longer.

" 'I always like to oblige myself,' he said, 'and really now, I cawnt see you just yet.'

"Lonsdale, who was attired in a tweed suit, a green necktie, and a horizontal scarf pin two inches broad, made quite a hit, as may be judged from this little remark."

And that, regrettably, is about all that is known of Walter Lonsdale, except that his face was chubby.

6

THE DOCTOR got the news from Whitney on September 26, the fifth day after his return. The cable read:

> STARTED FOR HOME ROOSEVELT. NOTHING ARRIVED FOR ME. PEARY WOULD ALLOW NOTHING BELONGING TO YOU ON BOARD. SAID TO LEAVE EVERYTHING IN CACHE ETAH. . . . SEE YOU SOON. EXPLAIN ALL. GOOD SHOOTING.

Although Cook did not say so immediately, Whitney's news disgusted him. In *My Attainment*, he wrote: "At the time I felt crippled; my feeling of disgust with the problem, with myself and the situation began."

The absence of his instruments meant only one thing: because he could not establish corrections for them, he could not present an accurate line of observations. Otherwise, his loss was not important. Polar observations can be faked, and observations made by only one man are almost meaningless. Early in the controversy this point was emphasized by scientists, but their remarks were buried in brief stories on inside pages. The most concise statement on the matter was made from Rome, where Signor Zappa of the Vatican observatory noted: "Astronomic observations in themselves would not be sufficient proof. Every calculation would be founded on bases of authenticity which have no other guarantee than Dr. Cook's word." Signor Zappa then identified the crux of the matter: "If Dr. Cook is not believed, one ought not to believe the others."[1]

Signor Zappa's point was firmly based. Because of the conditions under which polar work was done, the scientific world had no alternative but to take on faith the reports made by those who ventured toward the Pole. In Berlin Herr Baschin of the Geographical Institute found the attacks on Cook puzzling. "Hitherto it has not been the custom in scientific circles," he observed, "to attribute falsehoods to explorers returning from unknown regions. Most polar discoveries have been made by the explorer alone."[2] He added that the explorer was usually accompanied by some Eskimos.

Cook now faced an enormous problem, for faith is necessarily supported by a system. If something is to be believed, reasons for believing must be provided. Peary was backed by a huge machine, one that, as will be shown, was capable of creating, manufacturing reasons for believing that Cook was a fraud and that Peary was legitimate. But the Doctor was on his own. He was a loner, a classic instance of the individual confronted by established power. He was a loner involved in a small but definite event in the history of man's relations with the sphere he inhabits. He was a loner with one vexing weakness — demonstration.

He could demonstrate himself, for he was a convincing man. A writer who spent two hours lunching with him reported: "He is a man without personal magnetism; it is afterwards that the simplicity of his manner, his pleasant directness, the probability of what he says, comes back to the mind and makes it harder to believe that he lies than that he tells the truth."[3] And Captain Osbon, who had known Cook over many years, said: "I have yet to know of a single individual who formed an opinion antagonistic to Dr. Cook on the strength of a chat or interview with him. . . . Antagonism . . . was due to newspaper inspiration, not by reason of meeting the man face to face."[4]

Nevertheless, his weakness was demonstration, because except for himself he had little to show. He could not display his Eskimo boys, or present their testimony in translation. The only demonstration that he could exhibit, beyond himself, was his observations. Over a route distance of some 520 miles he had taken seven latitude observations, or one for every 78 miles, and seven longitude observations. At the South Pole, Amundsen took a latitude observation every 73 miles.

In *My Attainment* Cook wrote: "The value of all such observations as proof of a polar success . . . is open to such interpretation as the future may determine." Nevertheless, it seems probable that his thinking was similar to that of the English geographer J. Gordon Hayes, who in 1929 declared in his *Robert Edwin Peary:* "All reputable explorers, navigators and students of the subject are agreed that isolated observations made in one locality, at the end of a long journey, are of little value; but that their value is at once enhanced by a good series of observations taken with considerable frequency during the course of a journey. They should be like a ladder, the foot of which stands at the expedition's base, and which reaches the farthest point of the unknown by steps that are as regular as possible."

And so, although his observations were almost meaningless, it was reasonable for him to imagine that they would pull him through. Since they were so important to him, he was soon forced to edge away from the exact situation.

Sometime in the afternoon of the day Whitney's cable arrived, Walter Lonsdale told reporters: "Of course it is absolutely impossible for any man to prove absolutely that he has been to the Pole. Something must be taken on faith. It would be quite possible for a scientist . . . to make certain calculations and put them on paper as records of observations made on a trip to the Pole."[5]

A garbled version of this statement was reported to Cook, and in the evening he received a few newspaper men at the Waldorf and inquired of what Lonsdale had said. When Lonsdale's statement was repeated to him, and acknowledged by Lonsdale, the Doctor, according to the New York *World*, "looked more nervous than at any time since he had landed. . . . He made no comment, so this question was put to him:

"Wouldn't it be possible for a scientific man who has only got within a couple of hundred miles of the Pole to put down certain scientific figures which would indicate that he . . . reached the Pole?

" 'I can't answer that,' replied Dr. Cook, flushing and fidgeting on his feet. 'I don't think it is a fair question. My observations will be made public in due course and what they will show will then be open to everybody.'

" 'But isn't it a fact, Doctor . . . that in the last analysis something will have to be taken on faith, as Mr. Lonsdale put it. . . .'

"The Doctor swung around on one foot, then on the other, biting his mustache and fingering his watch chain, and replied after a moment's thought: 'I shall have to let the scientific men who examine my data answer that. I cannot undertake to do so.' "

The interviewers then asked some questions about Whitney. One was: " 'What did Whitney say when you first told him you had reached the Pole?'

"The Doctor thought for some time, then answered:

" 'I think he said: 'Well, I've been up here in a lucky year,' but I'm not exactly certain that those were his words. . . . You'll have to ask Whitney.' "

The final question was: "Have you made any arrangements for meeting Peary on his arrival here?"

Cook, much amused, said no.[6]

When America learned that Peary had refused to bring Cook's property south, its reaction was very unfavorable to the Commander. One paper observed: "In refusing to allow . . . the smallest article of Cook's on board the *Roosevelt*, the great explorer showed a petty meanness and spitefulness which can only be excused on the ground of temporary insanity from ambition and from the long strain of his journey." And in Philadelphia the *Inquirer* declared: "Mr. Peary insists that Dr. Cook prove his story, but it would seem as if Peary has been doing everything possible to hinder Cook and belittle him in the eyes of the public. . . . Why is it that men who have done really great things sometimes spoil everything by acting like cads." Only the New York *Times* defended Peary, saying: "Suppose Commander Peary had allowed the boxes to remain on board the *Roosevelt*, had brought them here and caused them to be delivered to the Doctor? What answer, what defense would he have had against a possible charge that records had been abstracted or instruments tampered with?"

On September 27, 1909, Peary left Portland by train to confer with General Thomas H. Hubbard at Bar Harbor, Maine. During the journey he was interviewed by reporters, including Barton W. Currie, who reported that the Commander "let drive with characteristic vehemence."

Of the several matters on Peary's mind, one was Cook's sledge. This was the stripped-down half a sledge used to carry the instruments and supplies when Cook left the underground den for Annoatok. Now it was lying on the rocks high above the beach at Annoatok, in a position where anyone could see it. Harry Whitney said of it: "The sledge was badly cut up. Some of the wooden strips had been slivered for firewood. . . . The base of the frame had been cut down for arrows. . . . The Eskimos had taken off the steel runners to make knives."[7]

But Peary, "with a smile that showed every one of his gleaming teeth and ruffled the bristles of his great, sandy mustache," chose different words. Earlier he had convinced himself that Cook's Eskimos had said that Cook had gone hardly any distance across the pack ice. Now he was convinced that what he had seen at Annoatok was not a wreck, half a sledge, but Cook's idea of a complete sledge, one capable of carrying him to the Pole.

" 'I examined that sledge. . . . Yes, I looked it over very carefully. So did Henson. So did MacMillan. They know sledges, I guess, and so do I. Was it anything like my Morris K. Jesup sledge? [Peary's shoulders shook, though at the same time he gritted his teeth.] I should say it was not anything like the Morris K. Jesup sledge.

" 'That sledge of Cook's was built along lines of no sledge I ever saw before. Why, I don't believe that sledge would last one day over Arctic ice with a standard load of 500 or 600 pounds.' "

Robert E. Peary was also concerned about Harry Whitney. On the previous day Currie had reported: "Whitney unequivocally is the Peary bugaboo in the present controversy." Currie added that Peary was very certain "that he can meet every iota of evidence that Whitney may advance in favor of Cook with a counter-charge that will be all the more dramatic in its effect."

Now, on the train to Bar Harbor, Peary began his counter-charge.

" 'I would like to know . . . why, if Harry Whitney knew the value of the instruments and proofs that Cook entrusted to his custody — the custody of a man who was practically a stranger — he did not sail back to Etah on the Jeanie for those things. Why did he come away from Smith's Sound and leave those treasures to the mercy of another arctic winter?

" 'Let me point out,' ran on Commander Peary, 'where the Jeanie was when I last saw Mr. Whitney. I picked up Harry Whitney at Etah on August 17 and we ran down the Sound about 100 miles to Saunders Island. Clear water and fair winds, fine going.

" 'At Saunders Island the Jeanie came along. We went into North Star Bay so that the Jeanie could transfer the coal she had for me to the Roosevelt. Then we ran out into open water again. Whitney was aboard the Jeanie. He was one day's sail from Etah. He had clear, free water along the eastern shore of the sound.

" 'Did Whitney run back to Etah for those immensely valuable records and instruments? He did not. He sailed directly west, where the ice was packed against the western shore. He wanted a bear. He cared more about a bear than he did about Cook's property. He would not cut out two days of his hunting to go back for what he says now he knew was Cook's proof of the discovery of the Pole.' "

Currie continued:

"Then, to add a touch to the intensely dramatic, Peary

related that whereas Dr. Cook had left his polar flag, his instruments and records to the mercy of a stranger at Etah, he [Peary] had sewn his flag into his undershirt, sewn his records into his clothing and taken every precaution . . . to guard his instruments against destruction.

" 'Why,' cried Peary with a savage sneer, 'I would not have entrusted those things to my father, mother, or brother or any human being. . . .'

"Peary had worked himself up to his first really passionate outburst against Dr. Cook and as he went on he poured forth a flood of information that sounded to his little group of interviewers like a series of short-arm jabs against the very vitals of Cook's claims. . . .

" 'I did not need any of Whitney's information. I did not want it. I didn't seek. I didn't need. Hadn't I seen and talked with every Eskimo in Eskimo land, and didn't Henson talk to them? Why, I know these Eskimos as a father knows his children. I won't say that they look on me as a god, but as a benefactor. . . . And after I had seen these Eskimos and talked to them what need had I to learn anything from Harry Whitney?

" 'Naturally,' said the Commander . . . 'I believed that when Whitney spoke of Cook's instruments that he meant superfluous instruments such as any Arctic hunter might carry. I never dreamed that Whitney meant instruments that had taken observations at the Pole. I never dreamed of a flag such as I had sewn to my body.' "[8]

For Harry Whitney, who hunted big game rather than hypothetical points on moving ice, the polar controversy was just dreadful. That he had failed Cook he surely regretted, but this was not his biggest worry. Like the Doctor, he was mainly concerned about the proofs of his Arctic deeds. The fact was, when Whitney transferred to the *Jeanie* he left his hunting trophies aboard the *Roosevelt*.

Barton W. Currie discovered this aboard Whitney's train. "The Commander has in his custody all the treasures Whitney gathered," Currie wrote, " . . . scores of immensely valuable skins . . . three or four hundred photographs, walrus tusks, narwhale horns."[9]

In this predicament Whitney handled himself honorably. He arrived at St. Johns, Newfoundland, on September 28 and, with Peary's scornful remarks about him in the news, talked with a reporter. "Mr. Whitney believes that Dr. Cook found the Pole and that Peary did the same," the reporter wrote. "In expressing this belief today he said . . . 'Dr. Cook's story seems to me truthful and probable.' So far as Whitney is aware, Cook's Eskimos never admitted that while with the Doctor they only progressed two 'sleeps' from land."[10]* In response to Peary's outrageous "I never dreamed that Whitney meant instruments that had taken observations at the Pole," Whitney said, the reporter wrote, that Peary "fully understood the kind of instruments he had and what other property of Cook's he had, and that Peary's refusal to take Cook's goods . . . was studied and deliberate."

Peary then toned down his aggressiveness. The *Herald* reported: "Mr. Whitney received messages from Mr. Peary complaining that he had not fully informed him about the nature of Dr. Cook's belongings. . . . Mr. Whitney says Mr. Peary is in error, as he informed him fully, and Captain Robert Bartlett saw all the things as he helped Mr. Whitney bury them at Etah."[11]

Later Peary would surpass himself by charging: "Cook's leaving of his records at Etah was a scheme on his part in which he would claim that they were lost or destroyed and so escape being forced to produce them to substantiate his claim."[12] Whitney then informed the press that he was certain that Cook would not have left his property with him unless he

* At heart Whitney was undoubtably pro-Cook. The Brooklyn *Eagle* for September 27, 1909, reported that Whitney had written his sister: "I saw Dr. Cook at Etah. He has accomplished a great thing and is bound to be a great man. He claims to have reached the Pole, and from evidence, I believe he has." On February 14, 1930, Sir Wilfred Grenfell, an Arctic missionary, wrote to Cook: "Harry Whitney on the Jeanie met me on his way back, and did a lot of wireless telegraphy from my ship, and was your very cordial friend" (Letter in the possession of Helene Cook Vetter).

felt certain that he, Whitney, would bring it back to America. He had previously told Currie: "I thought that a big ship like the *Erik* would come up for me. That is how I happened to have Dr. Cook's boxes. He said he could not transport them on one sledge and I offered to take them back."[13]

For Currie, Whitney was "not a man of quick decisions or very resolute purpose." Currie continued: "This young hunter, who would think nothing of pursuing a family of polar bear, palpably trembled at the mention of either Cook or Peary. It was more or less wildly . . . and with a tremulous hesitation that Whitney declared . . . that he considered Dr. Cook the gamest sort of explorer and believed his story."[14]

Whitney was extremely anxious to get down to New York and repossess his hunting trophies, but "He feared . . . to bump against Dr. Cook before he saw Peary," Currie wrote. "He did not want Peary to think he had first gone to Cook. At the same time . . . he did not want to offend Cook by first going to Peary."

It was just dreadful. "If only something will turn up," he told Currie, "that will make them forget me, I will be very happy. I have been dragged into this thing by the neck."

Meanwhile, Peary had come and gone at General Hubbard's summer home in Bar Harbor, from where Currie* had reported two items of special interest.

The first was that the president of the Peary Arctic Club had succeeded in silencing Peary. The Commander now "sat grinning and strangely silent in a big leather chair."[15] Hubbard had muffled Peary, it appears, by assuring him that the formal statement he had talked so much about issuing would absolutely annihilate Cook's claims. Consequently, Peary "seemed to feel more at ease . . . tonight than at any other time."

* Barton W. Currie of the New York *World* now passes, regrettably, out of this narrative. His stories constitute by far the best journalism done during the controversy. In later years he wrote a volume about book collecting and a bibliography of Booth Tarkington; further details of his life are lacking. *Vale* Currie!

And Peary had also changed in another way. General Hubbard having just given a reception in his honor — one hundred people attended — the Commander was "clad in a frock coat and immaculate as a popular pourer at pink teas." And in a sense he was very much at home in these clothes, Currie noted: "As suave as a Kentucky colonel." Yet he was still the same old Commander: "His muscles seemed straining to burst the seams. . . . he longed to burst out into a blue flannel shirt."

At Bar Harbor the talking was done entirely by Hubbard, who was even suaver than Peary. "With a barely perceptible smile and a nod in the direction of Commander Peary," Hubbard said with quiet emphasis: "I am satisfied that Commander Peary's statement contains facts and facts only, and it would be superfluous to add that the facts are true."

Hubbard did not repeat a statement about "competent authority" that he had made earlier in Bangor, where he had said: "Concerning Dr. Cook, I would say let him submit his records and data to some competent authority and let that authority draw its own conclusions from the notes and data taken in the field. . . . All that is wanted is the data and records made in the Arctic. [This was said at a time when Hubbard knew that much of Cook's data was still at Etah.] Competent authority will determine from them where Dr. Cook has been." He then added: "I may say that Commander Peary will also be expected to turn over his data and observations for the same purpose."[16]

Robert E. Peary's Property Revisited

> You must understand that the Pole is a theoretical point without length, breadth, or thickness.
>
> Robert E. Peary

Before the public the intensely interesting Commander, by nature so emotional and excitable, was a thoroughly "buttoned-up" member of the governing class, a man cunningly righteous for his reputation. The writer who ghosted most of his *The North Pole* found him maddening: "Peary was a dull man and it was impossible to get much lively human material out of him." But if Peary seemed dull to some, it was only because he had so much to hide.

Some of his secrets seem small — that he rode on a sledge instead of walking — but some of his secrets seem large.

It is not possible to study the North Pole controversy without considering that the unstable Commander may have been prejudiced in his identification of the North Pole. From land to the point where Bartlett turned back, the members of Peary's expedition paused only four times to locate themselves by taking observations for latitude, and until he was virtually at what he considered the Pole, Peary himself took absolutely no observations for longitude.* He traveled entirely by compass and the direction of the sun at noon.[17] In a situation where he would have expected to find large changes in the variation of his compass, he made no allowances of any sort for variation,[18] and so informed a congressional subcommittee.† But

* That Peary did take a sight just short of his Pole was mentioned by Matt Henson in his long statement in the Boston *American* of July 17, 1910. Many years later David Haig-Thomas, while in the Arctic, talked with Otah, one of the four Eskimos who accompanied Peary to the Pole, and reported that Otah said: "Peary looked at the sun. . . . The first time he said we were near the Pole, and the second time he said we had passed it. We had food for many days on the sledges." Haig-Thomas also reported that "Otah said Peary rode on the sledge a lot of the time." (*Traces in the Snow*, London, 1939, p. 142.) Thus both Henson and Otah, widely separated in time and space, agree about the circumstances of Peary's moves about his Pole.

† Admiral Sir Albert H. Markham wrote: "When a high latitude has been reached by a traveler, whose object is the attainment of a still higher latitude . . . there are only two observations to be taken that are of any importance. . . . These are for latitude, and . . . for ascertaining the variation of the compass. The latter is of great importance, for it enables the traveler to steer a straight and direct course toward the Pole. Observations for longitude are therefore unimportant, supposing, of course, that your departure has been made from a base whose latitude and longitude have both been ascertained before leaving. . . . sledging north I never bothered my head about taking any observations for determining my longitude, but I was very careful to check my course by

although he does not appear to have had any satisfactory means of determining his exact position at any time on the ice, he by his own account managed to hit the Big Nail right on the head.

So Peary had his small secrets, and he had his large secrets, and in the last category, especially, they were such that they were difficult for him to remember; all of which made it easy for him to demand that Cook "prove" his assertion, and even more easy to link his rival with Munchausen. Back in America, at a time when enough people had learned enough of his story — that portion that he acknowledged — Peary realized that certain details were difficult, and so he declared that the North Pole story was what it was, and not what people wanted it to be. There were reasons for his testiness, for in a quiet way his problems were and remain large and tenacious, being controlled by the most dangerous type of historical facts, the incontrovertible.

One such fact was the date when, returning from the Pole, he arrived back at the *Roosevelt*. Bob Bartlett had turned south on April 1, 1909, and had reached the ship on April 24. Twelve hours after Bartlett had headed south, the Commander and his party had started for the supreme target. They spent some thirty-three hours in its vicinity, and after returning to land, passed two days resting at Cape Columbia. And in spite of these delays, the Commander returned to the *Roosevelt* on April 27, only four days behind Bartlett.

Cook was the first man to comment on this large oddity. At a time when Peary's story was appearing in a magazine, and when the Doctor himself, in London, was emerging from hibernation, Cook told a reporter: "I see that . . . he says he returned only four days after Bartlett's return from the point fifteen miles south of the 88th degree latitude — that is about

constant observations for the variation of the compass" (*The Geographical Journal*, London, 1910, Vol. 35, pp. 303–304).

The reader should understand that there is considerable disagreement about this point. Captain Thomas F. Hall and others contend that without taking a sight for longitude, it is not possible to coordinate local noon, the sun's position, and a true north-south line.

135 miles from the Pole. Can it be believed that Peary . . . could have traveled 135 miles over an unbroken terrain and south 135 miles, making 270 miles in four days, less the time spent in observations? Why, he could not have done it without an airplane. . . . If Bartlett was sent back fifteen miles from the 88th degree and Peary reached his ship only four days behind him, what conclusion can you arrive at?" The Doctor then "made a motion of dismissal with his long arm."[19]

Peary did not respond to Cook's statement, but Henson said: "Bartlett was delayed all the time by leads, open stretches of water, from the time he left us. Once he was held up three or four days. We had good luck and met no such delays. The worst leads we found, when we had to ferry the sledges over one by one, detained us only a few hours. In addition we were making forced marches and Captain Bartlett was not. We kept on the march from eighteen to twenty-four hours a day against his ten to twelve. These are the reasons we gained on him."[20]

The free-speaking Bartlett had a chance to smooth over the situation when he wrote his autobiography. He refused. He said not one thing about being held back by leads, and restricted himself to stating that he had "a rough time before I reached the land. We lost the trail in drifting snow and I fell through young ice and nearly drowned."[21]

The situation is mysterious, but it is not really relevant to the question of whether or not Peary reached the Pole, just as the "fake peak" photograph is not really relevant to the question of whether or not Cook reached the summit of McKinley.

Although the Commander continues to be officially identified as the first man to attain the North Pole, the basis of this rank consists entirely of his own say-so, plus the political accomplishments of the Peary Arctic Club. Peary's polar diary is a restricted item, and his data has never been reviewed by any learned society or body of reasonably disinterested men.

Over the past sixty years, however, three independent investigators — Thomas F. Hall, J. Gordon Hayes, and Theon Wright — have worked their way through Peary's published data and have produced complex and impressive studies of it. These studies — published in 1917, 1929, and 1970, respectively — are the results of prolonged efforts, and these writers, historically, are Peary's true enemies. Although their separate accounts are confusing, and there is a divergence in the statistics that the three investigators display, plus the possibility that Peary never received any benefit of any doubt, all three examiners are united in their final conclusions: that Peary's record of his achievement is palliative and excessively tricky; and that the Commander, on the basis of his printed data, could not possibly have reached the Pole.

Hall, Hayes, and Wright are particularly interesting in their separate estimates of the daily rates of speed at which Peary would have had to travel in order to reach the Pole and be back at the *Roosevelt* on April 27. The conclusions of Wright and Hayes provide the principal sources in the following summary.

First, from the time Peary and his party left land to the time they reached latitude 87°47′49″N, the point at which Bartlett turned back,* Peary's speed was normal and unsensational. Wright observes: "From Cape Columbia to the Bartlett camp, a distance of 280 nautical miles, Peary averaged 13.3 miles per march on sea ice."[22] This was his daily speed over rough ice on which his advance divisions had broken the trail.

Second, after Bartlett turned back — or as Hayes phrased it, "after all responsible witnesses had been dismissed" — Peary's rate of speed increased phenomenally. From the time Peary left the Bartlett camp for the Pole to the time he returned to that same camp, according to Wright, he "covered 302 miles in eight days, at an average rate of 37.7 miles per day. . . .† No man in the history of polar exploration had ever achieved such sustained speeds, particularly over sea ice. Nansen and Johansen, on their polar journey, recorded about 12.5

* It should be recalled that Bartlett's observation was incorrect, and that they were actually six miles further south. This fact is not reflected in any of the figures which follow.

† The Brooklyn *Eagle* for October 19, 1909, reported: "Peary makes the point that in order to have reached the Pole . . . under the dates furnished by the Eskimos' testimony [Cook] would have had to travel at a rate of an average of twenty-one and one-ninth miles a day, which [Peary] says is an impossibility."

The figure 302 miles includes the 36 geographical miles Peary said he traveled about the Pole while taking his observations.

miles per march and never more than 20 miles. Shackleton, near the South Pole, recorded distances from 17.3 to 25.1 miles on five successive days sledging over land ice; and Scott, in the same area, reported an average of 13 to 14 miles per march. Amundsen averaged 15.5 miles on the way to the South Pole and 22.5 miles on the way back."[23] *

Hayes, for the same period, reported that Peary covered 341 miles of latitude in eight days, at an average speed of 43 miles per day.[24] Cook's fastest march was 29 geographical miles, which he achieved on one day only.

In *The North Pole*, according to Hayes, Peary "carefully abstains from mentioning a word as to the portentous distance he has done."[25] He avoided having to do so by restricting his report to minutes of latitude, and generalizations such as "A large party cannot be forced as rapidly as a small party." He made his most explicit statement at Battle Harbor: "Our speed was not unusual when you consider the favorable weather. . . . We were not vexed with cross winds. Instead of blowing east or west and filling up the trail . . . they came almost continually from the north. Thus they packed the ice still harder against the land of the southern shores of the Polar Sea and held it firm. We were not carried off course by the easterly drift. . . . Our equipment grew lighter and lighter. In going north we had used up two-thirds of the rations."[26]

Third, the statements of Wright and Hayes are based on their individual analyses of the data contained in *The North Pole*. In it, although Peary was traveling over drifting ice, he made no allowance for any kind of deviation from a straight-line course. "There was a tacit assumption," Hayes wrote, "that the pack-ice was motionless, and that pressure ridges and channels never caused any deviation."[27] Accordingly, the daily distances traveled by Peary are far more fantastic than they appear, being at a minimum twenty per cent greater than the previously quoted daily straight-line mileage figures indicate.

* Yet Sverdrup reported: "I have often covered more than twenty-five miles a day" (New York *American*, September 6, 1909). According to J. Gordon Hayes, Commander Cagni traveled from 28 to 29 miles on his best days (*Robert Edwin Peary*, London, 1929, p. 160). Cook averaged 15 geographical miles per day.

Hayes estimates thirty per cent for deviations. His figure for the number of route miles that Peary actually traveled from the Bartlett camp to the Pole, and back to the Bartlett camp, is 425 miles at an average daily speed of 53 route miles.[28] He stated: "Unless Peary and his party averaged over 50 statute m.p.d. for eight consecutive days over the pack-ice he did not reach the North Pole."[29]

Finally, Bartlett was thirty-four years old, and an experienced sledger. Wright notes that Bartlett "arrived at Cape Columbia late in the day on April 18, covering the airline distance of 280 miles in nineteen days, or at an average speed of 14.7 nautical miles a day."[30] Over the same distance, according to Wright, Peary's average speed was 23.9 miles per march."[31]

In no sense can any of the above be considered proof that Peary failed to reach the Pole. It is presented as one more indication of the oddities of the man who linked Cook to Munchausen, and as an illustration of why, in this narrative, so much attention has been paid to the statements of Matthew Henson.

Hayes believes that Peary, at his Farthest North, was still 118 statute miles short of the Pole.[32] Theon Wright's conclusion is much the same. He suggests that Peary might have turned back soon after Bartlett departed for land.[33] Both investigators take, and for far more legitimate reasons, a position similar to that which Cook's critics took when they charged that he had never gone out of sight of land. "My enemies credit me with a journey of 2,000 miles," The Doctor said, " . . . but then, to deny me my Polar achievement, keep me sitting here, on a sterile waste of ice, for three months. Would any man sit down there and shiver in idleness when the reachable glory of Polar victory was on one side and the . . . joy of game land on the other?"[34]

The logic of Cook's protest is impressive, as is the passion. Peary could say much the same thing. After Bartlett turned back, whatever perils lay ahead of Peary could not possibly be greater than those he had already passed through on his final expedition and its predecessors. Robert E. Peary had guts.

Matthew Henson had guts. If Bartlett's certificate is accepted as reliable, it becomes very difficult to believe that Peary turned back approximately one hundred miles from his life's goal. High courage demands respect and invites generosity. As the Reverend Bernard R. Hubbard, S.J., pointed out: "The important thing to remember is that anyone who accepted the challenge of the Arctic is worthy of the greatest consideration — whether he reached the Pole or not."[35] Such consideration has regularly been refused Cook, and there are indications that it is no longer being offered to Peary.

The polar expeditions of Cook and Peary can be regarded as events occurring within the world of sport, where the unbelievable, the impossible, and the unexplainable occur with a pleasing and dramatic frequency. The dubiousness of Peary's data, when subjected to statistical analysis, becomes much less dubious when one considers the many sportsmen who have accomplished the statistical impossible.

Whether or not Robert E. Peary attained the North Pole will never be known. One thing, however, is certain. He himself considered that he had done so, positively. After he had returned to land he spent two days recuperating at Cape Columbia. There the great explorer, silently gloating in his igloo, passed a portion of the time considering the honors he now deemed due him. Some of his ideas he recorded: "Monument for mausoleum? Faced with marble or granite, statue with flag on top; lighted room at base for two sarcophagi? Bronze figures, Eskimo, dog, bear, musk ox, walrus, etc. etc. Or bronze tablet or flag at North Pole and suitable inscription. Bust."[36]

Cook: Did He or Didn't He?

As Cook and Peary were the opponents in the polar debate, so was "Proof" the motto stitched across that controversy's banner.

Normally, in exploration, the traveler who has reached his goal builds a cairn of rocks and places inside it a handwritten message enclosed in a container. When the next explorer reaches the cairn he removes the original message, copies it, then places the copy in the container. The original message he brings back as evidence that both he and his predecessor have been to where they claim to have been.

But the North Polar Sea, the reader is reminded, presents a unique problem. The region consists of nothing but ice, ice that is constantly shifting position, ice that eventually drifts south and melts into the sea. In the absolute sense, proof is not possible. Nevertheless, the term was widely employed throughout the polar controversy, both by the public and by those who should have known better.

"Proofs, proofs, proofs was the incessant call, SOMETHING WHICH HAD NEVER BEEN DEMANDED OF A SINGLE ARCTIC EXPLORER," Donald B. MacMillan complained. "The explorer's word has always been accepted without question. In 1607 Henry Hudson came sailing out of the mists of the North with the claim that he had reached the high northern latitude of 81°30′. Who KNOWS that he did? In 1826, Captain W. E. Parry came struggling south over the ice pack with the claim that he had reached 82°45′. Who KNOWS that he did? In 1876 Commander A. H. Markham . . . in 1896 Fridtjof Nansen . . . in 1901 the Duke of the Abruzzi. . . . What absolute proof or conclusive evidence did each or any one of the above-mentioned men ever offer to verify or substantiate his claim? NOT ONE IOTA. Each one SAID that he did. His word was accepted. That was enough proof for Geographic and Scientific Societies the world over. Every one of the above records stands and will never be erased."[37]

So wrote the puzzled, indignant MacMillan. This amusing man approved of asking proof from Cook, but was appalled that such would be requested from Peary.

That cumbersome, ungallant word "proof" was in fact dragged into Arctic exploration by MacMillan's boss, the Commander himself. The event occurred when, as Peary was preparing for his final expedition, the Explorers Club of New York invited him to succeed Cook as its president.

In his reply the New York *Times* would report, Peary indicated, that he "did not care to serve unless the club could give him the assurance that, in the event of Dr. Cook returning and claiming the Pole, proper proof would be demanded of him. . . . Mr. Peary was prevailed upon to accept the presidency, the club acquiescing to the demands he made concerning proofs from Dr. Cook."[38] In effect, therefore, the officers and members of the Explorers Club agreed to a policy that was intellectually unsupportable.

In *The End of the Night* the American storyteller John D. MacDonald wrote: "Long days of testimony, of exhibits, objections, cross-examinations tend to focus the mind and the attention on trivia, so that the larger issues are forgotten."[39] That is what occurred during the polar controversy. The facts of the case were gradually obscured by a fog of bizarre and irrelevant trivia, and the world eventually accepted as truth "the frantic theory," as the geographer Balch called it, "that Cook's journey was largely fiction."[40]

Today, for the persistent investigator, the major points in the polar controversy are five in number. Four of these have been previously mentioned in this narrative. They are:

1. There was no proof tradition in polar exploration.

2. Unsupported astronomical observations, made by one man only, have no scientific validity.

3. The polar expeditions of Cook and Peary in 1908 and 1909 are most properly viewed as events taking place in the world of sport. Neither expedition had any real connection with science, and to judge them by science's strictures seems unscientific.

4. "If the next traveler corroborates the discoverer," Balch pointed out, "instantly the first man's statements are immeasureably strengthened." This statement can be supplemented by that made during the early days of the controversy by Professor W. D. McMillan, then head of the astronomy department at the University of Chicago. "I know of no . . . test which a sufficiently informed but unscrupulous explorer could not meet," McMillan said, "except a verification of his description of the country traversed by a second expedition."[41]

To these major points can be added one that has not been mentioned previously:

5. The basic historical documents of the controversy are Cook's and Peary's original accounts of their expeditions, their original descriptions of conditions at, about, and on the way to and back from the North Pole. These were written and published before the controversy began, and are incontrovertible. In each account each explorer appeared as witness and presented his fundamental testimony freely at a time when he could not possibly imagine — this applies particularly to Cook — the amazing situation that developed.

At the time, many people were impressed by the several parallelisms contained in the two original accounts. The explorer Anthony Fiala observed: "The most distinct impression I get from Peary's cabled account . . . is that it tends largely to corroborate, and in no way discredit Dr. Cook's first story. . . . Further, there is nothing in Commander Peary's account that would throw the slightest doubt or suggestion of improbability on Dr. Cook's statement."[42] Many people, such as Whitney, considered the situation obvious: both explorers had reached the Pole. But as the noise level and emotional content of the controversy zoomed upward and the "long days of testimony, of exhibits, objections, cross-examinations" began, this early awareness of the larger issues was engulfed by trivia; engulfed and forgotten.

Each explorer published three separate accounts of his expedition.

Cook's original account was his 2,000-word dispatch to the New York *Herald*, which that paper published on the morning of September 2, 1909. He then wrote a 25,000-word version of his great adventure. This the *Herald* ran serially on alternate days in October, 1909. His final report, the book *My Attainment of the Pole*, was published in 1911.

Peary's original account was 3,500 words long. Half of it was published in the New York *Times* on September 10, 1909; the remainder ran on the following day. In 1910 a much longer version of his story appeared in installments in *Hamp-*

ton's magazine. Enlarged once more, it was published as the book *The North Pole*, also in 1910.

In the present examination, only those statements that were included in the original dispatches will be considered, for the reason that the statements made in these dispatches were written before the controversy began.

Cook's first contact with the *Herald* was the cable he sent from Lerwick, in the Shetland Islands. It read:

> REACHED NORTH POLE APRIL 21, 1908. DISCOVERED LAND FAR NORTH. HAVE LEFT SEALED EXCLUSIVE CABLE OF 2,000 WORDS FOR YOU WITH DANISH CONSUL AT LERWICK FOR WHICH I EXPECT THREE THOUSAND DOLLARS. I GO STEAMER "HANS EGEDE" TO COPENHAGEN.

Portions of this message, and the 2,000-word dispatch in its entirety, were published upon receipt by the *Herald*.

Peary's original announcement came in a cable to the New York *Times*, which that paper published on the morning of September 7, 1909, five days after Cook's announcement. Peary's cable read:

> I HAVE THE POLE APRIL 6. EXPECT ARRIVE CHATEAU BAY SEPTEMBER 7. SECURE CONTROL WIRE FOR ME THERE AND ARRANGE EXPEDITED TRANSMISSION BIG STORY.

This cable was not immediately backed by any dispatch or elaboration of any sort. On the following day Peary sent the New York *Times* a 250-word itinerary of his journey, but nothing further. September 9 passed without any statement of any kind from him. His 3,500-word dispatch was not received until September 10, when it was immediately published.

It is most apparent, therefore, that Cook's account is the original account of conditions at, about, and on the way to and back from the North Pole. The Doctor's story was published eight days before Peary's and the Doctor's statements are his and his alone. In no way can it be suggested that he depended on anyone for anything contained in his 2,000-word dispatch, which covered not only his journey to the Pole but the whole of his entire adventure.

Peary's position is entirely different. He is merely the second man to report on conditions at, about, and on the way to and back from the North Pole. Not only is he the second man; he did see — before filing his own dispatch — a copy of Cook's story.

At some time during the two-day interval between when Peary sent his first cable to the New York *Times* and when he filed his 3,500-word account, the postmaster at Indian Harbor advised the perturbed editors of the *Times* that Peary was at his station "awaiting telegraphic news."[43] The nature of this "telegraphic news" is suggested by a story in the New York *Sun* on September 22, 1909. It was based on an interview that Peary gave at Sydney. "Another question was asked concerning Cook's first narrative of his trip poleward," the *Sun*'s representative wrote. "To this Peary replied that he had read nothing of Cook's writing save the first report sent from Lerwick and that was so full of errors in transmission that he did not consider it worthwhile to give it any attention."

The "first report sent from Lerwick" could only have been Cook's 2,000-word dispatch. According to the *Sun*, Peary saw it "while in Labrador." The Commander was a champion badmouther: the blue fox skins had been "wet, mildewed, and rotting"; the ivory horns had been "broken from knocking about"; the copy of Cook's report was "full of errors in transmission . . . not . . . worthwhile to give it any attention." Does it seem possible that the Commander did not read, in full, what the competition had to say?

Today, some sixty years after the event, there appears to be only one way of establishing the truthfulness of the statements included in Cook's original dispatch. It is by making a comparative presentation of those statements, in Cook's and Peary's original narratives, that are in broad agreement. Because the two explorers traveled along different routes at different times, this method is somewhat unsatisfactory. It is like comparing the journeys of two Californians who have gone to New York City, one leaving from San Francisco, the other from Los Angeles. The discrepancies in the Californians' accounts of their trips are bound to be large, but they should also contain a few observations in common, particularly when, as they draw closer to New York City, their routes begin to converge.

The following similarities have been noted in Cook's and Peary's original reports of their polar journeys:

About the 86th parallel both Cook and Peary reported improved conditions.

COOK: "Beyond the eighty-sixth parallel the icefield became more extensive and heavier, the crevices fewer and less troublesome, with little or no crushed ice thrown up as barriers."

PEARY: (beyond 85.48) "On the next two marches the going improved and we covered good distances."

Both Cook and Peary reported that it was colder between the 88th and 89th parallels than it was at the Pole.

COOK: "Observations on the 14th gave latitude 88 deg 21 min and longitude 95 deg 52 min. The pack here was more active but the temperature remained below 40, cementing together quickly the young crevices."

PEARY: "We stopped in sight of the 89th parallel, in a temperature of 40 degrees below."

At the Pole itself both men reported the temperature to be less intense. Cook reported the temperature at the Pole to be a minus 38 degrees Fahrenheit. Peary reported the temperature at the Pole to be a minus 32 degrees Fahrenheit.

Past the 89th parallel both Cook and Peary reported that the ice improved, but that the scene was monotonous and lifeless.

COOK: "The ice improved steadily, but still there was a depressing monotony of scene and life had no pleasures, no spiritual recreations, nothing to relieve the steady physical drag of chronic fatigue." (No exact latitude or longitude is attached to this statement, but it is obvious that he is past 89.)

PEARY: "Before I turned in I took an observation which indicated our position was 89.25. A dense, lifeless pall hung overhead. The horizon was black and the ice beneath was a ghastly white. . . . The going was better than ever."

At the Pole both explorers' psychological reactions to their success were quite similar: extreme disappointment.

COOK: "After all the observations had been taken with a careful scrutiny of the local conditions a sense of intense loneliness came with the further scrutiny of the horizon. What a cheerless spot."

PEARY: "It all seems so simple and commonplace. As Bartlett said when turning back, when speaking of his being in these exclusive regions which no mortal has ever penetrated before: 'It's just like every day!' "

On the return both explorers covered long distances quickly.

COOK: "With fair weather, good ice, and the inspiration of the home run, long distances were at first covered quickly."

PEARY: "We would try to double march on the return. As a matter of fact we nearly did this, covering regularly in our homeward journey five outward marches in three return marches."

On the return both Cook and Peary knew that the dangers would begin about the 87th parallel.

COOK: "Below the eighty-seventh parallel the character of the ice changed very much, and it became evident that the season was advancing rapidly."

PEARY: "Just above 87th parallel was a region fifty miles wide which caused me considerable uneasiness. Twelve hours of strong easterly, westerly, or northerly wind would make this region an open sea."

The explorers' reports concerning land at the Pole appear to be similar.

COOK: "No land, No life. No spot to remove the monotony of frost."

PEARY: "The first thirty hours at the pole were spent . . . studying the horizon with a telescope for possible land."

That there was only the barest possibility of land existing at the North Pole had been known for over ten years. Nevertheless, that bare possibility did exist, and in the minds of the public the fundamental question was: Any land at the Pole?

Cook's answer was extremely precise. "No land." The statement was firm; there was no hedging. Peary, however, did not specifically say that there was no land. His full statement ran: "The first thirty hours at the Pole were spent taking observations; in going ten miles beyond our camp and some eight miles to the right of it; in taking photographs, planting my flags, depositing my records, studying the horizon with a telescope for possible land, and searching for a practicable place to make a sounding."

In New York, originally, many people regarded Peary's statement as proving Cook's assertion. In Nova Scotia the three Cape Breton seamen who had been to the Arctic with both explorers found Peary's charges illogical. The Sydney *Daily Post* reported them as saying: "If Peary had gone north and found impossible conditions, then he might be troubled about Cook's story, but Peary proves Cook, at least that is the way we who have been north with Cook and Peary look at it."[44]

In the sixty-one years between 1909 and the writing of this narrative, a minimum of six parties, arriving by one means or another, have stood on the ice about the North Pole. These include the crews of three submarines (two American, one British) and one ski-equipped C-47 (American); as well as the members of the expedition led by Ralph Plaisted, of St. Paul Minnesota, which arrived at the Pole in snowmobiles on April 20, 1968; and the members of the British Trans-Arctic Expedition, led by Wally Herbert, which arrived on foot on April 5, 1969.

Unfortunately, the scientific data collected by these parties cannot be used to prove or disprove the statements made by Cook and Peary relative to conditions at the Pole itself. Scientists employed by the Navy are certain that there are no geophysic parameters that are definitive of the area about the North Pole; and that any description of sea temperature, air temperature, ice cover, wind pressure, and even drift at the Pole apply equally to the entire central Arctic. Cook would surely have agreed with much of this. Of the ice cover at the Pole he wrote in *My Attainment:* "The ice was nearly the same as it had been continuously since leaving the eighty-seventh parallel."

It should be noted, however, that naval research has taken place mainly from the air or under the ice, and that the ice cover itself, its actual surface, may be slightly different than such research indicates. For example: from the air, the ice about the Pole appears slightly rougher than farther south. This was first noted by Admiral Byrd in 1925. In 1969 Canadian pilots informed Wally Herbert that the ice about the Pole did not look too good. Yet Herbert found it otherwise. "Conditions got better and better all the time," he wrote. All who have walked to the Pole agree that the ice does get better, as was first reported by Cook.

That both Cook and Herbert, past the 89th parallel, observed and reported similar responses from their dogs, is worth noting. Cook wrote: "With the Pole only twenty-nine miles distant . . . even the dogs caught the infectious enthusiasm. They rushed along at a pace which made it difficult for me to keep a sufficient advance to set a good course."[45] And Wally Herbert wrote: "From latitude 89° to the Pole . . . the surface was so good that once or twice the dogs actually broke into a gallop, the first time they had done so during the whole journey."[46]

A modern estimate of Cook's report of conditions at the Pole was made in 1964 by John Euller, who wrote: "When Cook returned he described what he had seen: no land, a continuation of the polar ice pack, essentially a frozen ocean but in a state of continuous motion and upheaval. This was not profound, but it was original, and all subsequent accounts, including Peary's, agree with Cook's original description."[47]

Over the years Peary's charge against Cook — "the two Eskimos who accompanied him say he went no distance north and not out of sight of land" — has been repeatedly fertilized by the Commander's associates. Yet it appears that except when Peary was the authority on what the Eskimos said, a different story was told. On October 21, 1909, an account written by Knud Rasmussen, who had returned to Cape York to interview the Eskimos, was published in the New York *Times*. Although Cook's two Eskimo boys were away on a hunting trip, Rasmussen talked with members of their tribe, then reported:

"After they reached the polar ice and the little party had gone directly to the north, the two Eskimos knew that the goal was the Pole. . . . The friends of Ahwelah and Etukishook assert that the expedition had good ice and good weather and that the ice became better the further they came out on the Polar Sea. . . . Had Cook not taken a small canvas boat . . . the Eskimos think they should never have gotten home alive. . . . Cook's statements about how they got through the wintering, fighting musk-ox and walrus without ammunition, are also correct, compared with the statements of his companions. . . . I therefore reach this conclusion: That whenever Cook's statements are compared with the statements of his companions, they appear to be quite truthful. . . . The Eskimos have told their friends that they were very much surprised when Cook told them that the goal was reached, because the spot was not the least different from all the other ice they had passed over. They often had asked Cook to return, but that was only because they had a feeling that they were very, very far from shore and that they would never get back alive again. . . . The Eskimos, who have often seen the start of expeditions, had nothing but praise for the manner in which Cook reduced his equipment to the minimum. . . . To sum up, the Eskimos think that Cook reached the goal and that he during the voyage showed great nerve and energy."*

In addition to the fact that Peary did support Cook in seven instances, the following reasons can be given, *not as "proof" that Cook attained the Pole, but as evidence that his account of his attainment is truthful:*

1. Cook reported that coming south the drift of the ice carried him to the west. This puzzled him. Later, at Etah, according to Whitney, he said: "Conditions were very unusual in the Arctic that season."[48] His reason for believing that the ice would carry him east was that it had carried Peary east in 1906. At the time it was believed that there was only one system of currents in the Arctic. Today it is known that Cook's route fell within what is called the western Arctic gyral, in which the ice travels in a clockwise motion. Thus Cook was the first to report what has now been established as scientific fact.

2. Bradley Land, which he reported as "new land," is now interpreted as an ice island, a phenomenon unknown in his day.

3. No one has disagreed with any of his fundamental statements.

Once again, as on Mount McKinley, Cook is the man who breaks into the unknown. Once again, his report on the unknown is supported to a satisfactory degree by the next traveler, Robert E. Peary. Yet history's verdict is that Cook's account is dreamed up. The Arctic historian Jeanette Mirsky wrote: "It is impossible to dismiss him by simply calling him a liar. Rather it may be said that he is a great . . . fiction writer."[49] No other explanation of the parallels between the accounts of Cook and Peary has ever been offered, and that explanation is utterly impossible.

If history accepts as fact that Henry Hudson reached 81° 30′N in 1607, as it does; and that Captain W. E. Parry reached 82°45′N in 1826, as it does; and that Robert E. Peary

* The reader should be advised that after the Peary Arctic Club had established Cook as a fraud, Rasmussen reversed himself.

reached the North Pole in 1909, as it does; then it would seem that history should also accept Cook's assertion that he attained the North Pole in 1908. If Cook's word continues to be scorned, it would seem as if the whole of man's record of his efforts in the Arctic should be canceled and the region be designated a historic void.

Did Frederick A. Cook attain the North Pole or did he not?

He did.

But in the sporting sense only. He did not claim that he reached the exact mathematical spot. He understood that because he had been alone when he took his observations about the Pole, he could only make a relative claim to having attained the Pole or its approximate location. As a man can be in Manhattan without appearing at City Hall, so was Cook at the North Pole.

In the long run his great weakness, which he could not be expected to control, was that the next traveler, Peary, was an unreliable witness exceptionally open to statistical challenge, and lacking, today, the authority that would in itself automatically validate Cook's testimony.

That is the true scandal of the North Pole controversy.

The possibility of misrepresentation by the explorers on an occasion when their claims were not subject to physical proof is one of the controversy's most interesting problems.

We know that men, inheriting from the hominoid, and trapped in an intricate civilization, lie or distort or shade or omit the truth repeatedly each day. Men lie about small things, but do they lie about big things, such as the assassination of an American President? Men are ready to lie, it seems, about anything that threatens to disturb the pattern of ordered society and their own position in it. But both Cook and Peary had broken away from ordered society, and as they struggled toward the Pole, were on their own. They were following the urges of their private destinies, which had already led them to accomplish astonishing feats. The question of whether or not Cook and Peary attained the North Pole does not, finally, involve ordered society and its institutions, but only and entirely the consciences of the two great American explorers.

Their journeys were private quests. "The true explorer does his work," Peary once said in *Nearest the Pole*, "because the thing he has set for himself to do is part of his being, and must be accomplished for the sake of the accomplishment." Cook maintained that Peary had reached the Pole, saying of him: "He did what he had to do." Of himself Cook wrote in *My Attainment:* "I had proved myself to myself, with no thought at the time of worldly applause." He also wrote of himself when at the Pole: "That was my hour of victory. It was the climacteric hour of my life." He described his journey as "merely a personal achievement."

When all is said and done, only one attitude seems appropriate when contemplating the Arctic endeavors of Dr. Frederick A. Cook and Commander Robert E. Peary: a certain awe.

7

ON OCTOBER 3, 1909, the Brooklyn *Eagle* reported:

"*Portland*, *Maine*, October 2 — An animated conference lasting nearly an hour between . . . Peary . . . and General Thomas H. Hubbard . . . was held in the big train shed here this morning. . . . After a hearty shake of the hand the two men paced up and down almost the entire length of the train shed, under the yellow glare of the big arc lights. Now and then they stopped for a minute as the Commander laid stress upon some point. . . . At one of the pauses the explorer unbuttoned his navy blue sack coat and from it pulled what appeared to be a bulky envelope. Shortly afterwards he made several notes on a small piece of paper and handed it to General Hubbard. The general put both into his inside coat pocket. Finally the west-bound train began to move. General Hubbard grasped the Commander's hand cordially and, with a few words of parting, stepped aboard the express.

" 'I have no remarks to make,' said Commander Peary as he returned to his hotel. . . . 'It is entirely in the hands of General Hubbard and the members of the Peary Arctic Club.' "

There were eleven or less of them, great white hunters all, and owning the trophies to prove it, even if their spoils were not hides thrown on floors or heads mounted in halls. Normally, their grounds were about Wall Street, where they specialized in the law and banking, and the financing and management of railroads, insurance companies, and other inventions of earlier descendants of the hunting hominoid.

To the public they scarcely existed, although the papers would occasionally refer to them, in connection with, of all things, science. "There exists in scientific circles no closer corporation than the Peary Arctic Club," the New York *Herald* declared, "with a membership of 10 to 12 members, and a complete list of these would be difficult to obtain."

To their friends, the members of the club were not hunters but defenders, warriors assigned to protecting the dignity of the truth. But to protect the truth they had to demolish the lie, and so they hunted the liar. "Hunting is the master behavior pattern of the human species," W. S. Laughlin has written. ". . . Man evolved as a hunter, he spent ninety-nine percent of his species history as a hunter, and he spread over the entire habitable area of the world as a hunter."[1]

At the time there was no credibility gap to bother about, nor had anyone heard of overkill or the problems caused by "too much gun." There were no restraints, no restrictions on the club's aggressiveness. In older civilizations the members of the governing class, the weapons-bearing minority, had sharpened their claws by hunting lions and tigers; and the gentlemen of the Peary Arctic Club were not much different. Their prey was one of the governed, a brilliant, apolitical physician optimistic about mankind, whose only aggressions were geographic. He, however, did not regard himself as a lion or a tiger. After he had fled and had recovered from his mauling, he said: "I was like a deer that had been driven into a cold stream."[2]

Although the members of the club left behind, apparently, not one scrap of paper relating to the hunt, they must have had a bully time. And certainly they went first class. "Less than a dozen of Admiral Peary's friends have put up $350,000 to see him through in this matter," Herbert L. Bridgman would say. "I know because I am the treasurer of the fund."[3] So it was a grand affair, their whooping safari, rife with what Wall Street buff John Brooks calls "the thrill of battle, the call of the chase . . . the glamor of admission into a charmed circle

. . . and the social aura of association with the elect." Was not Robert E. Peary one of the great figures of the day? Men such as Andrew Carnegie thought humanity did not benefit from polar expeditions, but men such as Theodore Roosevelt disagreed.

Money was only a part of their arsenal, for they were also equipped with a masterly comprehension of propaganda and the desires of those subject to it; this being but a portion of their special sense of the world's realities and the imperfections of most of its inhabitants. Among the inhabitants they soon located a Montana guide with a wife and five children to support, and a Manhattan insurance salesman who liked to play the role of a man about town and had formed an alliance with a sea captain beached in Brooklyn. From these and others they purchased sworn affidavits. Eventually they owned a dozen such weapons, and these, skillfully exhibited in the newspapers, plus some aid from the naive victim, were just about all it took to transform a winner into a loser, a good guy into a bad guy wearing an abnormally large black sombrero.

Individually, they had much in common with those tycoons, residents of Wall Street, of whom Thomas Beer wrote: "Power had become their amusement, though journals talked of their mania for money. . . . They would spend a month of intrigue on finding a place in a government bureau for a widow out in Oregon, and the point was not that they liked the widow. They had never seen the woman. But it was something to do, a minute display of force and craft. . . . Most of them wanted nothing out of it save this thrill of making a point, an official had been created, or a bill, about which they did not care, had been killed in Congress. 'See,' one of them shouted to Stuyvesant Fish, 'I got my man in!' He had put a collector of customs in a trivial port . . . after spending ten thousand dollars on mighty dinners in Washington."[4]

They can be regarded as men with a strong sense of personal ownership of the present. And that they did own it, the part that immediately interested them, they proved beyond doubt. But they owned it without thought for the owners of tomorrow. That is: being glandular gentlemen who were not past what their leader called "the passionate period of life," and being men who *did* possess a share of the truth — which they had obtained so quickly and easily that they imagined that owning it they owned all — they did not comprehend that they could be wrong. They did not consider that they might be creating a historical slum, a mess which their heirs in matters geographic can only confront as best they can.

Yet the gentlemen of the club were not fools, nor boys or baboons. They were human beings, competent but limited operators whose potential for destruction was enormous. At their most efficient they suggest those men about whom one Wall Street observer wrote, in awed and disturbed tones: "Their resources are so vast that they need only to concentrate upon any given property in order to do with it what they please. . . . They are the greatest operators the world has ever seen, and the beauty of their method is the quietness and lack of ostentation with which they carry on. . . . With them the process is gradual, thorough, and steady . . . and there is an utter absence of chance that is terrible to contemplate."[5]

In the North Pole controversy Frederick A. Cook was the "given property" that the club "concentrated on." The campaign against him was "gradual, thorough, and steady." And there was indeed "an utter absence of chance that is terrible to contemplate."

At the time of the attack on Cook, the members of the club were:[6]

Henry Parish: Banker. President of the New York Life Insurance and Trust Company.

Anton A. Raven: Financier. President of the Atlantic Mutual Insurance Company.

Henry Fairfield Osborn: Paleontologist. President of the American Museum of Natural History, to which Morris K. Jesup, the founder of the club, had willed $6,000,000. Osborn was the son of the developer-president of the Illinois Central Railroad.

James C. Colgate: Broker. Senior member of James B. Colgate & Co., a firm founded by his father. Grandson of the founder of the Colgate Soap Company.

Herman C. Bumpus: Director of the American Museum of Natural History.

John H. Flagler: Financier. Founder of the National Tube Company, which in 1900 reported net profits after depreciation of $14,600,000. In 1901 Flagler sold out to the United States Steel Corporation.

Zenas Crane: Descendant of the founder of the Crane Paper Company.

Lewis L. Delafield: Lawyer. Partner in the firm that represented the American Museum of Natural History.

Benjamin Strong: Banker. Vice president of the Bankers Trust Company. In 1914 he would become the first president of the Federal Reserve Bank of New York.

Thomas Hamlin Hubbard: Corporate lawyer. Partner, Butler, Stillman & Hubbard. Brevet Brigadier General of United States Volunteers. President of the Peary Arctic Club and one of the two men whose membership is mentioned in their obituaries. "General Hubbard was in charge of Peary's side of the controversy," the New York *Times* reported on November 21, 1914. On occasions the General was a rather heavy-handed and superacquisitive man. Immediately after Peary had announced his attainment, Hubbard told the press: "The Peary Arctic Club is very jubilant. . . . As he was directly under orders from the Federal government there is no doubt that the Pole will become government property."[7]

Such reactions, however, were atoned for by his righteousness, his relentlessness, and his knowledge of the world. In addition to his military rank and his membership in the geographic peerage (Mount Thomas Hubbard; Cape Thomas

Hubbard), he owned the controlling interest in the New York *Globe;* was a trustee of Bowdoin College, Peary's alma mater as well as his own; and was a director of Western Union, Metropolitan Life, the National Bank of Commerce, Equitable Trust, and the Wabash Railroad. His good fortune started to rise, apparently, in 1885, when he represented English bondholders of the Wabash and became a member of the committee that reorganized that railroad. "After the death of Mark Hopkins," Hubbard's biographer wrote, "he undertook the management of the Mark Hopkins estate which included one-fourth ownership of the Southern Pacific Company."[8] For eleven years Hubbard was a director of the Southern Pacific and for five years its first vice president. Later Hubbard was president of the International Banking Corporation, the American agent for collecting the Boxer indemnity from China. In New York he lived at 16 West 58 Street.

Hubbard contributed at least $60,000 to Peary's expeditions. This figure includes the $10,000 he gave toward the construction of the *Roosevelt*, plus the $50,000 he added when he accepted the presidency of the club. It is possible that he also contributed an additional $50,000. Peary wrote: "General Hubbard accepted the presidency and added a second large check to his already generous contribution."[9] These sums do not include whatever amount he tossed into the pot set up to finance the attack on Cook.

Thomas Hubbard appears to have been concerned about legal ethics. He had endowed the Albany Law School with a chair for instruction in such. He had informed the law students of Union University: "It is safe to say of any able lawyer who has passed the passionate period of life, that he does not deem the verdicts he has won to have been successes, if they have been won by distortion of facts, by undeserved invective, by unjust aspersions of character or motive, or if their winning has taken from the opposing party something that should have been left with them."[10]

Talk of this sort may have been pleasant to hear in an age when Americans believed their country to be the most decent nation on the face of the globe. Today the best that can be said of Thomas Hubbard is that he was just another worldly but glandular man entirely adjusted to the concept that the end justifies the means. As the polar controversy began he *had* a reason for believing that Cook was a liar, and so, crying "False in One, False in All," he directed his forces adroitly. But Thomas Hubbard was not the first general to be brilliant but wrong. He led the campaign that tore away from Cook "something that should have been left." That campaign was founded on "distortions of fact . . . undeserved invective . . . unjust aspersions of character or motive." The modern investigator cannot regard the polar controversy as a study in stupidity. To do so would be to oversimplify the human condition.

Of Hubbard's person an acquaintance wrote: "There was in his appearance a sense of power, of dignity and integrity which inspired universal confidence in his character; and no man during the time of his life in New York, occupying so prominent a position at the bar and in business, has left a more stainless name. General Hubbard was a singularly handsome man in the best sense. Tall, erect, with a well-knit figure and splendid bearing, he was always a striking personage in any company."[11]

Herbert Lawrence Bridgman: Newspaper executive. Business manager and part owner of the Brooklyn *Standard-Union* from 1894 until 1924. Secretary of the club, and, today, its most fascinating member, mainly because he, the mastermind behind the assault on Cook, possessed qualities that would make him an ideal chief of the dirty tricks department of the CIA. He was a medium-sized, or perhaps small man with a cold face and a droopy mustache, reserved and with simple tastes. He had an exceptionally strong opinion of what life was all about and he backed his opinion with energy and cunning. After his death his wife discovered, to her surprise, that he was a millionaire.[12]

He was a native of Amherst, Massachusetts, and a graduate of Amherst College. After joining the staff of the Springfield (Mass.) *Republican*, where he rose to city editor, he went to

New York and worked for the Associated Press, *Leslie's* magazine, the New York *Press*, and the New York *Tribune*. In New York his interest in the affairs of his college fraternity, Psi Upsilon, was such that he became president of its executive council, a post that he retained for forty-one years. During this time he gave a hopeful hand to youngsters, and an even more hopeful hand, when allowed, to those alumni who were among the mighty great.

But Mr. Psi U was not Bridgman's only identity in masculine society in New York. Around 1891 he met Robert E. Peary. Since Bridgman's interest in travel and exploration was as genuine as his interest in potentially important men, they soon became intimates. At first Bridgman was simply Peary's press agent; only gradually did he become Peary's first friend. As a press agent he was superb. One of his greatest coups was the creation of the club itself, which Peary's daughter credits him with organizing: "It was foremost and primarily through the energy and organizing ability of Herbert L. Bridgman that the Peary Arctic Club came into existence."[13] Just how he brought this off is unknown, and formal credit for the establishment of the club continues to be given to Morris K. Jesup. The Pearys' original contact with Jesup was made by Josephine Peary, and it is possible that Bridgman pointed her at the tycoon.

As will be seen, the degree of ferociousness that the club showed in its attack on Cook was abnormal. Long after its victory was so total, officially, that the club had been disbanded — that is, long after, so far as its more casual members knew, its mission was accomplished — someone was still pursuing the Doctor, sporadically but successfully. It would seem, therefore, that someplace along the line Cook had had the immense misfortune of picking up a real and exceptionally competent enemy. It is extremely probable that that enemy was Herbert L. Bridgman.

Bridgman appears to have been the only member of the club, besides Peary, who knew Cook personally. Bridgman frequently visited Cook's office to talk about travel and exploration.* Bridgman also attended the social events in the Doctor's home on Bushwick Avenue.[14] The fourth floor of the house was a ballroom in which the Cooks entertained artists, writers, musicians, and explorers.

In the early years Cook regarded Bridgman as a friend. His telegram announcing his ascent of Mount McKinley was sent to Bridgman, as was the letter advising that he was going to attempt the Pole. It was after receiving this letter, brought south on the *John R. Bradley*, that Bridgman, apparently, became Cook's mortal enemy; not for personal reasons, probably, but simply because Cook was now a dangerous threat to Peary.

During the polar controversy at least one man, the Arctic explorer and writer Dillon Wallace, seems to have understood Bridgman's role. Referring to the Mount McKinley slanders, which began almost immediately after Cook's announcement, Wallace wrote: "They were inspired by persons . . . who have been hanging to the tail of Mr. Peary's kite for years, and who feared that they might lose their hold on the kite's tail and the financial backers of Mr. Peary should the expedition from which he is now returning have proved a failure. These men . . . gave [Cook] full credit . . . as an authority of high standing upon Arctic and Antarctic exploration until they learned that he was a dangerous rival of Mr. Peary for Polar honors. Then they forgot past friendships, and like a thief in the dark, tried to knife him in the back."[15]

Wallace's statement, eliminating all other members of the club — "financial backers of Mr. Peary" — points to Bridgman. In 1893, after resigning from Peary's second expedition, Cook attempted to organize an expedition to the South Pole. At the time Bridgman wrote in the *Standard-Union:* "The work of unlocking the great mystery of the South . . . could be trusted to no more competent hands than Dr. Cook's. Those

* Bridgman had gone to the Arctic in 1894 to see how his man was getting along. Later he made three more trips north for the same purpose. He also explored, on his own, the Mesa Encantada in New Mexico.

who know him know that he combines the patience, judgment and zeal of the explorer with thorough medical and scientific knowledge, added to the practical experience of priceless value gained with the Peary expedition."[16]

During the years of the controversy, and beyond, six bombs exploded under the Doctor, six actions by others that dramatically reinforced his image as a liar. Of these, as will be seen, three were tossed by men — Dunkle, Baldwin, and Houston — who had one thing and one thing only in common: they all knew, and were known by, Herbert L. Bridgman. As Ian Fleming wrote in *Goldfinger:* "Mr. Bond, they have a saying in Chicago: 'Once is happenstance, twice is coincidence, the third time it's enemy action.' "

For quiet, modest Herbert Bridgman, it all seems to have worked out beautifully. In 1910, soon after Cook had been bagged, he became chairman of the Publishers Association of New York, and continued as such until his death. He was one of the founders of the American Newspaper Publishers Association and served three terms as its president. In 1913 he was an American delegate to the International Geographic Congress in Rome. Amherst made him a Doctor of Laws. Meanwhile, being the interesting and energetic man that he was, he continued to travel. "At the age of sixty, Mr. Bridgman made a journey to the headquarters of the Nile," the New York *Times* reported in its obituary of him, "and penetrated into the interior of Africa, covering much of the ground that had been trodden by Livingston and Stanley." As he aged he became a mildly exotic citizen, the American bemedaled by foreign governments: from Belgium the Order of Leopold, from Bulgaria the Cross of St. Anthony.

At the time of his death in 1924, Bridgman was a member of the Board of Regents of the State of New York, a position that included certain luxuries, such as cruising to Europe on the New York State Nautical Schoolship *Newport.* It was aboard this ship that his tidy life ended. Of this superbly disguised man the captain of the *Newport* wrote: "His name, standing forever on the great cape at the extremity of northeast

Greenland, placed there by Peary in honor of his tireless co-worker, was pointed out by me on various occasions when foreign visitors were on board and the fine London *Times* map of the North Polar regions was spread on the cabin table. I have always suspected that Dr. Bridgman liked to have me do this. It was the one bit of vanity I was able to uncover in a nature altogether unassuming."[17]

Frederick A. Cook's crime can be described in many ways, one of which is to say that he was entirely different from the gentlemen of the club. He was not one of the boys. In the instance of a fabulous geographic prize, he ignored the whole of the American power complex, and proceeded as if the practice was, in America, that large matters were best accomplished as inexpensively as possible, and without fanfare.

8

THE HUNT built up momentum so swiftly that it seems certain that its directors had comprehended the Doctor's potential early and had made arrangements. A few years afterward the Mayor of Tacoma, Washington, would say as much, declaring that Belmore Browne, a distinguished Tacomian, and a man "exceptionally honored in the East," had informed him "weeks before Cook emerged . . . exactly what would happen and did. He would claim to have discovered the Pole, he would either be alone, or no responsible white man would be with him, and there would be an excuse about his proofs."[1]

The hunt began with a drive on Cook's most vulnerable spot, the gossip that he had faked his ascent of Mount McKinley. On September 6, 1909, only four days after Cook had informed the world of his attainment of the Pole, the New York *Sun* published a story from Butte, Montana, which stated: "Fred Printz, a well-known guide . . . takes the present occasion to charge Dr. Cook with fraud. In another part of his allegations he is supported by Ed Barrim [Barrill], another guide. . . . Both men alleged that Dr. Cook did not place a foot on Mount McKinley, but that the lower peaks were climbed and photos taken to deceive. . . . Printz . . . says: 'I'm just as sure as I'm living that Dr. Cook never saw the North Pole.' "

Two days later, in Seattle, S. P. Beecher, who as the cook on the second McKinley expedition had played no part in the ascent, confidently announced that the Doctor had not climbed the mountain. And on the same day, in New York, Herschel

Parker informed the press: "It is with great reluctance that I am compelled to say that Dr. Cook has not made a satisfactory explanation of Mount McKinley."* And so, six days after Cook's announcement had delighted the world, three of the seven members of the 1906 expedition had publicly agreed that Cook was a fraud. Today it seems obvious that the club's trackers had previously located the members of the expedition and routinely arranged for their availability. Eventually the club bagged the whole expedition.

In the Pacific Northwest such matters were directed by an experienced warrior, General James A. Ashton, now peacefully practicing law in Tacoma, where some knew him as "Slippery Jim." General Ashton acknowledged that a New York law firm had retained him to investigate, but informed reporters that the important thing was that he "does not know whether the information is wanted by Peary's adherents or friends of Dr. Cook's."[2] In New York the *Herald* soon revealed the damning truth. Jim Ashton and Tom Hubbard were partners "in the ownership of a large acreage of Tacoma tide lands on deep water."[3]

Meanwhile, Edward N. Barrill, the only important member, after Cook, of the 1906 McKinley expedition, was up in the Bitterroot Mountains of Montana. When he returned to his home in Darby, Montana, and caught up on the news of the world, he understood that for the first time in his forty-five hard years, he held the high cards. He smelled money.

For the moment, the air so fragrant about him, he was the one and only: the one man who had been with Cook at the summit, the only man who knew positively that Cook had

* In New York, in 1906, before Cook's attainment of the summit had been announced, Parker had been giving talks about McKinley. After the news of the ascent, Parker declared: "I do not believe he made the ascent of Mount McKinley." When Cook returned to New York Parker toned down his statements but continued to present himself as an expert on the mountain. He seems to have disgusted Cook, who in *To the Top of the Continent* (New York, 1908) revealed, to the close reader, that Parker had been a liability on the expedition. The result was that Parker was ardently pro-Peary.

reached the summit. But he was also the one man who knew that the "summit" photo was bogus; just as he was the only man who had his particular wife and his particular children, five, to think about. And since there had been some foolishness on McKinley, it was possible to wonder if there had not been more foolishness at the Pole. Also, he had climbed the mountain, just like the Doctor, and about the only thing he had actually gotten out of it was his name in a book, which he had showed proudly around town.

They called him "Big Ed," and for his times he was big, being six feet two inches tall, and weighing over two hundred pounds, with no fat on him. "A huge, upstanding hulk of a man," one reporter said of him. He had blue eyes, a sandy complexion, and a tawny mustache, drooping and frayed at the ends. A native of Buffalo, New York, he was of French-Canadian descent, and a tremendous talker. He was such a gabber that normally his listeners resisted him; "more or less skepticism around here," a reporter noted, "as to the exact value of the tales he tells."[4]

And there was a problem about his name. During those few days when, unexpectedly, he was the most important man in Montana, reporters from Missoula noted that at various times in the recent past he had been known as Edwin Barrill, Ed Burrill, Ed Brill, and Ed Barrim. In his affidavit against Cook, he signed himself Edward N. Barrill, and is so identified today.

Besides being large and loquacious, and careless about rather fundamental things, he was, it appears, a tremendous patriot. The *Daily Missoulian* reported that he "expressed disappointment and even disgust that Cook had come back from the north under a Danish flag and landed in Denmark instead of heading directly for his own country as Commander Peary did."[5]

At any rate, when "Big Ed" came down from the Bitterroot Mountains and smelled money, a strange thing happened. He shut up.

"He has developed a reticence," a reporter wrote, "not at all in accord with the reputation for talkativeness . . . hitherto enjoyed." The reporter then wrote, with captivating candidness: "His taciturnity goes with a shrewd business sense that seems likely to do him a very good turn before he is through with the present incident."[6]

But "Big Ed" did not shut up completely. After describing his position as: "This looks like a 'big mit' situation to me,"[7] he reminded the world that he himself had made no statement. To do so he had to repudiate the declaration of his buddy Fred Printz, and this he did easily: "Says that the Printz interview, in so far as it related to him, is not correct."[8]

When the Beecher and Parker statements were published, he belittled their importance. "I, of course, was the only man with Dr. Cook at the time in question," the *Daily Missoulian* quoted him as saying; "and the statements made by the other members of the party regarding the ascent of the peak were not made of their own personal knowledge."[9]

But otherwise he was quiet. "In regard to whether or not he believed Dr. Cook reached the north pole," the press reported, " . . . evasive in his answers."[10]

In the East the club's prey, with no idea that he was such, was encountering some of the minor eccentricities of civilization, an experience that bewildered him. As much as anything, he was handicapped by his belief that "I have, as I have said, absolute confidence in the good sense, spirit of fair-play, and ability of reasoning judgment of my people."[11]

From the beginning, in New York, he was the vulnerable man, wide open not only to the club, but to every variety of schemer, grafter, and unwelcome visitor. Across the hall from the entrance to his suite at the Waldorf was a reception room, and whenever he emerged to do what he wanted to do, he was besieged by those who had better ideas. A few of these individuals, such as the representatives of a sect of the times, the Hollow Earth people, were harmless. After congratulating him on his journey they — Internal Scientists — notified him that he had not attained the true Pole, and had probably not gotten any farther than the outer coast of the inner world. At the Pole itself, they assured him, there definitely was land, land that swarmed with new and superior people. If only he had journeyed a few miles farther. Other besiegers were more venial. One afternoon he was confronted by a vaudeville impresario who had learned that Peary had had a child by an Eskimo woman. The proposal was that Cook send north for the mother and child. A huge sum was offered for their services.[12]

At the time Cook was the public favorite. In newspaper straw poles the Pittsburgh *Press* listed 73,238 votes for Cook, 2,814 for Peary. The Watertown, (N.Y.) *Times* counted three to one for Cook. The Toledo *Blade* reported 550 for Cook, 10 for Peary.

Out on the lecture circuit the pace was destructive. In twenty-four days Cook showed himself at some seventy banquets and receptions, and gave innumerable press interviews. In city after city, crowds pressed about him. Each day, hundreds of people called on him. He himself was captured by the pace — "the excitement still ran like a fever in my veins" — and was so busy that he had no time to think. Meanwhile, wherever he went, he was disturbed by the fact that almost everyone seemed to accept as fact the absurdity that he had bribed his Eskimos with gumdrops. This myth, he eventually discovered, had originated with John R. Bradley. It seems that Bradley had tired of talking with reporters and had banned any further interviews. One reporter continued to pester him, however, and finally Bradley granted him a brief visit. It began with Bradley inquiring disgustedly:

"What is it you want to know?"

"Well, Mr. Bradley, I thought maybe you could tell us how Dr. Cook got the Eskimos to help him with his expedition, if he didn't have a lot of goods to trade them."

Bradley replied jeeringly: "Damn it, son, I thought you knew Doc had a barrel of gumdrops with him, and it's a settled fact than an Eskimo will follow you to the devil for a few gumdrops."[13]

The reporter rushed back to his office and pounded out his

story. It was printed as fact and grew as only a canard can. Gumdrop sales rose astonishingly, and wherever Cook went he faced comment about gumdrops, some of which was ill natured and aggressive.

He was too busy to read the newspapers, but he gradually realized that the press was attacking him ferociously. The charges and suspicions filtered through to him from reporters, and usually reached him in exaggerated form. He was particularly distressed by the fact that he was being attacked, not for unintentional error, but for deliberate falsehood.

In Washington he became the victim of a severe case of laryngitis, the first evidence that he was falling apart physically. "It got worse as I went to Baltimore and Pittsburgh," he wrote. "At St. Louis I was feverish and mentally dazed. Thereafter, day after day, my thoughts became less coherent; I, more like a machine." Although he was told that throughout his ordeal he smiled pleasantly, he was never conscious of doing so, and eventually wrote: "It is strange how, machine-like, a man can conduct himself like a reasonable being when, mentally, he is at sea." He wrote in *My Attainment*, "I have read a great deal about the sub-conscious mind; on no other theory can I account for my rational conduct in public at the time."

Altogether, he was passing through exotic territory, and although it had been viewed before, it had never been explored by a traveler whose situation was as remarkable as his.

When the Barrill stories began to appear in the eastern press, the Doctor sent his climbing partner $200 and asked him to come to New York for a press conference at which they would both tell their individual stories of the ascent. This did not appeal to "Big Ed." The *Daily Missoulian* reported: "He declares that he will pay his own expenses and be absolutely independent so that there can be no cause for suspicion."[14] Saying so, he kept the $200.

General James Ashton then entered the situation. He had secured the services of the photographer Walter Miller, who had been a member of both of Cook's Alaskan expeditions.* Now Miller came to Montana to bring Barrill west.

For eighteen years, in Montana, Barrill had been a blacksmith. Some months before the controversy began, curiously enough, his life-style had changed, and he was now in the real estate business in partnership with a C. G. Bridgford, who would soon swear in an affidavit: "The next communication I had with Mr. Barrill was the evening before he started for Seattle. He had told me a time or two before about getting a telegram from a man by the name of Miller; I think Mr. Miller is a photographer. . . . I went to him that evening and told him we had some men to take out to look at some land the next morning: he said to me, 'I cannot go; that party Miller from Seattle is in Missoula and I am to meet him there to-night. This means from $5,000 to 10,000 to me.'

"Mr. Barrill stated that he was at Mount McKinley when Dr. Cook made the ascent. . . . From what Mr. Barrill said I judged that Dr. Cook and he reached the top. . . . I judged as much from what other men told me as from what Mr. Barrill told me."[15]

But Barrill did not immediately go to Tacoma to see General Ashton. Instead, he and his buddy Printz† headed for Seattle. "He visited the office of the Seattle *Times*," Cook wrote later. "In the presence of the editor, Mr. Joe Blethen, he dickered for the sale of an affidavit to discredit me. He knew such an affidavit had news value. Indefinite offers ranging from $5,000

* In *The Shameless Diary of an Explorer* (New York, 1907), Robert Dunn wrote of Miller: "An utter stranger, he had . . . asked us to take him. The Professor [Cook] twice refused, not admiring his physique; but the night our horses and outfit were loaded . . . we still had not enough men. Miller appeared on the dock to see us off — and came with us . . . [a] youth of twenty-four, who did office work in the Seattle city hall." In the January, 1904, issue of *Outing* magazine, Dunn described Miller as "a pale, thin, slight youth . . . citified, uncouth, and low-voiced, as they are out on the coast."

† As Barrill was tall and powerful, so was Printz short and powerful. Belmore Browne described him as "a small, active man, as hard as nails, and probably as good a wilderness pack-train man as ever threw a diamond hitch."

to $10,000 were made.* Not getting a lump sum off-hand, Barrill, dissatisfied, then went to Tacoma. . . . That all this was done, was told me . . . by Mr. Blethen himself."[16]

On October 4, 1909, in Tacoma, Barrill swore out his affidavit. Its contents completely satisfied General Ashton, who later said of Barrill: "He may be nothing but a mountain guide but he is a type of our hard-working western man who will fight rather than lie."[17] Ashton also announced: "Barrill said the physician was a good fellow and he had not given the Mount McKinley matter a thought until the North Pole question came up. The guide said to me: 'Then I talked it over with my wife after you sent for me and we reached the conclusion that it was my duty to give the world the real truth.' "[18]

But for stubby Fred Printz the journey to Washington State was apparently profitless. He soon wrote Cook: "Friend Cook, I am sorry that I can't come at present. But will come and see you in 'bout 15 days if you will send me $350.00 and I will say that the report in the papers from what I have is not true. Hoping to see you soon, Your friend, Fred Printz."

To this Cook did not reply. The note itself was published in the New York *Times* on October 30, 1909.

At least one other man attempted to profit from knowing Cook in Alaska. The New York *Sun* published a dispatch from Tacoma which said that General Ashton's chief clerk had received additional information but would not reveal its substance. The dispatch continued: "About two weeks ago John Brigman arrived here from Alaska. He told friends that Dr. Cook and Barrill stopped at his camp. . . . He told John McMillan, an attorney, that he was willing to make an affidavit if well remunerated. Brigman told McMillan that he was employed by Dr. Cook . . . to go to a neighboring Indian village and bring back a squaw whom Dr. Cook wanted to interview."[19]

* In *The Case for Doctor Cook* (New York, 1961), Andrew Freeman noted that "C. B. Blethen . . . in an answer to an inquiry by the writer, supplied certain facts which he declined to make available for publication."

Meanwhile, the aldermen of the City of New York had voted to award Cook the finest honor in their keeping, the Freedom of the City. Lafayette had received it, so had Dickens and the Prince of Prussia, but it had never been presented to an American citizen. The ceremony was announced for the afternoon of October 15 at City Hall.

When the gentlemen of the club heard about it, they began to make their own preparations for the event.

On October 13 they released Peary's fourteen-point indictment of Cook. Although this document, in Peary's mind, presented the "proof" he had been talking about for over a month, it was in effect simply a series of screams. A story from Brussels would soon quote Adrien de Gerlache as observing: "Of the fourteen objections . . . there is not one of really convincing nature, and the majority would not carry the weight of a feather in a serious discussion."[20] But a serious discussion was not on the club's agenda. They were only interested in winning, and as they saw the problem, Peary's indictment provided a basis for asserting all sorts of things: such as that Cook was a faker because his Eskimos had told Peary that they had returned to land after traveling only "two sleeps" across the polar ice; that Cook was a faker because Peary had carefully inspected his sled and had recognized that it would not last even one day in the Arctic; that Cook was a faker because his leaving of his data at Etah was a deliberate scheme on his part to get out of having to show his observations; and that, finally, Cook was a faker because no man would have left a flag that had flown at the Pole with an utter stranger like Harry Whitney. All of this was presented to the public in the form of a 2,500-word document and map dressed up with a copyright.*

* Today only one of Peary's contentions seems worthy of attention. In 1906 he had been at Svartevoeg (Cape Thomas Hubbard) and had deposited a record in a cairn. In his indictment he stated that if Cook could show this record, he would accept it as proof that Cook had been that far north. Although Cook's time was so limited that he could not afford to give Bradley Land a close inspection, he attempted to locate Peary's cairn. "A great deal of careful search . . . was prosecuted about

Meanwhile, the club owned the Barrill affidavit, which by its nature would strengthen every statement in Peary's indictment. On October 14 the world was presented with "Big Ed" 's sworn testimony. The declarations by Printz, Parker, and Beecher had been tiny explosions, barely large enough to make a newspaper reader wonder; but Barrill's affidavit, the statement of the only man to accompany Cook on the mountain, was loud and dramatic. The story broke in General Hubbard's paper, the New York *Globe*, under a screaming headline and a conspicuous line of type that informed other papers that Barrill's statements were *not* copyrighted.

In his affidavit Barrill swore:

1. "I was with Dr. Cook continuously every day during the time he was attempting to ascend the mountain in the year 1906, and the nearest point to the summit of Mount McKinley which we reached was at least fourteen miles from the summit of that mountain."

2. That Cook's photograph of the summit of Mount McKinley was actually a photograph of a peak only 8,000 feet high.

3. That Cook had forced him to make false entries in his diary.

Barrill's diary played a prominent part in his affidavit, which the *Globe* published in two parts. The details of the diary were featured in the October 15 issue. "From and including the 9th down to and including the 18th of September," Barrill testified, "all writing in my diary is by me, but was made under the direction of Dr. Cook. I also changed the dates under his direction."

Although a portion of Barrill's affidavit has been demon-

Svartevoeg," he wrote in *My Attainment of the Pole* (New York, 1913), "but no such cache was found." In 1912 Donald B. MacMillan also arrived at Svartevoeg, where he spent a full day searching for Peary's cairn without finding it. The next day he moved out on the pack ice and finally spotted the cairn on a different headland altogether. After an immense amount of work, MacMillan succeeded in retrieving Peary's record.

strated to have been correct, the inference that Cook considered the control of the diary important seems improbable. As Andrew Freeman wrote: "If Cook . . . had anything to fear so far as Barrill's diary was concerned, it would seem that he would have found an excuse to procure the diary and destroy it long before he left Alaska. But there is nothing in the affidavit to show that he ever attempted to buy the diary or to bribe Barrill."[21] Those men, such as Belmore Browne, who had inside knowledge of the Barrill affidavit always disassociated themselves from "Big Ed." Once his affidavit had served the club's purpose, it was — with the exception of the map — discarded.

For the nation's newspapers, Barrill's affidavit was a sensation. On October 14, information about Barrill filled a full column on page 1 of the New York *Times* (which knew what was coming) and a half a column on page 2. On October 15 its coverage of Barrill's affidavit ran for a full column on page 1 and for two and three-quarter columns on page 2. By October 16 Barrill's affidavit was off the front page of that paper, but still rated two columns on page 2. Thus, in three days, the New York *Times* gave Barrill and his affidavit some seven full columns. This total includes almost six columns on what Barrill said in his affidavit. That paper's stories about what other people said about Barrill's affidavit filled an additional seven columns.

The man himself, "Big Ed" in the flesh, arrived in New York on October 14. There the club, at least Bridgman and Hubbard, got its first look at its star slanderer, who having no further need for caginess was once again, it would seem, his loquacious self. At any rate, the gentlemen of the club looked at "Big Ed," listened to "Big Ed," then hid "Big Ed." Although every reporter in New York knew that he was in town, they could not find him. A committee of the Explorers Club met hastily to receive his testimony, but he did not appear. The man of the moment, the man who over a three-day period was responsible for some fourteen columns of news and comment in the New York *Times*, slipped out of the metropolis and returned to Montana without being questioned by one single reporter.

The Doctor was lecturing in Atlantic City when the *Globe* broke its story about Barrill's affidavit. He learned of it from a reporter from the New York *Times*, whose editors had sent him down to show Cook a copy of the affidavit and observe and report his reaction. The reporter could only write: "Read very carefully through at least twice. Dr. Cook looked more and more surprised the further he got into the document." He afterwards told the reporter: "I never knew Barrill kept a diary. I never saw it. . . . The only thing I ever saw him do was make sketches."

He returned to New York the next day, October 15. The press found him at the Twenty-third Street Ferry. "The explorer, who is evidently greatly annoyed about the statements," the *Eagle* reported, ". . . did not depart from his usual attitude of reserve." But with every paper in New York carrying its own report about Barrill's affidavit, he understood that he had to say something, and so he declared: "It must be that money was used to induce him to sign such an affidavit."[22] And since he could not possibly acknowledge that a portion of Barrill's assertion was true, he was stuck with his small but deadly foolishness, and could only insist that his photograph showed the genuine summit. Later in the morning he for the first time sought legal advice. His choice was a reputable lawyer resoundingly named H. Wellington Wack.

Then came the ceremony at City Hall.

Several thousand people were awaiting his arrival. They gave him a mighty welcome. He smiled automatically, then the police broke a lane through the crowd and Alderman Walsh and Bird C. Coler escorted him into the council room. There he received more applause and cheers. Alderman McGowan rapped for order, then announced that the first business of the session would be the presentation of a gold medal from the Arctic Club of America. This was made by Dr. Roswell Stebbins, a veteran of the *Miranda* venture, who in his remarks said: "We hope it will call to your mind that your old shipmates have a warm welcome for you and a warm spot in their hearts for you."

As Dr. Stebbins was about to present the medal, "it slipped and fell beneath his feet," the *American* reported. It was quickly recovered and the presentation was completed.

Alderman Walsh then read a statement explaining why he and his peers believed that Cook deserved the Freedom of the City. In the light of today his statement shows that the politically sophisticated aldermen interpreted the North Pole controversy correctly. "The best proof of Dr. Cook's conquest, it seems to me, is to be found in the fact that his statement as to the polar conditions on the far north ice-covered sea is practically parallel to that presented by the other explorer. . . . Dr. Cook did not say, merely, that he found himself on a field of ice, leaving a loophole for escape should someone else report that land had been discovered at the Pole. He said that this field was drifting slowly over depths of sea, a fact which the other explorer has verified. . . . Under the circumstances, should we not do for him what has been done for other explorers upon presentation of far less evidence, and believe him? . . . If the other explorer really doubts Dr. Cook's word, why does he not challenge his statement as to climatic and geographic conditions? Why does he not assert that he believes no new land is to be found where Dr. Cook says it is? . . . Would a faker take chances in making unnecessary statements of alleged fact? To these questions, it seems to me, there can be but one answer."[23]

The presentation ceremony then took place. Once again, an odd and unfortunate incident occurred.

The New York *Sun* reported:

"Long before Dr. Cook arrived the Aldermanic chamber looked like a new oil field. A dozen towering camera tripods scattered about the chamber . . . greatly resembled so many oil derricks.

"Two of these contraptions were of the variety designed to take flashlight pictures. The tops of their derricks are enclosed in large square cotton bags, which are supposed to keep the smoke of the flash from choking off orators.

Harry Whitney.

Cook and his wife aboard the *Grand Republic* just before it docked in Brooklyn.

Peary and Bob Bartlett aboard the *Roosevelt*.

General Thomas H. Hubbard, president of the Peary Arctic Club.

Herbert L. Bridgman.

Lillian Kiel.

The cover of *Hampton's* January, 1911, issue. *Hampton's* forgeries have been called "the most dastardly deed in the history of journalism."

After 498 days in jail, Cook manages a smile as he leaves for Leavenworth.

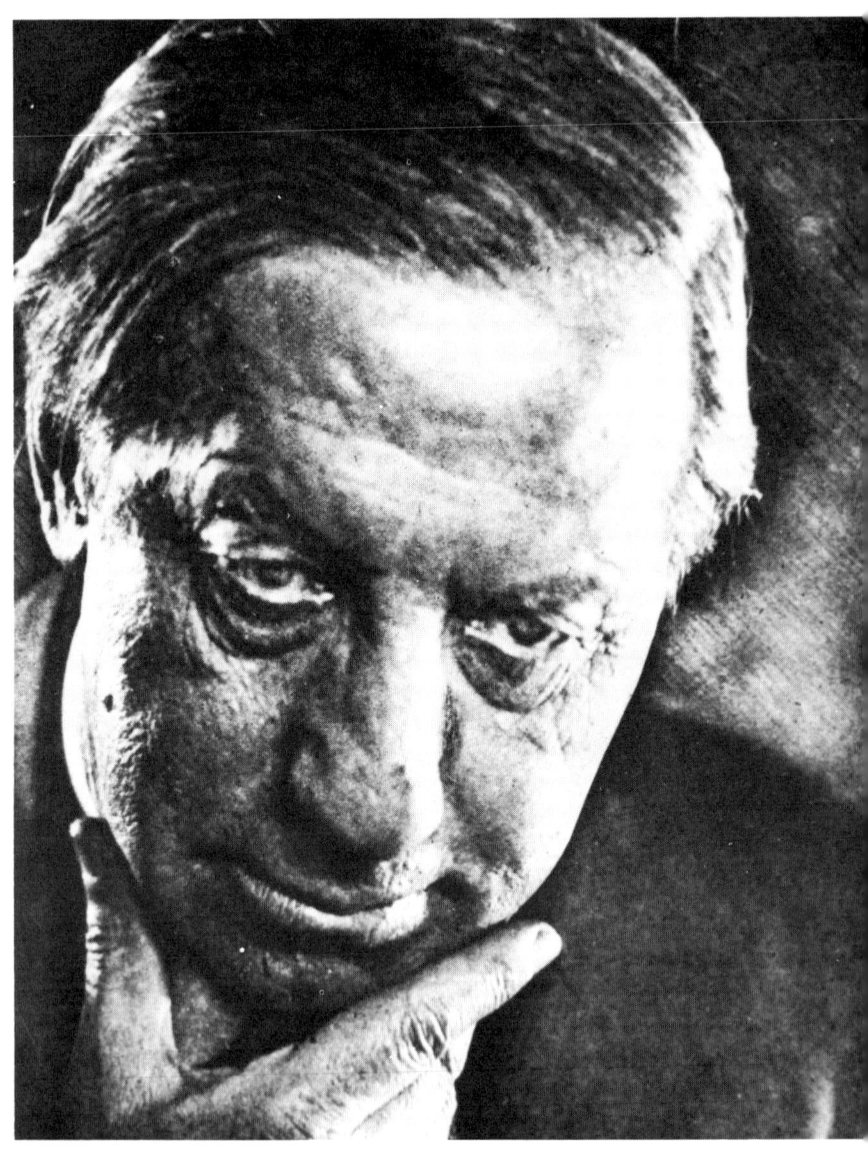

Frederick A. Cook in his late sixties.

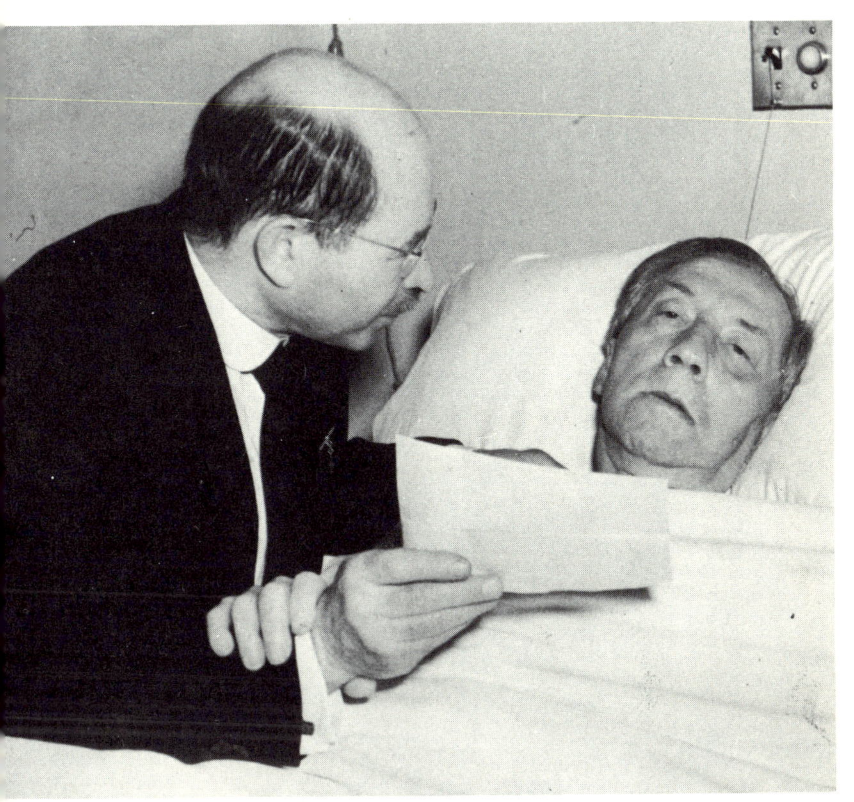

Cook after his stroke. Ralph Shainwald shows the Doctor the telegram announcing that Cook has been pardoned by President Franklin D. Roosevelt.

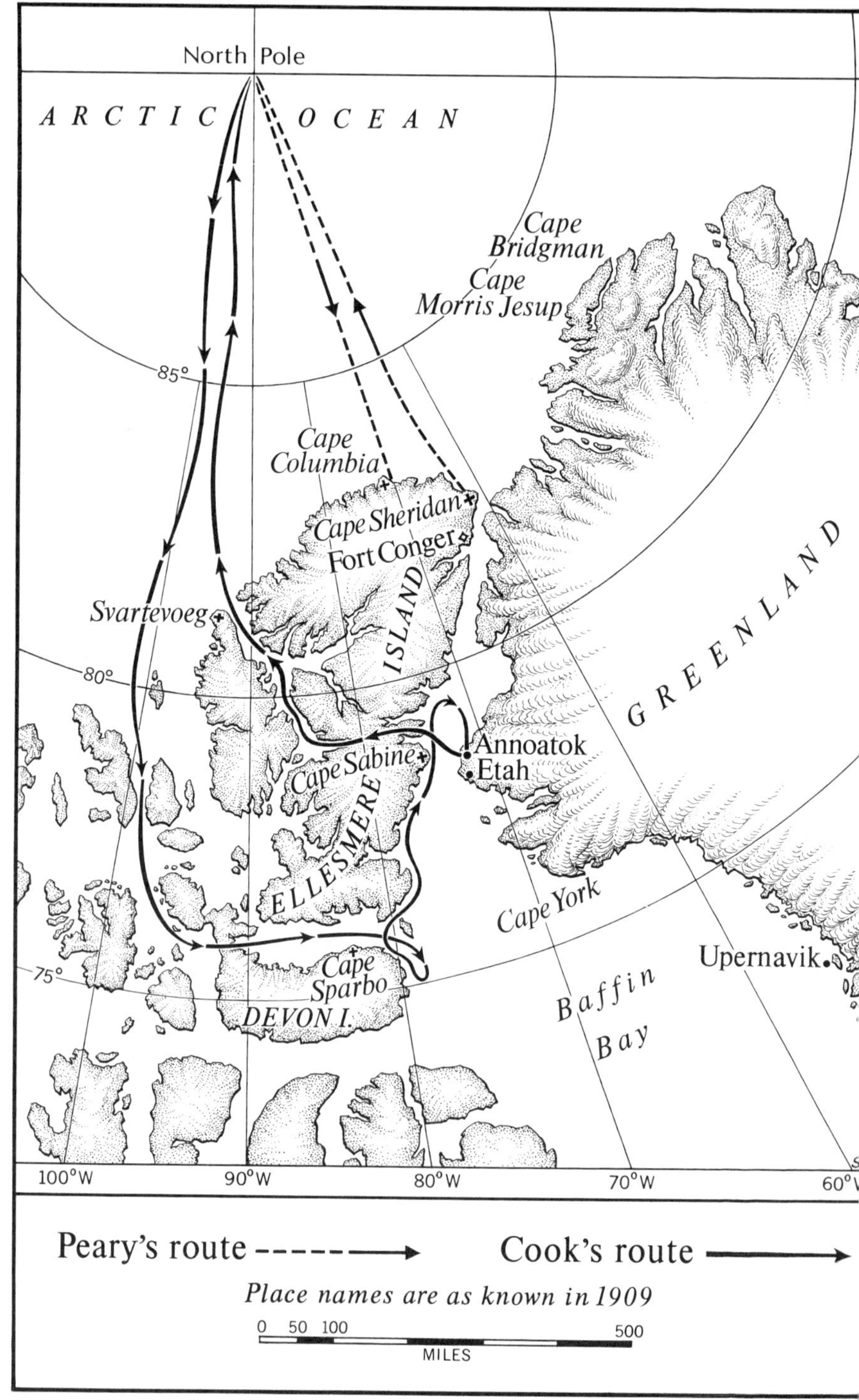
North Pole
ARCTIC OCEAN
Cape Bridgman
Cape Morris Jesup
85°
Cape Columbia
Cape Sheridan
Fort Conger
ISLAND
GREENLAND
Svartevoeg
80°
Annoatok
Etah
Cape Sabine
ELLESMERE
Cape York
Cape Sparbo
75°
DEVON I.
Upernavik
Baffin Bay
100°W
90°W
80°W
70°W
60°W
Peary's route
Cook's route
Place names are as known in 1909
0 50 100 500
MILES

"One of these flashlight bags at the top of its derrick was snuggled up against Swett's copy of one of Stuart's portraits of General Washington; that one . . . showing the General standing by the side of his white horse facing downstage with his accustomed calmness while a battle rages fiercely in the backdrop.

"When Alderman Walsh handed to Dr. Cook a beautiful mahogany box containing a scroll, he did so with a great deal of natural dignity. This did not suit the army of photographers. One of their number left the firing line, dashed up to the Alderman and the doctor, posed them carefully in artificial and unnatural attitudes, and then rushed back to the battery, gave a signal, and at once there was a flash and roar and the cotton tent snuggling to General Washington was instantly in a raging and ill-smelling flame.

"It was an awkward thing to handle, and before it could be lowered, still blazing, the General . . . had suffered a blister . . . as large as a man's hand.

"This was bad enough, but the second cotton tent also took fire, and between the two blazes the proceeding within a minute became so clouded that spectators could not see one another."

Neither of the unfortunate incidents made any impression on the robotlike Doctor, who wrote in *My Attainment of the Pole:* "I can recall the ceremony . . . but I was so confused and half ill that I was not in a condition to appreciate the honor." However, he did respond with a speech, which was frequently interrupted by cheers from the audience. "To feel that you have confidence in me," he told the aldermen, "amidst the unfounded statements and against the false affidavits published during the last few days creates a feeling of pride in me." The *American* reported that his words "seemed to work up the galleries to a frenzy," and that his denial branding Barrill a liar awoke "tumultuous cheering." The ceremony ended with the Doctor declaring that the Eskimos were made to say what they did not say, and that he would prove that this was so by bringing the Eskimos to New York.

Earlier in the day reporters had asked him about the Eskimos. According to the *Globe* he replied: "I will send a ship for them and when they come I will prove beyond all doubt that I accomplished exactly what I said I did." At City Hall he modified this statement by saying: "I will bring them here, not to prove my conquest of the Pole, but to prove the truth of this last statement of mine" (that the Eskimos were made to say what they did not say).

It seems probable that by this time he understood that, from the legal point of view, bringing the Eskimos to civilization was useless. The *Eagle* for October 4, 1909, had noted: "A writer in the current number of Bench and Bar on the 'legal' proof of this controversy places the testimony of both Cook's and Peary's Eskimos in the class of doubtful evidence. He quotes 'Moore on Facts' who says: 'Witnesses who are ignorant and occupy a low station in society are particularly liable to the influence of parties of superior intelligence and craft.' Again he says that the Eskimos 'occupied the relation of employees of Cook, and as such their testimony must be placed in the same category as the testimony of servants.' "

On the morning of October 16, with Barrill's affidavit still producing full columns of unfavorable publicity, the *Herald* attempted to protect the Doctor by breaking a scoop of its own. It announced that he was organizing an expedition, composed equally of his friends and his foes, to ascend Mount McKinley and retrieve the note deposited at the summit.

"This is his reply to the critics who have sought to wrest from him the fame of his exploit in Alaska," the *Herald* declared. It would be a nonpartisan expedition, the public was informed, and those who were for Cook and those who were against him would make the climb together. Its co-leadership was offered to Anthony Fiala, an explorer friendly to Cook, and to Herschel Parker, who opposed Cook. Both declined, and that was virtually the end of the idea.

It may be that no other man has ever endured the variety of stress that Cook suffered through. From the extremes of one sort of life he tumbled into the extremes of a life that was the exact opposite. For sixteen months he had eaten little but raw meat and pemmican. Now the rich food served at banquets gave him indigestion, and that made it difficult for him to sleep. Each day Cook's life became more chaotic. "I began to feel persecuted," he recalled later. "On every side I sensed hostility; the sight of a crowd filled me with a growing sort of terror. . . . I was pursued by reporters, people with cranning necks. . . . In the trains I viewed the whirling landscape without, and felt myself a part of it — as a delirious man swept through space."[24]

Meanwhile, although the noise of the controversy was increasing, the Doctor was not contributing to it. From the beginning he had guided himself by his belief that, as he wrote later, "In all history it has been shown that he who seeks to besmear others leaves the greatest amount of mud on himself." Accordingly, he did not refute the first trivial but widely discussed charges made against him. "Many of the attacks," he wrote later, "seemed so ridiculous that I felt no one would believe them — which was another of my mistakes." When Peary's charges appeared in the papers, Cook's friends advised him to fight fire with fire. He replied that such a course was distasteful to him; and that, moreover, the selfish, envious origin of Peary's charges was obvious. And at first, after Barrill's affidavit had been published, Cook was not able to recognize its importance. He considered that "fair-minded people would . . . see through this moneyed campaign of dishonor." But they did not. By October 19 the Brooklyn *Eagle* was observing that while Barrill's evidence could not be considered proof that Cook did not reach the Pole, "it is a contribution to testimony as to the veracity of the man. . . . it will go a long ways in destroying confidence in Dr. Cook and his words."

For the Doctor, life became more and more disgusting. "I felt what anyone who is not superhuman would have felt," he wrote eventually, "a sickening sense of helplessness, a disgust at the human duplicity which permitted such things, a sense of the futility of the very thing I had done and its little worth compared to the web of shame my enemies were endeavoring to weave about me."

As he whirled from city to city persons essentially friendly repeatedly advised him: "We will credit your attainment of the Pole if this Mount McKinley matter is cleared up." Each day it became more obvious that he had to do something; that some sort of exceptional effort was required.

No other episode in the continuously extraordinary polar controversy approaches the bizarreness of that affair's "high noon," which occurred in Hamilton, Montana, on October 28, 1909, when "Doc" Cook met face to face with "Big Ed" Barrill.

It was Cook's idea, his worst, by far, the final confirmation that the great explorer was lost in his native land. He imagined that if he could meet face to face with Barrill, whom he remembered as a good fellow, then what he assumed to be Barrill's fundamental decency would allow "Big Ed" to acknowledge that he had lied in his affidavit.

Hamilton, in the southwest corner of Montana, was only a few miles north of Darby, the hometown of Barrill and Printz, and possessed an opera house with a large auditorium. Its citizens learned that "Doc" was approaching when a Helena lawyer informed the press: "Cook authorizes me to announce that he will . . . lecture in Hamilton. . . . He will give his version of the Mount McKinley story, and will be glad to meet Edward N. Barrill face to face and answer any charges which his former guide cares to make."

In Hamilton Cook was preceded by his dude secretary, whose presence in the West was immediately spotted by Barrill and his cronies who, as Lonsdale wrote modestly, "noticed my arrival." He continued: "I . . . encountered a group of men standing outside a cafe . . . Barrill and Printz and their companions, evidently discussing . . . their course of action. At my hotel, shortly afterwards, I received a visit from these two guides. . . . They were very offensive in discussing Dr. Cook."[25]

But Cook's thought about Barrill's fundamental decency was only one portion of his naiveté. Since the end of the 1906 expedition, he had owed Fred Printz money. "Dr. Cook agreed to pay me $150 and expenses on the trip," Printz informed a reporter, "but he did not even pay my expenses and I had to borrow. . . . He paid my transportation to Alaska and as far back as Seattle. He agreed to send me my money in Seattle, but it came not."[26]

Cook was lecturing in Buffalo when reporters questioned him about his unpaid debt to Printz. "It is true that after the expedition was over there was money owed to several persons," he acknowledged. "I was not responsible for the bills but the society that had charge of the expedition must have overlooked these payments. When my attention was called to the bills I promptly paid them. . . . I invite the closest inquiry."[27]

Exactly what organization he was referring to is unknown. What is known is that he went to Alaska with the idea that Henry Disston would contribute a full $5,000. "We were to prepare a game trail for him," Cook wrote. "Something interfered, he relinquished his trip, and did not send the balance of the money promised. The result was that many checks I had given out went to protest."[28] It is also known that the property-damage judgment in Seward cost him $600. At the conclusion of his first expedition to Alaska, there were no financial problems of any sort.

Cook arrived in Missoula, Montana, aboard the North Coast Limited. After registering into a hotel, he gave Montana newsmen a disappointing interview. Perhaps someone had given him a severe lecture, or perhaps he himself had realized the dangers in the situation he had created. At any rate, the idea had changed. Instead of meeting Barrill face to face, he would simply "give my version of the Mount McKinley controversy and then leave my case in the hands of an honest jury — the people of the great state of Montana.[29]

The next day he motored to Hamilton and secluded himself in the Ravalli Hotel. Meanwhile, as the *Anaconda Standard* reported, "Ed Barrill and Fred Printz were about . . . all afternoon and evening, and their appearance on the street was always the cause of . . . sincere expressions of confidence and faith in them. . . . Disappointment was expressed . . . because Dr. Cook had decided not to make any fight. . . . That Cook had crawfished was the sentiment."

The following account of the big night in Hamilton will rely mainly on the notes of a stenographer who was present at the Logan Opera House. They were published in the *Anaconda Standard* two days later. Additional information will be drawn from the accounts in the New York *Herald*, the New York *Times*, and *Daily Missoulian*, as well as Hamilton's weekly papers, the *Western News* and the *Ravalli Republican*.[30]

"Long before the hour announced for the beginning of the lecture, the opera house was crowded to the doors," the *Daily Missoulian* reported; "hundreds of people . . . were unable to gain admittance. Most of these were local people; the adherents of Barrill and Printz . . . had taken care to get there early."

It was, decidedly, a wild night. The *Anaconda Standard*, protective of Montana's citizens, acknowledged that it was "stormy," yet insisted that it was "in no way 'rough house.'" The correspondent for the New York *Herald* thought otherwise: "During the entire discussion," he wrote, "the friends of Barrill and Printz hooted and screamed like . . . wild Indians." The *Daily Missoulian* reported: "In the presence of a hostile audience, which subjected him to insult and indulged in . . . churlish disregard for proprieties, Dr. Cook carried himself with . . . dignity."

The evening began with Mayor Drinkenburg presiding. He referred to the explorer as "our extinguished visitor." Barrill and Printz were sitting in what the *Western News* called "the dress circle." They were "just to the right and immediately in front of the stage, confronting the doctor at close range. Surrounding them were their lawyers and a group of personal friends."

After Cook had concluded his standard North Pole lecture, he referred to some notes, then said:

"At the time of my arrival in New York . . . when all America was rejoicing over the double discovery of the North Pole, there began a warfare to rob me of the glory of an achievement which was, and is, rightly mine. Confident that my rival had triumphed after nearly a quarter of a century in quest of the great unknown, I, with all good Americans, rejoiced in his success, and . . . I declared that there was glory enough for two. . . . My attitude . . . has not changed.

". . . the enemy began this flank movement on the climb of Mount McKinley: men with money to burn in the flame of infamy entered the arena. Men of this community whom I had previously believed to be honest, fell as victims. Their statements are absolutely untrue."

It must have seemed a fairly simple matter when, in Missoula on the previous evening, he had announced that the fight was off; but now the challenging statement had been made, and "High Noon," a most reluctant version, was on again.

Barrill's attorneys, Crutchfield and Wagner, stood up immediately. With all eyes centered on them, they challenged Cook's statement and declared that Barrill had the same right to be heard. Cook replied: "This is not a tribunal and I am not on trial, therefore I decline to enter into a controversy."

Then came cries of "four-flusher" and "quitter." Cook hesitated uncertainly. Meanwhile, Barrill's attorneys were stalking toward the stage where they were soon joined by United States Senator Joseph M. Dixon. But the editor of the *Anaconda Standard* was already on his feet and offering a resolution: "We, the people of Montana, having listened to the story recited by Dr. Cook . . . and having been informed that he came here to . . . defy his accusers . . . hereby declare . . . our abiding confidence in the integrity and uprightness of Ed Barrill and Fred Printz."

This was protested by Roland J. White, a San Francisco lawyer who was visiting relations in the region. For the rest of the evening he acted as Cook's counsel.

As reported by the stenographer, Senator Dixon now declared: "Mr. Chairman . . . I said to Dr. Cook a while ago . . . when he . . . announced he was coming . . . to confront Printz and Barrill, it was a direct challenge. . . . This man over here has been pointed out as Barrill. Stand up. If Mr. Printz is in the audience, stand up. (Both stand up.)"

By this time, according to the *Daily Missoulian*, "there were 20 people . . . on the stage, each trying to talk at once, and when Barrill reached the rostrum the scene was that of a New England town meeting divided on a road question."

But Cook was not among them. He had retired behind the scenes. "Dr. Cook remained in seclusion at the back of the stage," the New York *Times* reported. "Had he desired to leave . . . it was impossible for him to do so. There was no rear entrance."

This was surely one of Cook's most tragic moments. On an important occasion his whole world, his central idea about life, was crashing. Cook was a man totally committed to man. There is no evidence about whether or not he believed in God, but there is extensive evidence that he believed in man. "The only thing to be gained from reaching the Pole," he wrote in *My Attainment*, ". . . the lesson of its accomplishment, is that man, by brain power and muscle energy, can subdue the most terrific forces of a blind nature." He was a romantic whose trust in his fellow men was entire. "I have, as I have said," he wrote, "absolute confidence in the good sense, spirit of fair play, and ability of reasoning judgment of my people." He was an innocent, a sometimes careless and preoccupied gentleman who conducted himself according to his faith in man's natural goodness. "The people of this country," he once said, ". . . are clean, honest, and fair." By profession he was a healer who healed for brotherhood, a concept which meant the world to him. He described Peary's attitude toward Sverdrup as "unbrotherly." He and Barrill had fought their way to the top of a continent and there should have been a comradeship between them. As Shakespeare wrote:

For he today that sheds his blood with me
Shall be my brother; be he ne'er so vile
This day shall gentle his condition.

Afterward he, the adventurous instigator, had gone on to an even more tremendous victory, while the wilderness packer had turned into a real estate salesman whose most valuable property was his not completely immaculate climbing leader. Although Cook had recently become somewhat cautious, this sensationally direct evidence that his faith was badly founded must have been agonizing.

Backstage, Senator Dixon informed him that if he refused to face Barrill and Printz he might as well haul down his flag. When Cook returned to the stage, the *Ravalli Republican* noted, he "was the picture of dejectment. Beads of sweat stood out on his forehead, and it was plainly evident that he would rather have been anywhere else than in Hamilton just then."

The stenographic report continues:

"In response to Dixon's question whether he went to the top of Mt. McKinley Barrill said: 'We did not climb Mt. McKinley . . . fourteen miles from the top. . . .'

"From the audience: 'Let Dr. Cook cross-examine.'

"The questions were put for Dr. Cook by Attorney White:

" 'When did you make this affidavit?'

" 'I could not say.'

" 'About when and at whose instigation — at whose request did you make this affidavit?'

" 'The American people.'

" 'What part of the American people did you make this affidavit for?' (Calls for question) . . .

"Dr. Cook: 'Ladies and Gentlemen: First, let me say there has been a mistake in the statement of my coming here. I never stated that I was coming here to challenge these men. We cannot be held responsible for newspaper reports. Again I must tell you, as I told the mayor, I came here at his invitation to tell the story of our polar campaign. Now I see nothing to be gained by a discussion of the problem tonight. We climbed Mt. McKinley. I have already said we will organize an expedition to go to the top of Mt. McKinley to get these records. . . . When I say this to you, ladies and gentlemen, there is nothing further to be said on the problem and I cannot see that any resolutions that you may pass can possibly change that one way or another."

Then the dramatic moment came when Cook and Barrill directly confronted each other. But with neither of them, apparently, particularly enjoying the situation, it was not very dramatic.

Barrill said to Cook: "Will you say exactly where you left the records on top of Mt. McKinley?"

Cook turned to Barrill and said, according to the *Daily Missoulian:* " 'You have deliberately and willfully ——.' Then the doctor paused and skipped the hard word, ending his assertion with 'falsified.' "

Barrill responded: "You are another."

Cook said: "Your statement is untrue."

Barrill then turned to someone and asked: "Why doesn't he make an affidavit then?"

Cook said: "I will make one, if it is desired."

He then wrote out: "I, Dr. F. A. Cook, of New York, being duly sworn, do depose and swear that on September 16, 1906, I was on the top of Mt. McKinley and at that date I left the records of my climb deposited thereon, and that Edward Barrill was present at that time."

This affidavit he did not sign, as no notary was present with a seal.

The stenographic report continues:

"A stranger: 'Just one moment (after it was arranged that Barrill should tell the story and Dr. Cook should cross-examine). As a stranger here I want to see fair play, and I want to ask if Dr. Cook has submitted to this — let Dr. Cook say whether he is willing to stay here.'

"Senator Dixon asked Dr. Cook if he was willing to stay and hear Barrill's statement.

"Dr. Cook: 'I have stated — I have written it out, made an affidavit that we have been to the top of Mt. McKinley. After I have said that, the evening is at an end, and I do not care to stay any longer.'

"Dixon: 'If it were me and my reputation was at stake, I would stay here until morning.'

"Mr. Wagner: '. . . as a substitute for the resolution which was put here tonight . . .'

"Dixon: 'Let us hear the story first.'

"(Cries of 'Barrill! Barrill!')

"Dixon: 'Let Barrill tell his story.'

"Barrill: 'We went up a glacier — glacier — (turning to Cook) — name it.' (Dr. Cook does not respond.)

"Barrill: 'It makes no difference. We went up a peak. Practically a point of rock, and Dr. Cook said "that is good enough for Mt. McKinley." '

"Questions from the audience to Barrill:

" 'How high up was it?'

" 'Eight thousand feet . . .'

" 'Any discussion with him as to whether this was the top of Mt. McKinley? Why didn't you go to the top?'

" 'Too late in the fall and too cold; we could not go.'

" 'How long did it take you to get up there?'

" 'Seven or eight days.'

" 'How long would it have taken to reach the real top of Mt. McKinley? Was there any discussion there at that time whether any story would be put out whether you had gotten to the top of Mt. McKinley or not?'

" 'Yes. He said he was going to publish it as though he had been to the top of Mt. McKinley.' "

Barrill maintained that in a letter written from Labrador, Cook had written: "For God's sakes, keep still and when I come home I will bring you a chunk of the Pole." This letter, the guide declared, was now in New York. Cook denied that he had ever written any such letter. He acknowledged that in 1906 Barrill had written him about the money still due Printz.

By this time the wiser persons in the audience were leaving. The evening continued for at least another half hour, and without anything being accomplished by anyone. At one point Barrill admitted that Cook had recently sent him $200.

"Barrill: 'I got that to come to New York for a visit.'

"Mr. White: 'Why didn't you go after you got the money?' Did you use or employ that to go to New York, as Dr. Cook requested? Did you see Dr. Cook? Then you have money wrongfully in your possession."

Later Fred Printz arrived on stage:

"Dr. Cook: 'Did you make an affidavit and ask a thousand dollars for it?'

"Printz: 'He said he would give me a thousand dollars for it — he would have given a thousand dollars for it quick enough, if I had taken it.' "

It was an evening in which three outdoorsmen, each one of them a splendid performer in the wilds, stood up in front of the curious and — when it came to money, even Hamilton was too civilized for them — made grotesque fools of themselves. The Doctor indicated that he still owed Printz money. Printz denied that he had ever sent Cook the note in which he said that for $350 he would come to New York. The "chunk of the Pole" letter that Barrill declared Cook had sent him has never been published anywhere.

Nothing that occurred in Hamilton that evening faults the concept presented earlier in this narrative: that Cook and Barrill did reach the summit of the mountain, a fact that Barrill could not possibly acknowledge; and that Cook's "summit" photo was bogus, a fact that Cook could not possibly acknowledge. Neither man told the whole truth at the Logan Opera House. Both were frozen into their partial truths and could do nothing but prevaricate, which they did, apparently, with little enthusiasm. At some time during the evening Barrill appeared to be very certain that Mount McKinley could be climbed. The *Daily Missoulian* reported: "Barrill also announced that the mountain could be climbed."

At the close of the evening a second resolution was introduced: "We, the people of Montana . . . do declare our belief in the veracity of the statements of Ed Barrill and Fred Printz." This was modified to read: "We, the people of Ravalli County, Montana." Many in the dwindling audience refused to vote on the matter, but those who did supported Barrill and Printz and the resolution was passed as amended.

"Disgusted, with a heavy heart," Cook wrote in *My Attainment* "I left the hall. The oppression of my loneliness, defenselessness, and hopeless confusion rendered all sleep impossible that night."

In the morning he picked up one affidavit supporting him, "made by George W. Solleder," the New York *Times* reported, "a prominent farmer . . . living near the homes of Barrill and Printz. Solleder declared that Barrill, with whom he had been intimately associated for years, told him that he and Dr. Cook had climbed Mt. McKinley. Solleder avers that he and Barrill are now on friendly terms and have had no controversy."

At no time, it appears, was Cook aware that Barrill and Printz had gone to the editor of the *Western News* in Hamilton and informed its editor that in 1906 Barrill and Cook had attained the summit. Nor did that paper refer to this in its account of the big night. Its most positive statement about the Doctor declared that on stage he "throughout the trying ordeal, although visibly harassed, maintained his habitual dignity and stood most of the time regarding the audience with quiet composure."

In the evening he lectured in Missoula and received an entirely different reception. The *Daily Missoulian* commented: "His visit has been a distinguished honor. . . . There are two affidavits between which choice may be taken; one is Dr. Cook's and the other is Ed Barrill's. We know which we choose." Clearly, not everyone in Montana regarded "Big Ed" as a responsible person.

9

THE NET RESULT of this experience," Cook wrote of his misadventure in Hamilton, "was the conviction in my own mind that I was regarded everywhere, throughout the entire country, as a liar. For the first time, as a thing seen at night in a sudden flash of lightning, I perceived the perilous abyss on which I stood. . . . It became evident to me that what proofs I had must be immediately prepared for a report to the University of Copenhagen and for book publication to forestall eventual disaster.

"In this I had not a minute to lose," he said in *My Attainment*. "I decided to work day and night, and promptly canceled all lecture engagements, which at the time amounted to $140,000. I started for New York, and on the train made repeated efforts to begin writing. But when I tried to think, a rush of worries crowded my mind. I found myself unable to evolve a logical argument, to think of any subject consecutively. I gave up in despair, and a reckless desire to be rid of the whole thing swept through my mind. I hated the thought of the North Pole. Nothing was less desired than any glory attached to it."

In New York the Peary Arctic Club was working on a new angle. It now demanded that the examination of Cook's data take place not in Denmark but in America. Cook replied that he was sticking to his agreement with the university. The club, however, was determined to have a hand in the examination. Accordingly, its ally, the National Geographic Society, soon requested the University of Copenhagen to waive its first claim on Cook's data. The university refused. The society then proposed that its representatives be present at the examination of the data. Once again, the university refused. Why? Probably because, as Cook would point out, the National Geographic Society was "neither national nor geographic," being in fact a privately owned magazine and map-publishing concern that also functioned as a lecture bureau. Because this was little understood outside of America, any pronouncement by the National Geographic Society had undue weight in Europe.

In New York the *Times* protested the attitude of the university: "Commander Peary is suffering an irremediable injury from the delay in terminating the controversy which has arisen, and for that delay the University of Copenhagen is making itself in part at least responsible."

At the Waldorf-Astoria, meanwhile, the Doctor was continually pestered by the public. He was disturbed, also, by a new weapon that the club had added to its arsenal. It had hired private detectives, and not just two or three but a squad, from the Burns agency. Now, whenever he left the hotel, sleuths followed.

He attempted to improve his situation by moving to the Hotel Gramatan in Bronxville, but nothing could help him now, and the slide toward disaster continued. Weeks later his friend Charles Wake, an official at Equitable Life, commented on the situation in Cook's household: "[He received] numerous letters, from different directions, all telling in more or less plausible form of plots to steal his records and even murder him if possible . . . These letters, taken in connection with the vigorous effort which was being made to discredit him, finally caused me to share some of the apprehensiveness which was felt by Dr. Cook and his wife. I knew that sums of money which indicated an almost unlimited source were being spent in the fight against him. His telephone 'leaked' and he was constantly shadowed by detectives."[1]

One melodramatic letter, dated November 8, 1909, and mailed from Washington, D.C., told of a conversation that the writer had overheard accidentally. "He had been to call on a party at 1005 G Street," Walter Lonsdale wrote in a magazine article months later, "but finding no one in, had descended the stairs to return home. As he got to the bottom, two men rushed into the vestibule out of a shower of rain. . . . On hearing a disparaging exclamation from one . . . regarding Dr. Cook, the informant wrote that he had decided to act the part of a listener since it was dark . . . and he could not be seen.

" 'Yes,' exclaimed one, 'the train is all laid for the powder that will blow up Cook, and soon you will hear of his coming out in the papers saying he has been robbed of his North Pole data. . . . he will not be believed and will be proved the greatest knave and faker the world has ever seen.'

" 'That's so, Doc,' replied the other, 'and the best of it is, that even if he does get his data on board ship, it will never reach Copenhagen, for the man who carries it will be doped, or the express company that ships it will have no safe that cannot be cracked. . . .'

" 'If somebody has to be sandbagged,' was the reply.

" 'Oh, the old man has planned it alright, and the woman has never failed yet.'

"Just then a taxi cab came up, which they hailed and drove away."

Lonsdale concluded: "We did not treat this letter very seriously at first, but it was subsequently supported by such conclusive evidence that we were compelled to place some faith in it."[2]

And so, for Cook, a bad situation worsened. The Gramatan correspondent of the New York *Times* reported that a friend of the Doctor said he was in an excessively nervous condition: "It seemed evident that unless he took a long rest, he might suffer a collapse. He told me that he had been advised to go abroad. . . . He said to me, 'If this thing keeps up a few months longer I shall be in an insane asylum.' . . . He told me about the supposed conspiracy and I told him that it was all nonsense — that no one would think of trying to rob him. . . . It is a fact, though, that some of the doctor's advisors did succeed in convincing him that such a plot actually existed."[3] *

At the Gramatan, it appears, the Doctor was particularly puzzled by the presence of the club's detectives, whom he could only identify as not being employed by himself. The man from the New York *Times* reported that after a conference Cook and his advisers "decided that the sleuths were probably after the records. . . . Dr. Cook occupied rooms on the second floor of the hotel and his cabinet suggested that porch climbers would have very little difficulty. . . . It was agreed that the windows would be nailed down." Meanwhile, Lonsdale "was about at night looking furtively about him trying to espy the sleuths he thought were dogging his footsteps. Once . . . on the plaza of the hotel, he saw a sudden flash of light. 'There's a dark lantern,' he exclaimed. 'We're being watched.' "[4]

Throughout this period, just about everything Cook did became public knowledge. He was surrounded to the point where when he went to the Carnegie Trust Company and took out a foreign letter of credit for $15,000, the details were in the papers three days later. When it was all over Charles Wake told reporters: "The doctor and his wife evidenced an increasing anxiety to have me with them, and beginning with November 19 I spent every night at the Hotel Gramatan. So great was their fear for the safety of his original records that . . . I consented to the door between their room and mine being open."[5]

And at about the same time, Peary's life was proceeding splendidly. One afternoon he called at the White House and talked with President Taft. The New York *Times* reported:

* One of Cook's advisers was James B. Hammond, who had invented one of the first practical typewriters. By 1907 he was president of the Hammond Typewriter Company, and was worth over $2 million. Meanwhile, his brother Thomas was trying to have him declared insane, charging that James used "daily drugs and alcoholic stimulants." After examiners at Bellevue Hospital had declared James Hammond sane, he returned to his factory and received an ovation from his employees. James Hammond was often in the public eye and once, on a drive from downtown New York to Oyster Bay, scattered ten thousand new pennies to children.

"Commander Peary was closeted with the President for half an hour."

But as for Cook: "Looking haggard and ten years older than when he arrived from the Arctic," the *Herald* noted, "the explorer left his hotel . . . for a visit to New York. . . . The great change in Dr. Cook's physical condition has been noted . . . for more than a week."[6]

During these distressing times it seems probable that the harassed Doctor gradually came to understand his situation exactly. If so, he did not identify it for many. "Dr. Cook was a peculiar man," John R. Bradley said later. "He never told anybody anything. Never told me anything."[7] And Charles Wake described him as being, about this time, "even less communicative than usual." He was certainly aware of the unsettling fact that the polar data he possessed was not sufficient to be "proof" that he had attained the Pole. "Disturbed by the growing uncertainty of proving such a claim," he wrote later, "to the point of hair-breadth accuracy by any figures, despair overcame me."[8] On this point he was candid with Lonsdale, if no one else. "Dr. Cook was aware" Lonsdale wrote, "that he had not sufficient data for his report to Copenhagen, for he continually referred to his original field notes which he had left with Whitney at Etah. These, he said, he needed badly."[9]

But the aggressions of the National Geographic Society and the demands of the New York *Times* had focused public attention on the scholars at the University of Copenhagen, and the Doctor understood that he must submit something. And so he did. His report, which Lonsdale carried to Denmark, consisted of sixty-one pages of typewritten material describing the polar journey, plus a sixteen-page typewritten copy of his polar notebook.

Meanwhile, James B. Hammond had offered the use of his yacht, the *Lounger*, and it was possible for Cook to think about a voyage to Etah to recover his data and instruments. Two other friends had offered to pay for a sizable share of the costs, and he could cover the remaining expenses himself. He therefore wrote privately to Rector Torp of the university and after pointing out the problem of the missing data, suggested that the examining committee bring back an amiable verdict of "not proven." In such a case he would sail to Etah in the summer of 1910 and recover his property. But if the university's verdict was hostile, no such expedition would be attempted.[10]

On November 24, 1909, a day or so after the Doctor had completed his report, and one day before Lonsdale was to sail for Copenhagen, the two men left the Gramatan for New York. "On arriving in New York," Lonsdale recalled, "we were successful, for the first time, in shaking off our shadowers, and the doctor suddenly exclaimed to me, 'Lonsdale, here is a chance of getting away unnoticed, and I'm going to take it.'

"We ran after a street car, which was already in motion, boarded it and went with it as far as Thirty-third Street where we got off and entered the subway, making sure that we were not being followed. We left the train at Bleecker Street, slipping out just before the last door was closed, and from there we made our way, by a circuitous route, to the Pennsylvania Station. I bought, en route, at the request of Dr. Cook, a pair of scissors, a safety razor and some black paste for touching up the face. Entering a cafe the explorer took off his mustache and we then proceeded to a barber shop, where he had his hair cut short. In the meantime, I had bought a black slouch hat, and entering a second cafe, the finishing touches were put to the disguise. As things have turned out, these precautions might seem somewhat suspicious, but at the time, Dr. Cook only intended to get away and obtain a needed rest. Without a disguise of some sort, this could not be done, for his appearance was too well known and he could not have gone very far without being recognized. I said good-bye to Cook outside the Pennsylvania Railroad station and his last words were: 'Now I'll be able to get some sleep!' "[11]

Two months previously, Cook had arrived in the United States a world hero. Now he was vanishing into ignominious exile.

Three days later Marie Cook received a card mailed from

Toronto. After instructing her to meet him in Europe, Cook continued: "If the hounds are still pursuing you, put my original records in a safe deposit box and give the key to Mr. Wack; if they are not following you, bring the records with you. My life is of more importance than the polar matter, which can wait if necessary."[12]

He then went to Quebec and attempted to contact Captain Joseph E. Bernier, the skipper of the *Arctic*, the Canadian government ship that had carried the supplies Marie Cook had sent north to Etah. Cook apparently believed that Bernier might be able to collect the records Whitney had left at Etah. Bernier, however, could not be found. At any rate, a voyage to a point as far north as Etah could not have been made until the late spring and possibly would not have done any good anyhow. The Doctor must have understood that the campaign against him was as broad as it was energetic, and that his enemies would never overlook anything as fundamental as the data and instruments at Etah.

On July 25, 1910, the sealer *Boethic* became the first ship to call at Etah since the departure of the *Roosevelt*. The *Boethic* turned out to be under the command of Captain Bob Bartlett, the same Bob Bartlett who had skippered the *Roosevelt*, the same Bob Bartlett who had helped Whitney carry Cook's property ashore and pack it into a cache, the same Bob Bartlett who denied, in America, that he had ever done such a thing. When the *Boethic* returned to New York harbor a reporter interviewed Captain Bob, who baldly declared: "What use can Dr. Cook have in going back to Etah for 'Proofs' when there are none? The only articles belonging to Dr. Cook at Etah are some clothing and such like and possibly a sextant. But as for records, you can stake your life that there are none."[13]

He talked like a man who knew, positively.

In New York, after the Doctor had slipped away, rumors of plots and jobbery continued to dominate his household. Just before Lonsdale sailed for Copenhagen, H. Wellington Wack told an amused representative of the New York *Times* that Lonsdale's life was in danger and "that there was 'really in existence' one of the most diabolical plots that had ever been hatched against any explorer or any other man. According to Mr. Wack's information two women and a man have been hired by agents of some persons hostile to Dr. Cook actually to poison young Lonsdale. [They are said to be] loaded down with drugs that would do the despicable work for which they were engaged."[14]

But Lonsdale's voyage was uneventful. Carrying the records in a black iron box, he disembarked in Copenhagen on December 8, 1909, and was met at the gangplank by two Danish detectives. They escorted him to Landmans Bank and observed while the report was dropped into a safety vault. Lonsdale then went to the American Legation where he had a lengthy discussion with Minister Egan. Afterward Egan, according to the New York *American*, "stated that he was convinced that Dr. Cook had reached the North Pole."[15]

Although it was soon obvious that H. Wellington Wack was off in his details, it is just as obvious, today, that he was essentially correct when he talked about a diabolical plot.

Weeks earlier, while Cook was still resident in Suite 1095 at the Waldorf-Astoria, and an open target for his enemies, his household had been invaded by the Peary Arctic Club, temporarily represented by a brace of rascals named Dunkle and Loose.* George Dunkle, an insurance salesman, has been described as "thirty-four years old, well over six feet in height and exceptionally well groomed. He has every appearance of a prosperous man about town." Dunkle lived at 17 Livingston Place and had his office at 31 Nassau Street. His associate, August W. Loose, was a native of Norway, a graduate of the Navigational College in Bergen, and had commanded many seagoing vessels. By the time of the controversy, however, Loose

* When the reports about Dunkle and Loose finally appeared in the press the *Nation* observed: "Even the very names involved in the Cook affair are so strange as to seem to belong to the world of fiction rather than of fact. Not content with Wake and Wack, he must consort with Dunkle and Loose."

was an impoverished man and, according to Lonsdale, "completely under the influence of Dunkle."[16] It seems probable that his problem was alcohol. The episode in which these two men played the leading roles was and remains a collector's item for students of the diabolic and its chronology deserves attention:

1. In 1908, a year after Cook had sailed north aboard the *John R. Bradley*, the Arctic Club of America became concerned for his safety. Looking about for a ship to charter and send north, the Arctic Club of America approached a broker named George Lightfoot who owned a schooner, the *Emily B. Wright*. Lightfoot agreed to fit the schooner out as a relief vessel, and hired Loose as skipper. "Later Dunkle, whom I did not know then, came into the office to sell some insurance," Lightfoot told the Brooklyn *Eagle*. "We got to talking about the Cook relief expedition. He later entered my employ to secure subscriptions on a commission. The Cook relief committee gave us permission to collect money. Dunkle addressed the committee in the capacity of its representative and mine and the whole thing seemed settled when Dunkle was informed that Herbert L. Bridgman had made an offer to bring Cook back. Bridgman told the committee that he was fitting out the *Jeanie* to take coal and supplies to Peary; that if the committee would turn what money it had collected over to him he would also bring Cook back."[17] Although the story in the *Eagle* does not state that Bridgman met either Dunkle or Loose, it seems possible that he became aware of one or both during this period.*

2. About a year later, after Cook had returned to America, George Dunkle, the man about town, began to maneuver to meet him. "Dunkle approached me a short time ago," Anthony

* The negotiations with the Cook Relief Committee of the Arctic Club of America may have been handled directly by Bridgman, or they may have been handled by Henry Collins Walsh, secretary of the Explorers Club, in which Bridgman was a power. Lightfoot's statement included: "A man named Walsh was the one who made Bridgman's offer known. . . . The $995 was turned over to Bridgman, I understand, and that let us out of it." (Brooklyn *Eagle*, December 17, 1909.)

Fiala told a reporter from the *Herald*, "and asked me to introduce him to John R. Bradley . . . for the purpose of an insurance scheme on Cook. He wanted to insure the financial success of Dr. Cook's lectures. It didn't look right to me and I told him so. I refused to introduce him or have anything to do with it."[18] Dunkle also attempted to meet Cook through the explorer-writer Dillon Wallace. "When he talked insurance I told him I would not introduce him to Dr. Cook, as he wanted me to do," a reporter quoted Wallace as saying, "and said that I didn't want to have any dealings with him."[19] Finally Dunkle approached John R. Bradley. "I said I felt I ought not to be refused inasmuch as I had had a part in the original relief plans," Dunkle testified. "Mr. Bradley was very cordial and arranged to take me around to see the doctor."[20]

3. At the time, oddly enough, Cook was thinking about life insurance. "During my lecture tours threats from fanatics reached me," he wrote eventually. "I decided to protect my wife and children by life insurance."[21] The insurance companies, however, considered him too great a risk.

Dunkle's meeting with Cook took place on the afternoon of October 17, 1909, in the Doctor's suite at the Waldorf. "After Mr. Bradley had introduced me," Dunkle testified, "he engaged in conversation with some one . . . and that gave me the chance I wanted. . . . I had told Dr. Cook I was an insurance man. . . . I told him when he sent his records to Copenhagen it might be that he would want to insure them against loss. . . . I reminded him that an insurance man never missed an opportunity to talk business, and he replied that I was right, and that the suggestion to insure his records seemed a good one."[22]

Marie Cook was immediately suspicious of Dunkle and told her husband: "Don't have anything to do with that man. I don't like his looks." But the Doctor did not heed her.

After Cook had returned from his Montana misadventure, as he wrote later, Dunkle "seemed to be always around, and at every opportunity spoke to me. He gained a measure of confidence by criticizing the press campaign against me. I naturally felt kindly towards anyone who was sympathetic."[23] One day Dunkle arrived with August W. Loose. "Loose pointed out what I myself had been thinking," Cook wrote; "that all observations were subject to extreme inaccuracy. He suggested working mine out backwards to verify them." (Both Cook and Peary employed others to recompute their polar observations.) Cook accepted Loose's offer and paid him $250. "I told him to go ahead," Cook wrote, "using the figures published in the New York *Herald*."[24] Loose then moved into the Gramatan and went to work. Several days later he and Dunkle turned a set of observations over to Cook. As they did so Dunkle said: "Now Doctor, I want to advise you to put your observations aside. Send these to Copenhagen."[25] Cook studied the papers carefully and after identifying them as a complete set of faked observations, showed the two men the door. Soon afterward Cook went into exile and Lonsdale sailed for Denmark.

4. Dunkle and Loose then appeared in the office of the New York *Times* where they swore out affidavits declaring that Cook had agreed to pay them $2,500 for an original set of polar observations, plus a bonus of $1,500 if these observations were accepted in Copenhagen. They contended that the manufactured observations had been used by Cook in his report to the University of Copenhagen. They were revealing the truth to the world, they swore, because the Doctor had not paid them. For the *Times* the assertions of Dunkle and Loose were exceptionally printable. On the first day — December 9, 1909 — the story filled seventeen columns. On the following day that paper's Dunkle-Loose coverage began on the first page, occupied all the editorial space on the second and third pages, and almost all the editorial space on the fourth page.

The Dunkle-Loose affidavits followed the pattern established with the Barrill affidavit. Like Barrill, Dunkle and Loose presented themselves as self-confessed participants in an attempt to defraud. Like Barrill, they claimed that Cook had not paid them. Like Barrill, they inferred that Cook was a very stupid man.

Here is a brief sample of the testimony of Augustus W. Loose:

"We were discussing the azimuth, and I asked Dr. Cook what he understood that to mean. I had taken it from his discussion that he hadn't much of an idea.

" 'An azimuth?' he repeated. 'Well, just off hand, Captain, I can't explain it, although I have it somewhere in my books or papers.'

" 'Do you know how it is taken?' I asked him. He confessed that without looking it up, he was not prepared to answer."[26]

Loose also declared that Cook did not know either the longitude or latitude at either Annoatok or Svartevoeg.*

The New York *Times* had good reason to take anything derogatory to Fred Cook with intense seriousness. If the activities of the Peary Arctic Club took place behind the scenes, the *Times*'s patronage of Peary was public. That paper, on its way to being the institution that it is today, still faced a competitive struggle for power and could not afford a loss of prestige. Its association with Peary was so close that coming south the Commander had cabled its editor and requested his help in "issuing damaging statements against Dr. Cook."[27] In addition, beyond its yuletide "One Hundred Neediest Cases," the *Times* has rarely assisted the underdog. On the other hand, its coverage of the controversy was slightly more complete than that of any other newspaper, and on occasion it printed news detrimental to the cause of the Peary Arctic Club. Some of these items did not appear in any other paper.

That Dunkle and Loose had not acted independently, and

* For the month of December, 1909, the New York *Times*'s reports on Cook filled a minimum of eighty-three columns. He was on the front page fifteen mornings, usually in the lead story. An extraordinarily large percentage of this was garbage. The front page of the December 9 issue, in which the Dunkle-Loose exclusive was broken, also contained a story, attributed to the Boston *Traveler*, which declared that Cook was a patient in the Pine Tree Sanitarium at Wells, Maine. Thus, every story about Cook in the December 9, 1909, issue of the *Times* was based on totally false information, all of which was presented to the reader under the comic banner "All the News That's Fit to Print."

that there was a ruling mind behind the episode, is demonstrated by the timing of the rogues' affidavits. The Dunkle-Loose story was a brilliant instance of international bullying. Its target was not the American newspaper reader but the authorities in Denmark. The story broke after Walter Lonsdale had delivered Cook's report to the university, but before the committee of scholars had assembled to study Cook's material. At the time the position was this: if the Danes accepted Cook's report as evidence that he had been to the Pole, then the whole world would accept Cook, and the club's effort would be meaningless. The point, therefore, was to pressure the Danes. Dunkle referred to the situation in an off-hand way when he told the *American:* "We knew that the whole thing would be dead in a few days. The Copenhagen University might accept Dr. Cook's proofs, and after that happened nothing we could say would have any weight. We chose to make the story public before the Danes had a look at his records."[28] One way or another, the club was determined to be present at the examination of Cook's report, and mounted atop Dunkle and Loose, it arrived in the lowest possible style.

Dunkle insisted that the whole idea was his and Loose's. "There is no body of men behind this charge," he told the *American*, "and no man in the cut-up with Captain Loose and myself. We went into this thing solely for the money there was in it and there isn't much money when you cut it several ways."[29]

That from the beginning Dunkle and Loose had definite intentions of deceiving Cook is supported by one feature of Dunkle's affidavit. He carefully retained the physical proof that he had seen Cook. His affidavit stated: "Mr. Dunkle has the envelope which was sent up with his card. On one side of the envelope was stamped 'Tenth Floor, Nov. 3, '09, 2:45 P.M. Waldorf-Astoria.' On the other side was written in blue lead pencil, 'Dr. Cook, 1095' and in red ink was stamped 'Send up — 10.' " It seems probable that from the moment Dunkle began to maneuver to meet Cook, he was operating as an agent of the club. It had already demonstrated its mastery of timing, and was the only party to profit from the Dunkle-Loose affidavits.

In supporting its tremendous scoop, the New York *Times* reprinted editorials from other metropolitan newspapers. These included General Hubbard's *Globe* and Herbert L. Bridgman's *Standard-Union*. The editorial reprinted from Bridgman's paper was wonderfully righteous: "Every honest newspaper and every honest newspaper man owes the New York *Times* thanks today for a masterpiece, a straightforward, illuminating and conclusive piece of work, the final act of a drama which for daring and effrontery has never been equalled."

But not every paper agreed with the *Standard-Union*, and neither Dunkle nor Loose gained many admirers. The *American* reported: "Dunkle is in difficulty with his business associates over the exposure, and Captain Loose, who has heretofore borne a good name, must bear the odium of the charge that he stood ready . . . to forge a set of records for a man whom he believed to be dishonest in his claim that he had reached the North Pole. For Captain Loose there is the slight excuse of poverty."[30]*

5. Following the publication of its great exclusive, the New York *Times* continued to use large headlines to misinform its readers that Cook had used Loose's data in his report to the university. Finally, in a small story on an inside page, a story whose short headline did not mention the essential fact of the story itself, the *Times* acknowledged that Cook had not used Loose's figures: "Contrary to expectations, the observations fabricated by Captain Loose are not mentioned in the report."[31]

During the next thirteen years the readers of the *Times* heard nothing about these rascals, but in 1932, at a time when

* The New York *American* was published by William Randolph Hearst. In later years Cook would regret that he had not associated himself with Hearst. He recognized that Hearst, who was not responsive to the urgings of the establishment, was the one publisher who would have fought his case to a successful conclusion. In Copenhagen Cook had been steered away from Hearst by Minister Egan, who considered the Hearst papers disreputable.

Cook's fortunes were at their grotesque worst, an editorial in that paper called attention to his situation and in doing so did not forget Dunkle and Loose. "The story of how these worthies put their heads together to deceive the scientific world and relieve the doctor of some of his ill-gotten gains was printed exclusively in the New York *Times*."[32]

Although wrapped in grave typography, the affair of Dunkle and Loose and the New York *Times* was yellow journalism at its shoddiest and most disgusting. Yet on the level of international bullying it was a brilliantly cunning effort and, as shall be seen, a very effective one. Nevertheless, in the largest sense the episode can only be regarded as strong support for Mark Twain's estimate of the character of man: his contention that man was "most likely not even made INTENTIONALLY, and that his working himself out of the oyster bed to his present position was probably a matter of surprise and regret to the Creator."[33]

As the month of December began, a reader of American newspapers could regard Denmark as a conservative nation, solidly rooted in learning and unaffected by the nonsense out of New York. After the New York *Times* had cabled a synopsis of the Dunkle-Loose testimony to Copenhagen, its correspondent noted: "Cook's partisans in the press denounce it as an American bluff. . . . The Danish astronomer Burrau says Loose's testimony is fantastic."[34] An even more reassuring report appeared in the *Eagle*, which said that Professor Ellis Stromgren, chairman of the committee that would examine Cook's report, "indicated that the charges in the affidavit fall on their own weight when they assert Dr. Cook showed his ignorance of astronomical observations. He said before Dr. Cook sailed . . . the explorer talked with numerous Scandinavian scientists about the very things . . . his accusers charge him with being grossly ignorant . . . thoroughly satisfied the scientists of his competency."[35]

Meanwhile, Cook had surfaced momentarily in Marseilles and had mailed a letter to Lonsdale. "Though it leaves me in an unfortunate position," the Doctor wrote, "I prefer to submit the digest which you have as a preliminary report, asking the university to forego the final examination until the things are brought back from Greenland."[36] Rector Torp of the university had received a similar request.

But although he himself did not know it, the Doctor was now a domestic political problem in Denmark. The bizarre reports flowing out of New York, climaxed by the assertions of Dunkle and Loose, had provided the political opposition with a new and lively basis for criticism. The government, they charged, had acted far too hastily. One newspaper had suggested that the black iron box that Lonsdale had deposited in Landmans Bank contained nothing but a goldbrick. In addition, Cook was being criticized for starting his lectures before completing his report to the university. And finally, as the New York *Times* revealed, "the quarter in which doubts of Cook were first felt was the Royal Palace."[37] For such reasons the Danish government was not interested in anything preliminary. The problem of Frederick A. Cook had to be settled once and for all.

For the American newspaper reader, the first evidence that Denmark was vulnerable to the nonsense out of New York was very solid indeed. "Dr. Cook's data will be put under the microscope, turned inside out, and probed through and through," the Copenhagen correspondent of the *Times* declared, "and what is more important, unless he has furnished evidence sufficient to demonstrate beyond cavil that he has actually been to the North Pole, a verdict of 'not proven' will be rendered against him."[38]

And so, because of other people's fears, his fabulous sporting achievement was to be judged by the most rigorous scientific methods. Although every scientist on the examining committee surely understood that, in the light of every known fact, Cook's exploit was unprovable, the great explorer nevertheless would be required to prove, and prove beyond all doubt, that he had attained that magic point which, except in the minds of men, does not exist.

The decision of the committee of Danish scholars was announced in Copenhagen on December 20, 1909. After noting that the report as sent to them was the same as that which had appeared in the New York *Herald;* that the notebooks did not contain any original astronomical observations, but only results; and that the report was completely lacking in information that would prove that the astronomical observations therein contained were really made, the committee declared: "the material transmitted for examination contains no proof that Dr. Cook reached the North Pole."[39]

The next morning, December 22, 1909, a three-column headline on page 1 of the New York *Times* brayed:

COOK'S CLAIM TO DISCOVERY OF THE NORTH POLE
REJECTED, OUTRAGED DENMARK CALLS HIM
A DELIBERATE SWINDLER: HAVING NO ORIGINAL
OBSERVATIONS, HE USED LOOSE'S FAKES

In its news and editorial columns, that paper now referred to Cook as "monster of duplicity," "shameless swindler," "infamous wretch," "sneak thief," "reprobate," "greatest imposter of all time," and "king of the thimble-riggers."[40]

Early in the controversy the Peary Arctic Club had sponsored the thought that Cook was insane. Now its president abandoned that idea. "Dr. Cook isn't an insane man," General Hubbard declared as soon as the Copenhagen decision had been announced. "On the other hand I think him a mighty smart man." Herbert L. Bridgman had "nothing more to say as the outcome speaks for itself."

It so happened that in Manhattan that evening an organization known as the New England Society was holding its annual banquet. After the tables had been cleared the society's president, General Thomas H. Hubbard, arose and introduced the guest of honor, Robert E. Peary. In an atmosphere that the press described as "amid prolonged cheers," the Commander stood up and bowed. Earlier in the day, after seeing the first dispatch from Copenhagen, he had declared: "Three months ago, from the Labrador coast, I sounded an explicit and deliberately worded warning to the world, based on complete and accurate information in regard to Cook's claim. In doing so I accepted the responsibility devolving upon me and fulfilled my responsibility to myself and the world."[41] Now, before the New England Society, his mood was grander: "The greatest of the earth's trophies has been won for the United States and for New England," he declared. ". . . And now it would seem a fitting sequel to that if . . . the Stars and Stripes might wave at both ends of the earth's axis . . . I would be glad to aid in any way in the promotion and organization of an American Antarctic Expedition."

The next day, December 22, 1909, a friend of Cook's made a suggestion. "Reaffirming his complete confidence in Dr. Cook," the *American* reported, "Rear Admiral W. S. Schley, retired, called publicly upon Commander Peary to submit his proofs that he had reached the North Pole to some scientific body other than the National Geographic Society. . . . 'The Danes are the best posted body of men in the world on Arctic matters,' he said. '. . . The University of Copenhagen should . . . examine the Peary proofs, for in that way they would be submitted to the same test that was applied to those of Cook.' "[42]

This suggestion alarmed the National Geographic Society. It had gone through the motions of examining Peary and his proofs, as will be recounted presently, and had announced itself entirely satisfied that he had attained the Pole. Schley's suggestion, accordingly, ". . . has raised a storm at the . . . Society," the *World* observed. ". . . The leading members argue that American scientists would demean themselves if they should acknowledge that their findings needed verification. . . . 'Nothing can be gained by submitting Commander Peary's data to the University. . . .' said Prof. Gannett, chairman of the committee that passed upon Peary's proofs, 'and I see no reason why he should do this. The committee which passed on his papers is fully qualified to arrive at an unbiased conclusion.' "[43]

Minister Egan then arrived in New York, bringing with him

a piece of news that solved the problem neatly. The New York *Times* for December 25 reported Egan as saying: "The University of Copenhagen accepted the word of Commander Peary that he had reached the Pole and the verdict of the National Geographic Society without having any desire to examine his proofs."*

Meanwhile, in Denmark, a comedy of disassociation was being performed. Throughout its run, it appears, the Danes — who had been so splendid — made not one reference to the fact that Cook had volunteered to submit his data to the university; or to the fact that Cook had satisfactorily answered every question put to him by the scholars from the university; or to the fact that Cook had requested that the university regard his report as preliminary.

Professor Ellis Stromgren was the first comedian to appear on the boards. His opening line was: "Cook's treatment of the university is shameless." His longest speech ran: "We have been hoaxed in a most shameful manner, and hoaxed by a man through whom we thought to honor a great nation. For Doctor Cook was supported by the American Minister Egan, and furthermore, received the congratulations of President Taft. We have been hoaxed."[44]

In the background the government was preoccupied with the dignity of the throne. It was pointed out that not for one moment had King Frederick been fooled by Cook. Had his majesty ever presented, personally, any medals to the imposter? Never.

With Cook unavailable, some Danes identified Knud Rasmussen as the leading villain. He had recently announced that he had read Cook's original diary and had found it "correct and satisfying in every detail." Now, when he got his chance to

* Years later J. Gordon Hayes wrote of the Copenhagen decision: "They gave the only possible verdict: that such figures were no scientific proof of his [Cook's] attainment of the Pole. But, in the wretched controversy of that time, the equally certain verdict on Peary's observations was never sought; though, if his figures had been submitted to any other independent authority, *no other verdict was possible*" (*Robert Edwin Peary*, London, 1929, p. 188).

speak, he declared: "The university would not call on me at first because I was one of Dr. Cook's strongest supporters. Later, however, I was invited to the investigation and when I saw the observations I realized that it was a scandal. . . . No schoolboy could have made such calculations. It is a most childish attempt at cheating. Cook had killed himself by his own foolish acts." It seems possible that the Danes, in their embarrassment, grossly exaggerated the condition of Cook's data, and that Rasmussen was particularly guilty. Exactly what observations for the altitude of the sun at the Pole Cook sent to Denmark is unknown, but it is probable that they were identical with those that he gave on page 302 of *My Attainment of the North Pole*.

Walter Lonsdale, who played no part in the comedy, must have been a lonely man. He said: "I still believe in Dr. Cook, but I am less sure than yesterday."

Minister Egan, then still on the high seas en route to New York, believed that Cook "thought" he reached the Pole, the press reported.*

In New York those most closely associated with Cook had to do some explaining. The New York *Herald* declared: "The opinion of the university is that Dr. Cook's claim is *not proven*, which is not precisely the same thing as declaring that he did not reach the Pole, although some esteemed contemporaries hasten to give it that interpretation, while others still go further and declare him to be 'a fraud.' The *Herald*'s only interest in the matter throughout has been that inspired by its well-known habit of being the first among newspapers to get the news, whatever it may be, and the first to publish it. . . . With the purpose of supplying the data upon which intelligent readers may form their own opinion the *Herald* . . . has given, and continues to give . . ."

* In 1911 Egan wrote Captain B. S. Osbon: "I have never for a moment doubted the honesty of Dr. Cook. . . . This whole matter has been treated in such a sensational manner that I think it ought to make all Americans blush for the lack of regard to scientific truth, which I used to think was a characteristic of my fellow countrymen" (Osbon, "Cook and Peary," *Tourist*, September, 1911, p. 211).

John R. Bradley acknowledged: "Well, the best of us get fooled once in a while. He fooled the King of Denmark, didn't he? And all those foreign scientists, he fooled them too. There isn't anything to do but stand up and be a good sport and take your medicine. . . . We've all been fooled by the biggest thing of the kind that ever happened. I'm going to be a good sport and take my medicine."[45]*

Except for Rear Admiral Schley, only two newsworthy persons appear to have retained a feeling of kindness for Cook. One was Benjamin F. Trueblood, secretary of the American Friends Society. He told reporters: "On the surface the case looks very gloomy for Dr. Cook, but I am not ready to renounce and denounce him." The other was Minister Egan's daughter Carmelita. She found the Copenhagen decision difficult to accept. "He was such a nice man," she told a reporter. "I can scarcely believe this news. I certainly trusted him, and I think every other woman in Denmark did also."

And so, in a game that the great American sportsman could barely recognize, masculinity being a many-layered affair, the club had won. But its victory was not complete. Its prey was not dead, only grievously wounded. The hunt, therefore, went on.

* This was Bradley's position publicly. Privately, however, he felt otherwise. Some weeks before the Copenhagen decision, according to information supplied by a descendant, Bradley had had a private confrontation with Cook, during which he had asked Cook to tell him the truth. The gambler was convinced that he could tell when a man was not telling the truth, and Cook replied in a manner that convinced Bradley that he had attained the Pole. This belief Bradley retained permanently, despite the disasters that trailed the Doctor thereafter. For Bradley, Cook was a remarkable explorer and an honest man. At the same time, he regarded Cook as naive and trusting, totally unsophisticated in matters concerning the great world.

10

THE ABILITY to transform a winner into a loser was only one of the talents in the club's equipage. It was just about as deft in turning a loser into a winner, especially when joined by an ally as crafty as the National Geographic Society. Before the public the society was as much or more involved in the affairs of Peary as was the club itself. The society had contributed $1,000 to the costs of Peary's final expedition. It had also, as Cook wrote, "as a lecture bureau . . . retained Mr. Peary to fill an important position as its principal star for many years."

Nevertheless, the society did not immediately identify Cook as a fraud. A day or so after he had announced his attainment of the Pole, the society's president said: "I regret that there has been, in some quarters . . . an attempt to revive the discrediting of his ascension. . . . Our society had Dr. Cook lecture before it on . . . Mount McKinley, and . . . we would not have invited him if there had been the slightest doubt of his integrity, courage, and ability."[1]

That the society had readjusted its thinking did not become noticeable until it announced, as its basic policy, that it was the "usual course" that an explorer must bring back proof of his accomplishments. This had never been so, previously, in Arctic exploration. The society had not asked Peary for "proof" before awarding him, in 1906, a medal for his Farthest North. Until the unique polar controversy began, it seems that, as Cook wrote in *My Attainment of the Pole*, "The National Geographic, like every other geographic society, had previously rated the merits of an explorer's work by his published reports."

Be that as it may, the job of "proving" Peary's claim to the Pole was cunningly accomplished by the National Geographic Society. From its own membership it appointed a three-man subcommittee to determine whether or not Peary had attained his goal. The central figure was Colby M. Chester, a retired rear admiral who had been superintendent at Annapolis and commander-in-chief of the Atlantic Squadron.* The other members of the subcommittee were O. H. Tittman and Henry Gannett. Tittman was chief of the Coast and Geodetic Survey, the agency to which Peary had been assigned while drawing full pay on his 1908 expedition. Gannett was a geographer occasionally employed by the survey.

Sometime around the end of October, 1909 — about the time Cook was approaching Montana — this subcommittee met in Washington, D.C. Although the occasion was formal in that it was the subcommittee's one and only meeting, and that the Commander attended and presented his "proof," it was informal in that it was held in the home of Admiral Chester, and was a pleasant, clubby afternoon. Exactly what material Peary presented as "proof" is not known today, but according to Captain Thomas F. Hall, it was in the form of "some 'loose leaves' purporting to have been torn from his log book or diary, together with other 'loose leaves' said to contain his observations of the sun and computations thereon."[2]

Whatever it was, it impressed the subcommittee, which reported: "Commander Peary has submitted to this subcom-

* Of Chester, Captain Bradley Osbon wrote: "By marriage [he] is identified with the man who has been and is sales agent of Peary for the disposal of the latter's furs, skins, walrus tusks and narwhale horns, brought down from the Arctic. . . . The resident members of this committee are also possessed of many trophies of the Peary hunting" (*Tourist*, September, 1911, p. 210). In his article Osbon quoted from an affidavit sworn to by a Joseph G. White, a member of the crew of Peary's supply ship *Erik* in 1908. White testified: "Most of the time Peary and Matt Henson . . . were busy trading with Eskimos and making big profit on the furs and ivory, and giving the Eskimos very little . . . coffee, bisquits and candy."

mittee his original records and record of observations, together with all his instruments and apparatus. . . . These have been carefully examined by your subcommittee, and they are unanimously of the opinion that Commander Peary reached the North Pole April 6, 1909."[3]

Later, Cook, who was a lenient man, observed in *My Attainment of the Pole:* "I have no objection to Mr. Peary's friends endorsing him — a friend who will stretch a point is not to be condemned."

But pleasant, clubby afternoons sometimes have unpleasant consequences. Almost a year later — after the club had decided to have Peary promoted to the rank of rear admiral, then retired at the highest possible pension — Peary was called before members of the House of Representatives Naval Affairs Subcommittee and quizzed about his memories of the afternoon at Admiral Chester's. He could hardly remember anything.

The questions were put to him by Congressman Ernest W. Roberts, who presumed to think that the society had accepted a grave responsibility when it investigated Peary's claim. The public, the Congressman declared, had a right to know how the society had reached its decision.

ROBERTS: "What did you do while there with the committee? I want to find out how the examination of the proofs was made. . . ."

PEARY: "There again, as the members of the committee are accessible, I would prefer to have them take that up."

ROBERTS: "No; I want to have your recollection. . . ."

PEARY: "I can recall that I was there at Admiral Chester's house with the members of the committee, and some others, I think, came in addition to the members of the subcommittee; and I remember too that I was there until sometime in the evening; I could not say how late."

ROBERTS: "Have you exhibited to the subcommittee that original memorandum that you have shown us? Did they read it?"

PEARY: "How much the different members of the committee read I cannot say."

ROBERTS: "And you submitted the data of your astronomical observations?"

PEARY: "That is my impression. I had it there with me, and I presume they saw portions of it, perhaps all of it.

ROBERTS: "Did they verify any of the computations in your presence . . . ?"

PEARY: "The only thing I can say is that I think Professor Gannett was making some figures. Whether he carried out the full computation I cannot say."

ROBERTS: "Do you recall Admiral Chester going over the astronomical computations?"

PEARY: "I remember Admiral Chester having a chart showing the projection of the sun."

ROBERTS: "How many hours would you say, as the best estimate you can give, you were with the committee?"

PEARY: "Well. I should say I was there the greater portion of the day."

ROBERTS: "Do you recall when it was . . . the month or the day?"

PEARY: "It was sometime in October, I should say."

Among the facts that hesitatingly emerged was that the society's examination of Peary's sextant and other instruments — "carefully examined by your subcommittee" — had been even more farcical than its study of his observations.

ROBERTS: "Did you bring with you to Admiral Chester's house your instruments?"

PEARY: "No."

ROBERTS: "Where were they?"

PEARY: "They were at the station."

ROBERTS: "Did the committee see these instruments?"

PEARY: "They did."

ROBERTS: "Where . . .?"

PEARY: "At the station."

ROBERTS: "Did you go with them?"
PEARY: "I did."
ROBERTS: "Do you recall what time you got to the station?"
PEARY: ". . . it was pretty well along in the evening."
ROBERTS: " . . . after dark?"
PEARY: "It was after dark."
ROBERTS: ". . . How did the instruments come down?"
PEARY: ". . . in a trunk."
ROBERTS: ". . . what did you and the committee do with regard to the instruments?"
PEARY: "I should say that we opened the trunk. . . ."
ROBERTS: "That is, in the baggage room of the station?"
PEARY: "Yes."
ROBERTS: "Were all the instruments taken out?"
PEARY: "That I cannot say. Members of the committee will probably remember better than I."
ROBERTS: "Well, you do not have any recollection of whether they . . . examined them?"
PEARY: "Some were taken out, I should say; whether all were taken out, I could not say."
ROBERTS: "Was any test of those instruments made . . . to ascertain . . . the instruments were accurate?"
PEARY: "That I could not say. I should imagine that it would not be possible to make tests there."
ROBERTS: "Were those instruments even in the possession of the committee other than the inspection at the station?"
PEARY: "Not to my knowledge."[4]

Afterward Congressman Roberts wrote: "A perusal of . . . Peary's testimony shows his recollection of the . . . day . . . delightfully vague and uncertain. The occasion was a most momentous one in his career, for the report of this committee was to settle in the public mind the mooted question of his having attained the Pole, and the fact that the incidents of the day made no sharper impression . . . is very conclusive evidence that the examination was anything but minute, careful, or rigorous."[5]

But such embarrassments were minor in comparison to the benefits that the society could provide. Late in December, the National Geographic Society awarded Peary its Grand Gold Medal "for the discovery of the North Pole." The ceremony, which took place at the society's annual banquet, contained a full measure of the oddness that characterizes the polar controversy. "The medal was handed to the Commander in a somewhat tentative way," the New York *Times* noted; "or rather it was not handed to him at all. What he got was the box it was supposed to come in. This is because the . . . society . . . is waiting to review the findings of the Danish experts on Dr. Cook's records."[6]

At any rate, the National Geographic Society's endorsement, and only that, as Captain Thomas F. Hall would observe, was "the sole foundation upon which the entire super-structure of Peary's claims and honors have been built."[7] These honors included medals from a dozen nations.

So that was it. Demanding "proof" from Cook, Peary himself had nothing to offer. The only "proof" he possessed that he had attained the Pole was that the National Geographic Society said it was so.

Matthew Henson, about this time, was also attempting to profit from his acquaintance with the North Pole. During the expedition he had been paid $50 a month. When the *Roosevelt* arrived in New York, he and every other member of the exploring party had received a bonus of $250 awarded by the club. In the meantime his wife, imagining that he was going to make a fortune, had quit her job as a menial in a bank. When Henson showed up with not much more than his bonus, she was forced to ask for her old job back. She was rehired.

For a time, it seemed as if his situation might improve. William A. Brady, a theatrical manager, invited him to make a lecture tour. His first appearance was in Middletown, Connecticut. Although he was greeted by the Mayor and a brass band, the public did not respond. Brady then booked him into New York. He opened at the Hippodrome on Broadway on October 17.

"The negro was received with much enthusiasm," the *Eagle* said. ". . . His voice did not carry and shouts of 'Louder' came from the gallery. He explained that he had spent the greater part of his life in driving Eskimo dogs in a region where people did not talk much. 'That's all right, go ahead, old man,' a voice shouted."

Up on the stage Henson, who was wearing tails, soon made some anti-Cook remarks that angered the audience. Numerous people began throwing questions at him. A gray-haired gentleman whom the press identified as a Cornell professor named Alfred H. Walker, the author of *Christ's Christianity*, insisted on asking Henson technical questions about observations, artificial horizons, and refractions. "With a warning finger the veritable auditor led the negro pole-hunter from one slippery question to another," the *American* said. "Finally Henson said, 'Now sir, Commander Peary is going to tell you about that. . . . you just get all that fine scientific business from the Commander." As the questions became more and more numerous, the lights were turned on and William A. Brady dashed onstage with what he insisted was a "genuine" picture of the North Pole. The lecture ended with Henson surrounded by questioners. To clear the stage the management had to turn out the lights. Although the Hippodrome seated five thousand, only five hundred attended the opening. For all intents and purposes, Henson's effort to profit from his tremendous deeds was finished.

His signed article on the relations between himself and Peary at the Pole appeared in the Boston *American* on July 17, 1910, and has been largely ignored ever since. Despite the fact that so much of what Henson said contradicted Peary's story, the club did not hurry to placate him. Some sort of understanding was reached, however, and in 1912, when Henson's *A Negro Explorer at the North Pole* was published, Peary wrote the introduction and gave the publisher $500 to use advertising the book. Of it Captain Thomas F. Hall wrote: "I place little or no credence in Henson's book because manifestly it is censored in an endeavor to have it agree with Peary's story as to matters of fact north of the Bartlett camp."

Eventually a black politician secured a federal appointment for the man who said of himself at the Pole, "then I lead a cheer for Old Glory." He became a messenger boy at the United States Custom House in Manhattan, at an annual salary of $900.

It was an evening — February 8, 1910 — that began brilliantly and became grander and grander. The scene was the Metropolitan Opera House, the finest auditorium in New York City; and the event itself, formally sponsored by the Peary Arctic Club, was the National Testimonial to Commander Peary. The house was packed, everyone was happy, and each time Peary's name was mentioned the audience cheered. Up on the platform the polar hero was surrounded by the members of his club, by some of the members of his last expedition, and by an honorary committee of thirty-one millionaires.

Cook's name was never mentioned, and there was only one direct reference to him. That occurred when Charles Evans Hughes, the Governor of New York, apologized for the delay in honoring the Commander and stated that "circumstances were not within our control." The New York *Times* reported that "the audience laughed and cheered at that and Peary nodded and smiled." When Peary got up to give his lecture the audience rose and cheered and the band played "Hail to the Chief." Meanwhile, sitting behind him on the stage, and ready to applaud at the proper moments, were the thirty-one millionaires, representing in the flesh what one of Peary's biographers described as "his wide circle of influential friends." They included: [8]

Charles B. Alexander, lawyer; director, Equitable Life Insurance Company

William Henry Bliss, lawyer; associate counsel, Northern Pacific Railroad

Andrew Carnegie

Hugh J. Chisholm, president, International Paper Company

Henry Clews, banker, author of *Twenty-Eight Years in Wall Street*

Robert J. Collier, editor, *Collier's Weekly*

R. Fulton Cutting, director, American Beet Sugar Company; president, Citizens Union; president, Association for Improving the Condition of the Poor

H. P. Davison, partner, J. P. Morgan & Co.

Cleveland H. Dodge, director, New York Life Insurance Company, National City Bank; president of the board of directors, YMCA

Stuyvesant Fish, banker; president, Illinois Central Railroad; trustee, New York Life, Mutual Life Insurance Company

Henry C. Frick, chairman, Carnegie Steel Company; director, Pennsylvania Railroad

Algernon Sydney Frissell, banker; president, Fifth Avenue Bank of New York; trustee, Greenwich Savings Bank

Elbert H. Gary, chairman, U.S. Steel Corporation

Archer M. Huntington, president, American Geographical Society

Adrian H. Joline, lawyer; president, Missouri, Kansas & Texas Railroad

Otto H. Kahn, banker, Kuhn, Loeb & Co.

Seth Low, former Mayor of New York; president, Columbia University

John G. Milburn, lawyer; trustee, New York Life Insurance Company; president, Pan American Exposition

Henry Morgenthau, lawyer; chairman, Democratic Finance Committee

Norman B. Reame, director, U.S. Steel Corporation, Baltimore & Ohio, Erie, Chicago, Burlington & Quincy, Pierre Marquette, and Sea Board Air Line railroads

John Harsen Rhoades, banker, Rhoades & Co.; trustee, Greenwich Savings Bank

Jacob H. Schiff, banker, Kuhn, Loeb & Co.

Isaac N. Seligman, banker, J. & W. Seligman; trustee, United Hebrew Charities; member, Committee of Nine for Police Investigation

Theodore P. Shonts, president, Toledo, St. Louis & Western, Interborough Rapid Transit Company (IRT) of New York, St. Louis & Western, Minneapolis & St. Louis, and Iowa Central railroads

Paul M. Warburg, banker, Kuhn, Loeb & Co.*

Among themselves, these men had collected a purse of $10,000, which they would present to Peary at the end of the evening. They were awarding him this sum because they believed it was the decent thing to do. Their attitude, surely, was similar to that which had been expressed in an editorial in the New York *Times* immediately after the Copenhagen decision. "The pity of it is that his triumph should have been clouded," that paper said of Peary, "and his just pride tinged with disappointment and vexation. . . . It can never wholly be made up, but certainly now reparation should be made in every appropriate way. Imposture has met its doom; merit should have its full reward."

So that was the way they saw it — "reparation should be made in every appropriate way." They believed that the Commander should have $10,000 contributed by themselves; they believed that he should be promoted to the rank of rear admiral and retired at the highest possible pension. They had joined him on this public occasion, and were making their display of

* General Thomas H. Hubbard and Henry Fairfield Osborn, both members of the club, were also on the honorary committee. Others included William C. Demorest, Albert Lewisohn, and Egerton L. Winthrop, Jr.

approval, in order that Congress should be aware of their interest in Robert E. Peary.

After the $10,000 had been presented, the Commander delighted all by announcing that he would deposit it in a bank as a joint contribution to fit out an expedition to go to the South Pole. The applause was tremendous, and the evening ended with everyone in a splendid mood. For at least once, in New York City, imposture had met its doom. Now merit was beginning to receive its full reward.

The recomputation of Peary's polar observations was nicely accomplished, the job being done by Hugh C. Mitchell, assisted by C. R. Duvall. Both men were employees of the United States Coast and Geodetic Survey, whose chief, O. H. Tittman, had been one of the three members of the National Geographic Society's cozy subcommittee. As one student of the controversy soon complained, "Practically, the relation of employer and employee exists between him [Tittman] and Mr. Mitchell." As private individuals Mitchell and Duvall were hired by Peary, who paid them $300. After yanking Peary's observations about, changing something here, fixing something there, Mitchell and Duvall put aside their "private individual" hats and picked up their "government employee" hats and appeared before the House Naval Affairs Subcommittee. There they certified that on the basis of their recomputation of Peary's observations, the Commander had definitely reached the North Pole.

Although Peary had been most willing to show his records to the friendly clubmen of the National Geographic Society, he had originally refused to show the same records to the Naval Affairs Subcommittee. The official explanation of his attitude toward the representatives of Congress was: "Commander Peary and his friends say that contracts signed months ago with his publishers render it impossible to make his records and scientific data public now. . . . It would be breaking faith with his publishers, which he is unwilling to do under any circumstances."[9]

In December the National Geographic Society certified his

attainment of the Pole by presenting him with, if not its Grand Gold Medal, at least "the box it was supposed to come in." February saw the Night of the Thirty-one Millionaires. Soon afterward Peary and Bob Bartlett departed on a European tour during which they were honored with boxes *and* medals, gold for Peary, silver for Bartlett, by all the major European geographical societies except those in the Scandinavian countries.

Buttressed by such awards, Peary finally presented himself before the Naval Affairs Subcommittee. Although Congressman Roberts questioned him closely, as has been seen, about his memories of the afternoon at Admiral Chester's, and found "his recollection of the events of the day . . . delightfully vague and uncertain," the majority on the subcommittee appeared willing to accept just about anything as long as it looked all right and was not crammed down their throats. But except for the recomputations the Commander seemed to favor blatancy.

Among the data that he submitted to the members of Congress was a diary. Concerning it Congressman Roberts remarked: "If the members of the committee care to, I would like to have the book examined particularly with reference to its condition and state. It shows no finger marks or rough usage; a very cleanly kept book."[10]

Congressman Helgesen also commented on the appearance of the diary. "It is a well-known fact that on a long arctic journey ablutions even of the face and hands are too luxurious for the travelers. Pemmican is the staple article of food. Its great value lies in its greasy quality. How was it possible for Peary to handle this greasy food and without washing his hands write in his diary daily and at the end of two months have that same diary show 'no finger marks or rough usage'?"[10]

Such material, presented by Peary as proof that he had attained the Pole, exasperated Congressman Butler, the otherwise sympathetic chairman of the subcommittee. At the end of Peary's testimony Butler turned to him and said: "We have your word for it, and we have these observations to show that you were at the North Pole. That is the plain way of putting it, your word and your proofs. To me, as a member of this committee, I accept your word; but your proofs I know nothing about."

Years later, according to John Edward Weems, Peary's most recent biographer, Josephine Peary wrote: "No one will ever know how the attack on my husband's veracity affected him, who had never had his word doubted in ANY thing at ANY time in his life. He could not believe it. And the personal grilling which he was obliged to undergo at the hands of Congress . . . hurt him more than all the hardships in the Arctic regions and did more towards the breaking down of his iron constitution than anything experienced in his explorations."

An amended version of the Peary Bill was passed by the subcommittee by a vote of four to three.*

A spokesman for the committee majority indicated that the decisive factor in the testimony was the certification by Mitchell and Duvall.

A member of the minority wrote: "the more I investigated and studied the story, the more thoroughly convinced I have become that it is fake pure and simple."

In the bill originally offered before Congress, Peary had been described as the "discoverer" of the North Pole. In the bill as amended this was struck out and Peary was credited with simply "reaching the North Pole." The bill was signed by President Taft on March 4, 1911, after which Peary was placed on the retired list of the Navy's Corps of Civil Engineers with the rank of rear admiral and an annual pension of approximately $6,000.

Meanwhile, the newspaper-reading world had no real idea of the Doctor's whereabouts, although as the weeks went by press

* Fitzhugh Green wrote: "On February 11, 1911, General Thomas Hubbard took a hand in the proceedings. He had a good friend in D. S. Alexander, Representative of New York in the 61st District, and chairman of the committee on rivers and harbors. He proved a medium through which the Peary Arctic Club could keep its finger on the pulse of the Investigating Committee" (*Peary, The Man Who Refused to Fail*, New York, 1926, p. 337).

agents for resorts, hotels, and sanitariums from Michigan to Maine reported his presence at their establishments. Actually, he had turned south at Marseilles, had paused in Portugal, then entered Spain. He and Marie were reunited in Algeciras, the noisy but cheerful waterfront town opposite Gibraltar. "Since she had no address for him and did not know his assumed name," Andrew Freeman wrote, "they wandered around the streets looking for each other. Finally they met in a small park."

From Algeciras they continued south. Cook had spent some twenty months in the Arctic. He had put in a fall and early winter in the United States. Now he wanted heat. There are no polar bears in Paraguay, and there is where he finally halted.

Of his situation at the time he wrote, most impressively:

"Few men in all history, I am inclined to believe, have ever been made the subject of such vicious attacks, of such malevolent assailing of character, of such a series of perjured and forged charges, of such a widespread and relentless press persecution, as I; and few men, I feel sure, have ever been made to suffer so bitterly and so inexpressibly as I because of the assertion of my achievement. So persistent, so egregious, so overwhelming were the attacks made upon me that for a time my spirit was broken, and in the bitterness of my soul I even felt desirous of disappearing to some remote corner of the earth, to be forgotten."[11]

Even when he was in hiding his enemies continued to construct their slanders, their elaborations on his awfulness. On the morning of May 20, 1910, the New York *Times* presented the world with fresh news about its candidate for World Champion Scoundrel. The one-column headline was terse yet horrified:

COOK TRIED TO STEAL PARSON'S LIFE WORK

It seems that sometime around 1870 a young missionary of the Church of England, the Reverend Thomas Bridges, had been sent to Tierra del Fuego, at the southernmost tip of South

America, to convert the natives to Christianity. His first task was to learn the native language, which his predecessor had defined as "a very poor means of educating them for a higher life, as it is sadly wanting in definite terms for ideas which the natives have never entertained."

After twenty-five years in the area, Thomas Bridges abandoned his missionary effort, but remained at Tierra del Fuego as a rancher and retained his interest in the language of the Yahgans, the Indian tribe native to the place. During these years he published some twenty monographs on the Yahgans, and within a tiny circle of scholars was known as the sole authority on the Yahgan language. By 1897, when the *Belgica* expedition arrived, Thomas Bridges had compiled a Yahgan dictionary containing 32,000 words.

The basic account of the dictionary affair, as seen from the point of view of the plaintiff, was written by Thomas Bridges's son, Lucas. "I took the scientists to Haverton," he wrote in *Uttermost Part of the Earth*, "and introduced them to my father. Dr. Cook was most interested in the Yahgan-English dictionary on which, by then, Father had spent over thirty years of work and thought. Publication was discussed. . . . Dr. Cook . . . offered to take charge of the dictionary then and there, but Father promised to hand it over to Dr. Cook on the return voyage of the *Belgica*."

By the time the *Belgica* reappeared at Tierra del Fuego Thomas Bridges was dead. "Dr. Cook came down in a cutter . . . with the intention of securing my late father's dictionary," Lucas Bridges wrote. "We remembered how Father had given his assurance . . . so we entrusted that brisk young American surgeon with the priceless dictionary and grammar."

After Cook returned to America the New York *Times* reported: "Besides medical and anthropological reports, Dr. Cook will make a notable contribution in the shape of an extensive vocabulary of the Yahgan language." A reader of the item could assume that Cook had put the dictionary together all by himself. Eight years later the charge was made that such had been his deliberate intention.

Once again, the assertion was made by a snugly established

member of ordered society. He was Charles H. Townsend, director of the New York Aquarium. His charges were substantiated by Professor Franz Boas, a Columbia University anthropologist friendly with Henry Fairfield Osborn and others at the American Museum of Natural History. "Dr. Cook came to me with a copy of the dictionary," Professor Boas wrote. "He intimated to me that it was largely his work and that he wanted to consult me." Boas testified that Cook had never once mentioned Bridges's name.

In *My Attainment of the Pole* Cook wrote of the dictionary: "Although this was of little use to anybody, it was a scientific record worthy of preservation. In a friendly spirit towards the late Mr. Bridges and his Indians, I persuaded the Belgians at great expense to publish the work. It was written in the old Ellis system of orthography, which is not generally understood. Working on this material one year without pay, I changed it to ordinary English orthography." He stated that he had written an introduction to the dictionary, that it was his understanding that the introduction had been published in Belgium, and that in it he had said: "The credit of collecting and making this Yahgan Grammar and Vocabulary belongs solely to Mr. Bridges, who devoted most of his time during thirty-seven years to recording this material."

Years later Lucas Bridges was informed that the Observatoire Royal in Brussels was printing the dictionary, and that it was being advertised as the work of Dr. Frederick A. Cook. Bridges went to Belgium and discovered that this was true. A proposed cover not only credited the work to Cook, it described him as "Dr. of Anthropology." Near the bottom of the proposed cover a line of small print stated that the Reverend Bridges had been "instrumental in collecting the words." Lucas Bridges discussed the situation with Belgian officials and was able to have the credit lines reversed. Later, in an appendix to *Uttermost Part of the Earth*, Rosemary H. Moeller declared that the Curator of the Observatoire Royal "was not ignorant of the work's real authorship" and that the real authorship "was already known in the scientific world"; both of these charges being inferences that not only had Cook attempted to defraud Thomas Bridges, but that Belgian scientists had knowingly conspired with him to do so, and were, accordingly, willing to risk their reputations over such an absurd matter.*

Today the contention that Cook stole the dictionary, that after a stay of six weeks at Tierra del Fuego he attempted to palm himself off as having in that limited time collected 32,000 words of the Yahgan language and written a grammar in addition, seems very strange. He was already the hero of the *Belgica* expedition. He would soon be rewarded by the King of Belgium. The affair seems packed with that special variety of trouble that sometimes overwhelms those who put themselves out to help others. The Doctor was within his rights in submitting the dictionary as part of the scientific collection of the expedition. That the writer of the original story in the New York *Times* misunderstood the situation is possible. Professor Boas's memory of an event ten or more years old could be faulty. It is doubtful that Cook was a party to anything that described him as a "Dr. of Anthropology." It is also doubtful that any Belgian scientist would risk his reputation by conspiring with him. But in this most human world all things are possible, and perhaps the resourceful Doctor imagined that a time would come when having a reputation as an authority on the Yahgan language would be handy. If so, he was wrong. In 1825, when Charles Darwin visited Tierra del Fuego, the Yahgans numbered about three thousand. But by 1932 the population of the tribe, including half-breeds, was down to forty-three.

* The absurdness of such charges was originally brought out by F. J. Pohl in his unpublished article "Defense of F. A. Cook," The Stefansson Collection, Dartmouth College Library, Hanover, N.H.

II

MEANWHILE, living the life incognito in drowsy Paraguay, Cook pondered the immense problem of reestablishing his correct identity. By the late summer of 1910 he had recovered from his mauling, and so Marie Cook returned to the children and he traveled to London. He registered into a prominent hotel as F. A. Cook, then settled down to write his story. After a month or so, he felt ready to begin his comeback. Although one New York newspaper had offered his brother William $1,000 for his address, and the New York *Times* had offered just about anything for his first exclusive statement, he simply contacted the correspondent of the New York *World* and declared himself alive.

At the moment his situation was like this:

Even those who would like to believe in him found it difficult. "He has been his own worst enemy," Anthony Fiala would soon declare "for he did much by his flight towards confirming the opinion that he was a fraud. Had he remained and faced the music he would have held his old friends and gained new ones and he would have been in a better position than he is now to enforce his claims."[1]

He himself was a sturdy but medium-sized man with blond hair, blue eyes, and a large yellow mustache. His appearance was pleasant but unglamorous. When his friends had last seen him in America he had been "highly nervous, continually clasped his hands over his stomach, and complained of gastric distress."[2]

Now, some eleven months later, he appeared before the London correspondent of the New York *World:* "He stood tall and robust, wearing dark apparel and a black derby hat, carrying grey gloves and a walking stick. His countenance was suntanned and rounded in the cheek lines. He waited, hat off, smilingly contemplating the scrutiny of his interviewer."

The first thing the man from the *World* wanted to know was: Why did you vanish?

"I was like a deer that had been driven into a cold stream. I simply had to get away from the perturbing conditions. The circumstances that surrounded me . . . the great weariness, mental fatigue, and the disgust that had come over me — the disgust at the conspiracy that was despoiling me of the results of my life's work — these things caused me to suddenly leave New York. I left for anywhere — anywhere that I could be absolutely alone."

The reporter wanted to know: What were his plans for the future?

"I have simply been awaiting the time when my health would permit me to return to the United States. I did not run away from my task, but from the intolerable conditions that were created to ruin it and goad and harass me. What I so dearly earned may have been filched from me, but only temporarily. It will come back to me just as I shall come back."

The man from the *World* seemed to wonder how Cook had ever gotten into his present situation:

"Every world achievement has aroused envy and engendered intrigue."*

* The *World* story ran some five thousand words. In it the reporter noted that soon after arriving in England, Cook learned that Peary was going to lecture before the Royal Geographic Society. Accordingly, he attended. " 'I stood twenty yards from Peary,' chuckled Dr. Cook, 'and none recognized me. . . . I was very much interested in Peary's lecture and heard it very comfortably.' " He was unrecognized because he had grown a beard and changed the styling of his hair and his mustache. "The beard cut Van Dyke and grizzled at the sides," the *World* reported; "the mustache, instead of being closely cropped . . . has been allowed to grow long with flowing ends drooping on either side of the sharply pointed beard." (During his months in Paraguay, Cook had amused him-

The story broke in New York on October 2, 1910. Visitors appeared at Cook's door almost immediately, but large adventures did not evolve until the arrival from America of T. Everett Harré, an associate editor of *Hampton's*, a popular magazine of the day. Mr. Harré had a proposition to make: *Hampton's* had published the Robert E. Peary story serially, but the articles had not contained any really sensational developments and circulation had not improved. Now *Hampton's* wanted to publish the Frederick A. Cook story. Its editors were certain that it had the makings of a great human document.

The Doctor was interested, for he saw the publication of his story in a magazine as the first move in his comeback. Despite the fact that one magazine had made him a standing offer of $10,000 for anything he had to say, while *Hampton's* could only offer him $4,000, the idea of his story appearing in *Hampton's* had special attractions. "The opportunity of addressing the same public," he would say later, "through the same medium as Mr. Peary . . . strongly influenced me."

But even at the start the magazine's offer contained a catch. Its editors had done some thinking and had come up with an idea which, if acceptable to Cook, would make his story an even greater, even more human tale than it was already. All Cook had to do was to announce, in *Hampton's*, that he was relinquishing his claim to the Pole.

"I was to go secretly to New York," Cook wrote in *My Attainment*, "submit myself to several employed alienists who should pronounce me insane, whereupon I was to write several articles in which I should admit having arrived at the conclusion that I had reached the Pole while mentally unbalanced."

The idea did not attract the Doctor, nor did it warn him. Being the sane and rational man that he was, however, he was

self by developing a remarkably and comically long blond mustache. In England he had clipped its tips, but it was still extremely long.) "He has also changed the fashion of wearing his hair," the *World* continued. ". . . Now it is closely clipped and brushed forward, forming a sort of bang over his forehead." (Among mid-twentieth-century hair styles for men, Cook's resembled that worn by Laurence Olivier in *Hamlet*.)

willing to concede, as Harré told Andrew Freeman years later, "that neither he nor Peary could claim to have reached the mathematical pole. . . . As both he and Peary had been alone in taking their observations, both could only make a relative claim to getting to the Pole or its approximate location."[3]

But otherwise, the offer from *Hampton's* interested him, and he agreed to return to New York incognito for further discussions. There he and the magazine's executives soon came to an understanding that guaranteed that his story would receive the widest publicity. He would write the articles, then return quietly to England, and make his formal return to America in late December. The January issue of the magazine would be carrying the first installment of his story and his arrival would promote its sale.

But nothing worked out as he had imagined. The fact was, the Commander's contract with *Hampton's* stipulated that it could not publish anything derogatory to Robert E. Peary. In addition, the Doctor, that supremely unbusinesslike gentleman, signed a letter from *Hampton's* which stated that they were making "no editorial guarantee whatsoever." And so, after he had completed the articles and had returned to London, he made an agonizing discovery. The unimaginable worst had happened. It was so bad that even the most worldly of men would have been dazed.

The editors of *Hampton's* had taken his small concession regarding the impossibility of his attaining the exact mathematical Pole, and had inflated it into the really sensational revelations that they required. "Did I get to the North Pole?" *Hampton's* advance press release quoted Cook as saying. "Perhaps I made a mistake in thinking I did. Perhaps I did not make a mistake. After mature thought I confess I do not know exactly whether I reached the Pole or not. . . . Fully, freely, and frankly I shall tell everything — and leave the decision to you. If, after reading my story, you say: 'Cook is sincere and honest; half-crazed by months of isolation and hunger, he believed that he reached the Pole; he is not a Faker,' then I shall be satisfied." And in addition, the magazine's promotional people were announcing that he had confessed that his journey to the Pole was fabricated, and in extenuation was pleading insanity.

All of this was being announced lustily in the newspapers. The New York *Times* gave it a full column on the front page. As for Cook, "I felt impotent, crushed," he would write. "In my very effort to explain myself I was being made a cat's-paw for magazine and newspaper sensation."

Such was the first incident in our great victim's comeback. As a character in Hemingway's *Islands in the Stream* said of another matter: "I kept waiting for truth and right to win and then somebody new would knock truth and right right on its ass."

In the story of Frederick A. Cook the *Hampton's* confession series is the definitive event. The modern corporate state has been defined, by Charles A. Reich in his *The Greening of America*, as "an immensely powerful machine, ordered, legalistic, rational, yet utterly out of human control, wholly and perfectly indifferent to any human values." That is a perfect description of *Hampton's*. In Cook's life that magazine and its insane editors, more so than the club, figure as the corporation confronting and crushing the lone citizen. The definitiveness of the *Hampton's* episode, however, does not lie in such a contrast, but in the fact that it was the only incident about which, years later, individuals involved came forward and revealed the truth, and so demonstrated exactly how far others were willing to go in order to profit from Cook's situation. Edward Barrill had certainly lied for money. George Dunkle and Augustus Loose had lied for money. And *Hampton's* also lied for money — "to boost newsstand circulation."

The full story of the "confession" series was not revealed until January 1915, when Lillian Kiel, a secretary at the magazine during the period when the series was prepared and published, appeared before a congressional hearing.

All of the material derogatory to Cook had been manufactured by the magazine's editors, Lillian Kiel testified. Each galley proof had been initialed by Cook, but afterward "we of the editorial staff . . . cut through the galley proofs and inserted what has been known to the world as Dr. Cook's confession of 'mental unbalancement.' . . . We issued a 'statement to the press.' That was done in order to make a magazine story appear authentic and also — and really ahead of any other motive — to boost newsstand circulation . . . or just to make a few men more wealthy than they previously were."

Lillian Kiel provided some interesting information on the background of Peary's series in *Hampton's:*

"When the story was first concocted, Mr. Peary had no story, he had no data, he had nothing to present to *Hampton's* Magazine, but he was under contract . . . to produce something. When he appeared before the committee of Congress they asked him for his proofs, and he made the statement that he was 'under contract' with *Hampton's* Magazine to have his proofs appear first in *Hampton's* Magazine. They engaged a public stenographer to do the work, and Mr. Peary merely answered questions. From these notes Mrs. Elsa Barker made up the story. . . . She was a personal friend of Mr. Peary's. . . . I took the story from the time he left the ship up to the point where he was supposed to reach the Pole. There were no proofs, and consequently *Hampton's* Magazine was all in a furor. My services were discontinued for about two weeks. Then I received a letter from Mrs. Barker telling me that she had just finished the 'observations'; that they were too technical to dictate to me, and she recalled me to finish the story."

The information about Peary's contract with the magazine, which guaranteed him a minimum of $50,000, came out during Miss Kiel's testimony before the House committee:

MISS KIEL: "They were under contract with Mr. Peary not to print anything that would be detrimental to Mr. Peary."

MR. TOWNER: "How do you know that?"

MISS KIEL: "One day I was standing in the hall . . . and

when we knew that we were going to get Dr. Cook's story Mr. Long came along and grabbed Mr. Hampton by the arm and said, 'We can't do it; we're under contract with Bob.' Mr. Hampton said, 'Never mind, we'll fix it up with Bob.' When I upheld Mr. Peary in office 'confabs' the head stenographer told me that I did not know 'everything.' "

MR. TOWNER: "This is the contention: Dr. Cook's story as originally written for *Hampton's* Magazine would have defended Dr. Cook?"

MISS KIEL: "It would have."

MR. TOWNER: "And in order that it should not do so these insertions were made?"

MISS KIEL: "Exactly."

It was toward the close of her testimony that Lillian Kiel testified that Cook had signed *Hampton's* "no editorial guarantee whatsoever" letter. At the completion of her testimony the chairman thanked her: "We certainly have been very much entertained by your interesting story." Lillian Kiel replied: "I did not come here, gentlemen, to entertain you. I merely came to show you one of the many wicked methods which were employed to denounce Dr. Frederick A. Cook. . . . I am here simply in the interest of justice."[4]

The unbelievable had happened. The Doctor had won a hand. But it had required four years, and had been scored against determined opponents. "The original transcript of the hearing was destroyed," Theon Wright has written. "Thus . . . Miss Kiel's testimony . . . would have been lost to history except for the efforts of one Congressman, who kept a copy of the minutes of the hearings."[5]

Years later, in New York, T. Everett Harré, no longer employed by *Hampton's*, swore in an affidavit dated January 21, 1944:

"I am making this affidavit, now, to clear up certain distortions of fact of which I have personal knowledge. The so-called 'Confession' of Dr. Cook . . . was a trumped-up fake. . . . Dr. Cook freely admitted that no explorer could determine the position of the North Pole with mathematical, 'pin-point' accuracy. (Neither can a sea-captain locate the position of his ship within feet or inches.) Dr. Cook consistently insisted that he had reached the North Pole as closely as he could determine. Working with Cook, I studied and handled his personal diary and films. The notebook was time-worn, stained and greasy from close contact with his body. The copious, tightly written entries were mute evidence of having been written through a long and arduous experience. After Dr. Cook had OKed the galley proofs . . . they were altered without Dr. Cook's permission and without my own knowledge, to change the entire meaning."[6] *

But in London, in December, 1910, Cook could provide no explanation for "Dr. Cook's confession" and was faced with the ordeal of returning to America. He sailed from Bremen aboard the *George Washington* and arrived in New York on December 22, 1910, a year and a day after the announcement of the Copenhagen decision. On the following morning a story on his experiences with his fellow passengers and their reactions to him was published in the New York *Times:*

"It was left for a girl passenger to draw from him a confession of his identity.

" 'Are you Dr. Cook?' she asked archly at his elbow on the second day out.

" 'Yes, I am,' he replied with a pleasant smile.

" 'Are you the Dr. Cook who went to the North Pole?" she asked again in blissful ignorance of the 'confessions' published on this side of the water.

" 'I suppose I am,' the Doctor replied.

* In 1937 Harré had given a memo covering the situation to Charles Driscoll, who in his biography of the columnist O. O. McIntyre wrote of the *Hampton's* incident: "Ruthless exploitation of reputations was not uncommon in the mad race for circulation . . . but this was something more than exploitation. This was deliberate misrepresentation and chicanery." For Driscoll the *Hampton's* forgeries were "the most dastardly deed in the history of journalism" (*The Life of O. O. McIntyre*, New York, 1938, p. 222).

"In spite of his bold face Dr. Cook, other passengers said, was worried and uncertain how he would be received. They relate this incident. . . .

" 'The first night out after his identity had been established,' said one, 'Dr. Cook was in the smoking room playing cards with some of the passengers and drinks were brought in. Dr. Cook was plainly nervous, fearing someone would refuse to drink with him, and so . . . he proposed that all should drink to the Stars and Stripes.'

" 'Of course,' continued the narrator, 'no one could refuse to do this, and so the ice was broken.' "*

During the voyage he was particularly pleasant to the children aboard, some of whom perched on his knee while he told them fairy stories. "In almost every instance the women were on Dr. Cook's side," the *Times* reported. "It was said that Dr. Cook had been particularly courteous to some of them and even playful with the children aboard. . . . 'Dr. Cook has been a perfect gentleman, modest and agreeable,' all the women said who said anything at all."

At Quarantine the reporters came aboard and the drama heightened.

"The Doctor's arrival," the report continued, "was chiefly notable for a row over him among the passengers. Between Quarantine and the pier in Hoboken the whole Cook controversy was on again, just as hot as it was a year ago. In 20 minutes the scene in the ship's drawing room was so promising of at least half a dozen fist fights that the oldest and most blasé ship news reporter hugged himself with delight at the prospect. Men called each other liars to their faces, shook their fingers under each other's noses, and broke friendships which seven days on the ocean in hourly contact had served to cement. Women stood on chairs and joined vociferously in the arguments shouted by the men on both sides of the question of whether or not Dr. Cook had reached the Pole and whether or not he had been ostracized on his 'return from Elba.' . . .

* Cook was a light drinker, preferring wines. He started smoking cigarettes while in London.

"The first man seen, W. C. Sprague . . . asserted with emphasis that Dr. Cook had not been ostracized at all but cordially received everywhere. He said he had joined in the games and made himself extremely agreeable.

"While Mr. Sprague was reeling this off, up walked a tall, dark man with a monocle stuck in his eye. . . . He said, 'Never mind my name. . . . You are reporters aren't you? Well, you ought to be policemen to arrest this fellow Cook. He stole Peary's honors from him. Coming over the passengers haven't had a thing to do with Cook. . . . There is hardly a decent man on the ship that has associated with him.'

" 'Who are you?' demanded Sprague. 'I have never seen you a single time coming over. You have been sick all the time and haven't been out of your stateroom. . . .'

"It turned out that Mr. Chance, as he was called, had kept to his room pretty closely, but he was pugnacious to the last, following the reporters all over and denouncing Cook at every turn.

" 'I am a friend of Peary's,' he said, explaining that he wasn't a personal friend, but simply indignant at the way Peary had been treated. . . .

" 'I'll bet that fellow,' he said in a high voice, referring to Sprague, 'is a press agent of Cook's.'

"Siding with this man was . . . W. J. Harkness, a prosperous businessman of Rochester, N.Y. He said Dr. Cook had been avoided by the other passengers. . . .

" 'Mr. Sprague says he was everywhere warmly welcomed,' said the reporters, and Mr. Sprague was right on the spot to back up what he said.

" 'What that man said isn't so,' said Harkness. Then he turned to Sprague, shaking a finger in his face, adding: 'You know it isn't so. No gentlemen have been his companions.'

" 'It is so,' said Sprague. 'I have been with him myself.'

" 'I said "gentlemen," retorted the dignified Mr. Harkness, and added, glaring at Sprague, with his finger under his nose:

" 'What you said about Cook is false, and you know it is false.'

"By this time their voices, raised to a high pitch, had attracted practically everyone in the room to a circle about the men. . . . Some of the more timid men began shouting 'Remember there are ladies present.' The man called Chance was much excited and slipped on his hat.

" 'Take off that hat, you man who said Cook wasn't a gentleman,' shouted several, including some women, and with a rather sickly smile he removed his offending headpiece."

Meanwhile, the Doctor was in his stateroom conferring with someone from *Hampton's* who had come aboard with the reporters. When he eventually left his cabin he said: "I am through with exploration. I have had enough. I am here to settle down as an American citizen." He continued to follow his disastrous policy of modesty and candidness. "I still believe I reached the Pole, though I am not sure I did," he said, meaning that he was not sure in the scientific sense. "I am not a navigator, but I can handle instruments." He told reporters: "I was in the United States less than a month ago." He explained the purpose of his visit, then said: "I was registered under an assumed name because I was very busy." He was described as "looking like a health advertisement for a physical culture demonstrator."

One evening not long after his arrival, Cook had the unanticipated privilege of an hour in the company of Robert Dunn, the author of *The Shameless Diary of an Explorer*. In his autobiography Dunn wrote: "One night I walked into the Waldorf's old square bar, deserted but for one man alone at a table sipping champagne. I went over; Doc beamed placidly. 'Hey, Doc. Put it over on the world, didn't you?' I greeted him. An hour we must have talked, his stream of words repeating his published story. Whether or not he believed what he said, I couldn't tell, but his justification of his claims grew pathetic. I never saw him again."

Before long, Knud Rasmussen was back in the news with a statement that followed what was by this time a smoothly established pattern. In it Cook, who had previously been charged with faking his claim to the top of the North American continent, faking his attainment of the North Pole, stealing a dictionary that a parson had labored over for thirty-seven years, and employing two rascals named Dunkle and Loose to concoct a false set of astronomical observations, was charged with swindling his Eskimo companions, Etukishook and Ahwelah, by never paying them what he had promised, a knife and a gun apiece. This the Doctor denied. He said they had been paid before they started.

His talent for defending himself was almost nonexistent. At least a part of the story of his efforts to see that his boys were treated generously had already been told by Harry Whitney. It seems that just before leaving for Upernavik, Cook had told Whitney about a region where musk ox was plentiful, and had arranged that Etukishook and Ahwelah be members of the hunting party. Out in the field Whitney and the Eskimos came across a cache established by Cook more than a year earlier. Of its contents Whitney wrote: "Everything was carried down to camp, and there, in accordance with Dr. Cook's request, I divided between his two men Etukishook and Ahwelah, such things as I did not need myself."[7]

The Peary Arctic Club can be called some awful things, but it can never be described as half-hearted. Its dedication to the task of making life difficult for Cook was total. In 1910, when its prey was still hiding, the club attacked him by sending an expedition to Mount McKinley. It was lead by Belmore Browne and Herschel Parker, and its task was to find the "fake peak," duplicate Cook's photograph, and thus establish Barrill's affidavit as utterly truthful. Barrill was not a member of the party, but was represented by the map that was part of his testimony. Once they had completed their photography, Browne and Parker made a modest effort to climb the mountain, but soon turned back, and after naming a peak for General Thomas H. Hubbard, retired to New York.

The publication of their attempt to duplicate Cook's photo did not solve anything. It seems probable that although Browne and Parker were in the right area, they photographed the wrong peak, and after returning to New York had to touch up their photograph. E. C. Rost, a photographic expert who supported Cook, described it as a "combination photograph-drawing-painting," and Edwin Swift Balch, after examining the photo, politely declared that Browne and Parker were mistaken.[8]

In 1912 the club again assaulted Mount McKinley. Now the goal, for one reason or another, was the summit itself. The magnificently equipped expedition was guided by an extremely able man named Merl La Voy. This time Browne and Parker and their party got to within a few hundred feet of the summit before storms made further climbing impossible.

Cook's first task was to stay alive, his second to keep talking, his third to pray for a miracle. That it would require a miracle to clear his name in his own lifetime he seems to have understood. "Within my bosom there is the self-satisfying throb of success," he declared in 1911. ". . . That throb remains, it will always remain, and it is the only reward that I expect. . . . My reward will come with the reward that our children's children will give."[9]

No daily record exists of his movements in 1911, 1912, and most of 1913; but in general, here is what he did.

He wrote *My Attainment of the Pole*, which was marketed by his own organization, the Polar Publishing Company. A minimum of sixty thousand copies was printed. In it he said: "If you have read this book, then read Mr. Peary's 'North Pole.' Put the two books side by side. When making comparisons, remember . . . that my narrative was written and printed months before that of Mr. Peary. . . . Since my account was . . . first, the striking analogy apparent in the Peary pages either proves my position at the Pole or it convicts Peary of using my data to fill out and impart verisimilitude to his own story."

Afterward he traveled the country telling his story face to face. Since the newspapers were almost entirely opposed to him, he told his story from the lecture platform. For a time, after the *Hampton's* fiasco, he had trouble getting bookings. Finally the Chautauqua Association made a thorough investigation of his contentions, then accepted him on its lecture circuit. He soon became its star attraction. He also appeared in vaudeville. He appeared anywhere and everywhere that he could get a hearing.

And everywhere he went, the club was there ahead of him. "In nearly every town where he spoke," Andrew Freeman wrote, "Cook found the newspaper editor and a number of residents in possession of a voluminous and anonymous press sheet containing the Mount McKinley affidavits, the so-called Eskimo statements, distorted reports of the Copenhagen decision, and copies of editorials vilifying him. While he was in Des Moines, Iowa, the *Evening Tribune* of that city said: 'Whatever else Dr. Cook may be right or wrong about, he is certainly right about the efforts that are being made to suppress him and his contention over the North Pole. The *Evening Tribune* is in receipt of a mass of printed material about the doctor sent from no acknowledged source, that in the preparation must represent weeks of labor and hundreds of dollars of expense. The question that naturally suggests itself is why such an effort should now be considered necessary to discredit the doctor and who is financially interested enough to go to the expense.' "

The club described those who attended his lectures as "credulous" people. Once in Florida, as Freeman has recounted, three of this sort came up to shake Cook's hand. They were John Burroughs, Thomas Edison, and Henry Ford. "Doctor, I've read everything you've written and I'm with you," Ford told Cook. Since no lectures were scheduled for the next two days, Cook accepted their invitation to join them at Edison's home. Later they drove him to his next engagement. "Keep up your fight," Ford advised him, "and stand on your own feet."

For Robert E. Peary, the evening of April 6, 1912, was most congenial. It was the third anniversary of his arrival at his North Pole. It was the night when the club honored him with a testimonial dinner. During this affair he received a special trophy, one made in part out of material that he himself had stolen from the Eskimos.

The anthropological classification of Hunting People is reserved for that portion of humanity that survived into the nineteenth century without agriculture. Among these people, the Greenland Eskimos were the only group fortunate enough to be able to make their weapons out of local iron. Their main source was three meteorites that had fallen near Cape York at some unknown time. During Peary's 1894 expedition, for the bribe of one rifle, an Eskimo showed him the location of the meteorites. Soon afterward, because he had so little to show for his twenty months in the Arctic, he seized the two smaller meteorites and brought them to New York as trophies. In 1897 he made a special voyage north and secured the remaining meteorite. After it had arrived in New York, a team of forty horses hauled it up Broadway to the American Museum of Natural History. Soon afterward the wife of Morris K. Jesup purchased the three meteorites for $50,000, then donated them to the museum.

Fifteen years later, at its testimonial dinner, the club honored him with a special medal shaped like a five-pointed star. Each of its points was made of iron chipped from the meteorites, and each point was inscribed for one of his deeds: "The Crossing of Greenland, 1892; Securing the Great Meteorites, 1897; Insularity of Greenland, 1900; Farthest North, 1906; The North Pole, 1909."

It was a unique award, bestowed on a remarkable occasion, for the evening marked the formal disbandment of the Peary Arctic Club.[10] For most of its members, the hunt was over. Robert E. Peary, was a rear admiral. His attainment of the North Pole had been certified by Congress. He had medals from virtually every important nation in Europe. He had medals from every geographical organization in America. Could the dignity of the truth have been protected more diligently, more decisively? Could they not say, "See, we got our man in"? Peary surely agreed. Besides, he still retained the support of his friend, the inventor of the club, Herbert L. Bridgman.

For the most part, 1913 was an anxious year for the New York *Times*. Thirty days into the year trouble surfaced far to the west in a region where metropolitan information was not easily available. The fact was, the natives of Tacoma, Washington — and the *Times* strove to identify the tribe correctly: "the simple Tacomese — or Tacomites, or Tacomans" — were behaving improperly. ". . . are listening to the Doctor with credulity, are applauding his preposterous tales, are actually inviting him to public banquets in recognition of his greatness and consolation for his wrongs." The *Times* was puzzled. "Can it be that they have never heard or read of what has been proved against the man to the absolute satisfaction of everybody fair enough to examine his record and intelligent enough to understand it?" And in case its readers had forgotten, the newspaper reminded them of the party line: "Just as he pretended to have reached the Pole when he never went within hundreds of miles of it, so he pretended to have climbed Mount McKinley though he never ascended more than its foothills."[11]

And as the year went on Cook continued to improve his position in regions far from Times Square. Now, at his lectures, the audience received circulars describing his situation as "the American Dreyfus Case." Attached to each circular was a postal card which could be forwarded to Senators and Congressmen. By early December, according to the *Times*, "the postal card campaign had been carried to a stage whereby Senator J. Hamilton Lewis of Illinois and Senator Miles Poindexter of Washington were daily expecting to receive the Cook memorial."

To the *Times* and its friends the situation was intolerable. A full scale congressional investigation? Two United States Senators ready and willing to support Frederick A. Cook? He had to be stopped.

Captain Evelyn Briggs Baldwin was, in 1913, a veteran of five Arctic expeditions, including the Baldwin-Ziegler Expedition of 1901, which he had commanded. In earlier years he had worked for the United States Weather Bureau, and had served in the Army Signal Corps. He made his first trip to the Arctic in 1893 as meteorologist on Peary's second formal expedition, and was one of eight disgruntled explorers who returned to America at the end of the first year of the two-year expedition. During the voyage south on the supply ship *Falcon* one of his shipmates was Herbert L. Bridgman, who had come north to see how his man was getting on. A year or so later, in *Northward over the Great Ice*, Peary implied that Baldwin and the others had lacked guts: "[They] discovered that arctic work was not entirely the picnic they had imagined."

Baldwin, therefore, had no reason to like or favor Peary. At the same time, he was not very friendly with Cook, whom he suspected of interfering with his relations with the millionaire Ziegler. Nevertheless, Baldwin had written a three-thousand-word statement, "Positive Proof of Dr. Cook's Attainment of the Pole," which Cook had published in the appendix of *My Attainment of the Pole.* "I was not upon particularly cordial terms with Dr. Cook at the time," Baldwin said in 1912, "but a comparison of certain vital points in the stories told by the two men leaves no doubt in my mind."[12]

By 1913, however, Baldwin's relations with Cook had improved and the Captain had decided to enlarge his early statement into a book. "I took up the work," Baldwin eventually informed the New York *Times*, "expecting that I would be able to complete a volume that would help Dr. Cook's cause."[13]

Sometime in October, 1913, Cook left New York on a lecture tour. During his absence he allowed Baldwin to use his quarters. "Dr. Cook offered to let me work in his rooms at the Prince George Hotel," Baldwin told the *Times*, "and to make use of his two stenographers. . . . I in turn gave him completed portions of my manuscript to read while he was in the west."[14]

Early in December Cook, then in Cleveland, sent Baldwin a package that the Captain later said contained a four-page typed memorandum plus the first half — two hundred pages — of

Baldwin's manuscript. Attached to the memorandum was the message "Baldwin, This is to be an outline of the report to Congress. I prefer to send it over your signature: therefore, look it over and change it as you wish, but make it brief as possible. F. A. Cook."[15]

In addition to believing that Baldwin would not object to sending the material over his own signature, Cook anticipated that Baldwin would help him prepare the memorial itself, for — still in Cleveland — he sent Baldwin a second note: "I will get to New York Thursday evening and we must lock ourselves up and complete the report for [Senator] Poindexter. He is in a hurry for it."[16]

Some two weeks previously, however, Baldwin had contacted or been contacted by Herbert L. Bridgman. On December 6, when Baldwin dined with Cook's old trail-mate Ralph Shainwald,* he was in an anti-Cook mood. Shainwald reported that "he seemed very much wrought up and referred to the McKinley matter as if he had never known before that this had been questioned. . . . said he had heard a lot of things about Cook which he was at a loss to understand." Later that evening Shainwald and his wife accompanied Baldwin to Cook's suite at the Prince George where Baldwin, after criticizing one of Cook's photos in *My Attainment of the Pole*, said he was going to show them the original negative.

"We anxiously waited to view the negative," Shainwald wrote, "and Baldwin fumbled through a box of negatives and finally admitted that he forgot that he did not have this picture there. . . . I wondered how Baldwin would come to remove . . . Dr. Cook's property. . . . I asked him whether he had spoken to anybody else about the picture. He said, 'Yes, the enemy knows about it too.' After a time I suddenly said to Baldwin, 'When did you see Bridgman last?' 'About three weeks ago,' he replied. A little later Baldwin admitted that he had seen Bridgman several times. . . . I simply said to Baldwin, 'Be very careful about Bridgman.' His reply was,

* By this time Shainwald had become president of his family's firm, the Standard Paint Company.

'You don't need to worry about me, Bridgman is the biggest faker I know.' "[17]

By the time Cook returned to New York, Baldwin had vanished. On December 13, the Doctor dined with the Shainwalds and mentioned Baldwin's absence. "We had a full talk," Shainwald wrote. ". . . Cook was loath to believe anything wrong about Baldwin. We suggested, however, that on returning to his rooms he investigate to see whether any of his material was missing. At about midnight we were called to the phone and Dr. Cook, laboring under great emotion, informed us that not only was the film missing . . . but in addition a film taken of Peary's Eskimo son and one or two other films. But even more astonishing was the fact that a great many pages dealing with the northern journey had been clipped from Dr. Cook's note books."[18]

The next day Shainwald called on Cook and viewed "one note book in which it could be seen from the numbers on the pages that about 60 pages had been removed. Another book showed the loss of about 15 pages. . . . All this matter had been in Dr. Cook's trunks in his rooms, but the Doctor had not taken the precaution of locking them."[19]

Weeks previously, as Baldwin knew, Cook had signed a contract to appear on the English vaudeville stage beginning January 1, 1914. On the day before Cook sailed, Baldwin returned to the Prince George to pick up the second half of his manuscript, and in response to close questioning, maintained his original position: he would continue to assist Cook with his claim.

Of this meeting Baldwin said, the New York *Times* reported, "When I did meet Cook for the purpose of demanding back the rest of my manuscript he said to me: 'You have been to see Bridgman.' "[20] This Baldwin denied.

On December 28, while Cook was on the high seas, a story in the New York *Times* demonstrated that in spite of that paper's previous anxiety, the year 1913 was concluding splendidly. Yes, Captain Evelyn Briggs Baldwin had investigated Cook's report of his polar expedition. Yes, the Captain had anticipated that the book he was writing would help Cook's cause. But what was the final result of Captain Baldwin's research? The result was, Captain Baldwin now declared in the New York *Times:* "I absolutely convinced myself from documentary study that Cook never went near the top of Mount McKinley and never got within hundreds of miles of the North Pole."[21]*

What had happened, the *Times* explained, was that Baldwin, "after consulting a number of friends, including George B. Cortelyou, president of Consolidated Gas Co., who was in President Roosevelt's cabinet," had gone to Washington, presented himself to Senator Poindexter, and charged that Cook wanted to send his memorial to Congress over his signature, and that he, Captain Evelyn Briggs Baldwin, repudiated this. He had further charged that in 1911 Cook had written in over his shoulder the last three paragraphs of his three-thousand-word statement, "Positive Proof of Dr. Cook's Attainment of the Pole," and that ever since then he, Baldwin, had been trying to get Cook to acknowledge this.[22]†

* The furthest development of the party-line nonsense did not appear until 1927 when W. S. Barclay wrote in *Land of Magellan:* "During the *Belgica* expedition Cook stayed comfortably ashore in Harburton [Tierra del Fuego] while the rest of the ship's company went south, picking him up on the return" (New York, 1927, p. 208).

† On January 3, 1914, on the stationery of the New York Yacht Club, Baldwin wrote to Fred High, general manager of the Chautauqua Association, and applied for a job as lecturer: "For more than three and a half years I have practically sacrified my life for a man whom I believed to be a victim of unjust attack. . . . It is now our obvious duty to . . . reveal the whole wretched confidence game, and to set ourselves right before our countrymen and women and their children. . . . For three years you have given Cook the right of way. But has he not had his day? Verily, 'Falsehood makes a league while truth is getting on his boots.' "

High replied: "I see that you now claim that Cook interpolated the last three paragraphs. . . . I published this article as signed by you, and you came to my office and thanked me. . . . Why did you try to get me to further this work if you knew that this was a fake? . . . Explain why you timed your treachery, and bit the hand that fed you, when it would do him the maximum of harm . . . your Judas-like stunt of betraying your friend and benefactor" (Letters in the possession of Helene Cook Vetter).

And finally, Baldwin charged that despite the fact that Cook had written a six-hundred-page book on his expedition, he planned to use Baldwin's manuscript, which he had not seen a complete version of, as the basis of his appeal, and that he, Baldwin, repudiated the use of his manuscript for such purposes.

Despite the flimsiness of Baldwin's charges, and the fact that they were unsupported, his widely published statements destroyed our great victim's drive for a congressional investigation. The charges were effective because they were supported by the previous statements of Barrill, and of Dunkle and Loose. "Dr. Cook up to his old tricks," one newspaper headline advised. It was a matter of an associate of Cook advising the concerned, through a United States Senator, that he had learned through sad, personal experience that Cook was just as bad as his enemies said he was. The charges were effective, also, because they were made at a time when Cook was out of the country and could not reply.

"Captain Baldwin was asked," the New York *Times* reported, "how he had ever managed to stay so long in the ranks of the Cook defenders, and how he felt about the proposition as a whole. 'I am glad to strike my flag and surrender,' he said. 'I feel a lot better out of that proposition.' "[23]

The New York *Times* then interviewed Herbert L. Bridgman. "I was most interested in the *Times* story," he declared, ". . . for I was aware of the extensive postal card crusade being worked up in the Northwest, and of the fact that a considerable number of credulous people were accepting the appeals of Dr. Cook's circular and pamphlets and were attempting to obtain the active interest of Senator Poindexter. I think this movement will now collapse." Bridgman maintained that "he had not seen Captain Baldwin for years, although they were bunkmates in an Arctic expedition years ago." He identified himself as simply a spectator. "I had no knowledge of what it was that destroyed the confidence in Dr. Cook until I saw the *Times* on Sunday."[24]

Meanwhile, Baldwin's repudiation was being published

around the world. In London Cook had been booked for eight weeks at the Pavilion at $1,000 a week, and for nine weeks in the provinces. When he opened at the Pavilion very few people were in the audience, and they snickered when he spoke of his Arctic adventures. Between his first and second appearances his agent advised him to appeal to the British sense of fair play. Cook, however, rejected this advice. He preferred to speak in terms of Christianity. At the end of the day the tour was canceled.[25]

It may be that there is no more difficult position than that of an explorer, such as Baldwin, on the beach, growing older and possessing, possibly, not much interest in civilization itself, nor any method, perhaps, of obtaining funds except by ratting on other explorers. At any rate, Cook's friends reported, Captain Evelyn Briggs Baldwin soon paid up a thousand dollars in personal debts and came forth in a new wardrobe, acting the part of a well-to-do gentleman.[26]

Even Peary's friends, at least one of them, found Baldwin disgusting. In April, 1914, the secretary of the Explorers Club of New York told a reporter: "Baldwin! That scoundrel? Why, he's a downright crook! The scum of the earth."[27]

Perhaps so, but in an anxious year, he had been a fine friend of the New York *Times*.

1914 — the great dispute was now in its fifth year, yet it continued to be lively. Both Cook and Peary were in demand as lecturers, and in a parochial era were features of the American scene. Cook had been grotesquely wronged, and was in the business of letting people know about it. The controversy was his whole life. It was also a good living. Although he had ignored many opportunities to profit financially, he had nevertheless earned $200,000. He was one of the most celebrated men in the nation, and it does not seem possible that he did not at least partially enjoy his dramatic situation. America's leading underdog had grown into his role and was playing it with skill.

"I know popular feeling is strong against me," he told a

reporter in one city, "and everything that has been said detrimental to my character has been due to the machinations of one man. I am visiting cities and towns to lay my claims before the people and have them sign a petition which in time I hope will give me the show that I have never had: a detailed investigation, unbiased, of my records. In the last several years I have spent $200,000 acquired through my own efforts to substantiate my claims. I have no backing whatever."[28]

His opening phrase deserves a second glance — "I know popular feeling is strong against me." It is possible that he was not as unpopular as he claimed. He was detested by the governing class, who had established him as entirely disreputable and were not about to change that identity. But he was not unpopular, it would appear, among the governed, who could be impressed by his tenacity, and identify with him. Bad publicity was as much a part of his environment now as avalanches had been on Mount McKinley, and isolation on the way to the Pole. He accepted everything and continued on — a man in motion. And besides, every once in a while he had a little fun.

On April 2, 1914, he arrived in Pittsburgh. Peary was scheduled to lecture on April 3 at the Presbyterian Church in the Bellevue section of that city, and on the following day he himself was to lecture at the Methodist Episcopal Church in the same section of Pittsburgh. After checking into the Fort Pitt Hotel he called in the reporters. The next morning the Pittsburgh *Sun* reported: "Dr. Frederick A. Cook reiterated all his charges against . . . Peary between puffs of a cigarette . . . 'I am going down to Bellevue tonight,' said Cook, 'to hear what Peary has to say.' "

In Bellevue that night the Presbyterian Church was packed. The Doctor entered and was loudly applauded. He chose a seat one pew from the front and to the right of the pulpit. Earlier in the day he had announced: "I shall not say anything back tonight. Tomorrow night will be my night." The intensely dramatic, accordingly, did not occur; but the situation remained interesting. "Peary's lecture was well delivered," the Pittsburgh *Press* reported, "and was illustrated by many interesting pictures. He emphatically said that the expedition headed by himself was the only one that ever reached the north pole."

What happened at the conclusion of the lecture was also reported by the *Press:* "Admiral Peary slipped out of the church by a rear exit; Dr. Cook went out the front way and was followed by a crowd of admirers."

The next night, at the Methodist Episcopal Church, the Doctor received what the *Press* called "a highly flattering reception." During his lecture he referred to the National Geographic Society as a "scrub association." He described its three-man subcommittee as "three scrub politicians in Washington, not one of whom had ever seen a piece of Arctic ice." He declared that Peary had been passing the hat for twenty-five years and had promoted a fur company from which he and his friends had made $1 million. He announced that the pastor had received a thirty-six page pamphlet that was signed "Veritas" and dated from New York. He was referring to one of the mailing pieces that the club sent out by the thousands. Printing costs absorbed much of the club's $350,000 war chest.

Out in the Northwest, meanwhile, Cook's admirers were not impressed by Baldwin's unsupported declarations, and continued to appeal to Senator Poindexter. On April 30, 1914, in the Senate, Poindexter introduced a resolution calling for the recognition of Cook as the discoverer of the North Pole. It was referred to the Committee on the Library, and was thereafter forgotten.

Frederick A. Cook was a man eager to accomplish uncommon things. At the same time he was apolitical. Because he was so adventurous, ordered society's guardians regularly encountered him, and being politically hypersensitive themselves, constantly misjudged him. In 1915 he dropped the controversy and soon became involved in a situation that, although small when compared to his previous adventures, was fantastic by ordinary standards. It was the one episode in his life that, since he emerged unharmed, can be regarded as comic.

It began when his friend Frank P. Thompson, a Chicago

physician, proposed an expedition to climb Mount Everest. Cook agreed immediately and around the twenty-second of May they departed from Chicago. At the time the war in Europe was accelerating and foreign agents were operating throughout the United States. The passengers on the train to San Francisco included a group of Indian revolutionaries. Cook, who was interested in languages, spent some time with them. This was noted by agents of the British Secret Service.

On May 27 Doctors Cook and Thompson sailed from San Francisco aboard the *Mongolia*, on which the Indian revolutionaries also sailed in steerage. During the voyage Cook again sought them out, as was noted by the British Secret Service. In Honolulu Doctors Cook and Thompson spent one night with the German Consul, who was an old acquaintance of Cook's. This, again, was noted by the British Secret Service.

When they arrived in Penang, Malaya, which was British territory, they were arrested, then released and permitted to sail to Rangoon. There they purchased postcards to send to friends. Some of these cards contained scenes taken in the vicinity of the fortifications in Rangoon, and were stamped "Made in Germany." These purchases were observed by the British Secret Service, and once again Doctors Cook and Thompson were arrested. After their release they continued on to Calcutta where they were placed under guard at the Great Eastern Hotel. They then learned that they would not be permitted to go to the Himalayas. Meanwhile, neither Cook or Thompson had been able to discover why the British were interested in them. A few days later they asked permission to go to Sudharam to hunt tigers. It was refused. It was then discovered that on the day when Cook and Thompson had made this request, Indian revolutionaries had attempted to land forty thousand Mauser rifles near Sudharam. This, also, was noted by the British Secret Service. Later, Cook acknowledged that he knew of this event, having read about it in the newspapers.

Eventually Cook and Thompson learned that they were suspected of being involved in a German scheme to stir up a revolution in India. When they were finally permitted to leave

India, they went to Borneo, and then spent two months sailing the southern seas in a twenty-eight-foot boat. They then traveled to Manila, and afterwards to Yokohama. In neither port, because of the war, could they pick up a boat to San Francisco. They finally returned to America via Siberia, Russia, and Copenhagen.* By offering their services as surgeons, they were able to sail on the liner *Kristianiafjord*, and arrived in New York on January 23, 1916.

But the comedy was not over. As it turned out, the British Secret Service had a reason for being concerned about Cook. But it also turned out that, as in each of his other encounters with the guardians of ordered society, the British Secret Service was one hundred percent wrong in its interpretation of him. Cook was not interested in helping the Germans: the Germans were interested in murdering him. On October 18, 1917, at a conspiracy trial in Chicago, the German agent George Paul Boehm acknowledged that he had planned to murder Cook. He would then, Boehm testified, assume Cook's identity and travel about India stirring up trouble among the natives.

Not even the club had thought of that one.

In 1916 Cook was criticized for accepting Dr. Thompson's invitation to attempt Mount Everest. Over the years Congressman Henry T. Helgesen had been very critical of Peary, and by September, 1916, he had decided that Cook was equally suspicious. "In 1915, when matters looked as though a hearing might be granted him," Cook had gone to the Orient, Helgesen complained in a lengthy series of remarks in the *Congressional Record*. "The present year, on the more or less plausible excuse of a Chautauqua lecture tour, he went West, at a time when, with a little extra effort on his part, his friends hoped to secure for him a hearing which he has so long professed to desire."

The fact is, Cook understood that Peary's friends could not

* Of Cook's reappearance in Copenhagen Maurice Egan wrote: "It astonished us all when he returned. . . . His lecture occasioned a very unpleasant fracas, although his friends were in the majority in the lecture hall" (*Recollections of a Happy Life*, New York, 1924, p. 272).

possibly afford to allow him a congressional investigation. Peary's position was too weak, and they knew it. They could not permit the case to be reopened, and they had the means to stop it. Although there were occasions when the Doctor was carried away by his minor successes, in the back of his mind he understood that time, and only time, could alter his reputation.

But in 1915 and 1916 time still favored Peary. Cook had every right to defend his identity, and the logic of his situation required that he call for a congressional investigation; but he had already gone virtually the full distance on that route, and had been betrayed by Baldwin. Now he had other friends and associates. Could he ignore the possibility that, for a large or urgently needed sum of money, and on a dramatic occasion, one of them would be treacherous? The operative phrase is "three-time loser." He was that doubled. Each of his defeats had been extremely public, and on a large scale. It seems possible that he had had about all he could take.

So it is not surprising that he chose Mount Everest and another round on the Chautauqua circuit over the Congress of the United States. He had been telling his story for five wearying years, and his situation had not really improved. The important people continued to disregard him. After five years he still did not know anyone except Henry Ford, whose advice and good wishes had not seemed much different from anyone else's. Nor was there any indication that the National Geographic Society and the New York *Times* had become less powerful.

Lecturing was an honorable living, but not much else. As yet, no alternative career had been discovered, and particularly nothing that included the tremendous, the colossal, the stupendous.

12

A sliding scale up and down in the wild gamble for oil is part of my experience.

Frederick A. Cook

HIS ROUND-THE-WORLD-FRIEND Dr. Thompson owned some oil leases in Wyoming, was curious about their value, and asked him to investigate. "I had in my explorations," Cook wrote, "acquired a good working knowledge of geology, and I knew something about oil formations. So I accepted the mission."

In 1916 a man did not have to know much in order to be knowledgeable about oil. Because many of the early discoveries had been made along creeks, oil men were students of creekology. They also employed oil smellers, fortune tellers, wigglestick operators, and persons with X-ray eyes. Anyone who for any reason might have a nose for oil was in demand, and in the fields about Casper, Wyoming, this included Cook, who was soon put in charge of field work for the New York Oil Company.

Twenty-seven years or so earlier, as a young doctor, he had entered ordered society in a normal manner. Then exploration had pulled him away from the ordinary, and since 1909 he had been an exotic freak whose situation differed from that of anyone else in the world. Now, late in 1916, he dropped his lonely, exhausting identity and, fifty-two years old, reentered ordered society as a hunter in the world's most exciting industry.

"I became actively and continuously engaged in a search for new fields," he testified in 1923, "in the unexplored and undeveloped fields of Mid-Wyoming. There are three fields there that are more or less to my credit, and the names I gave those fields are the names by which those fields are known today. The first is the Hamilton Dome in the Big Horn Basin. The second is the Red Rose Dome, which is not yet fully proven for either oil or gas. The third is Hidden Dome, also in the Big Horn Basin, which has developed into one of the most important gas fields in Wyoming, and is still a prospective field for oil."[1]

In order to develop the sites that Cook soon filed claim to, Frank G. Curtis, president of New York Oil, organized the Cook Oil Company. He made the Doctor president and gave him a block of stock. Oil was brought in and the Doctor prospered. For the rest of his life he would be proud of Cook Oil. "[It] is today a highly successful company," he wrote in 1936, "and it bears my name."[2]

It was a prosperous company, but it was not a tremendous company. The tremendous, so far as oil was concerned, was not part of the scene in Wyoming. It was concentrated in Texas where the Ranger and Burkburnett oil booms were running full blast and the miraculous occurred daily. And so, in December, 1918, Cook Oil's president sold his stock for $40,000, then resigned and departed for the tremendous.

"I first traveled over the state a good deal," he said later, "examining various fields and prospective fields, making myself familiar with the oil and oil possibilities of the state. In the meantime I had acquired a number of leases and then I came to Fort Worth."[3]

Optimism has always been the lubricant in oil, and in Ranger and Burkburnett the cheerfulness was extraordinary. A good gusher was worth $1 million a month. Small farms were selling for $250,000. The owners of a 150-acre site had refused $7 million. The merchants were tearing down their stores to make room for more derricks. In Fort Worth, the city nearest the boom towns, thousands of men boarded the trains every morning and rode out to Ranger or Burkburnett. In the evening they poured back into the city. There shopgirls and secretaries who had formerly spent their lunch periods chattering about their boyfriends now talked mostly about their purchases of oil stock.

The Mid-Continent Oil Boom, as it was called in the eastern magazines, was a regional extravaganza that had attracted national interest, and although many Texans had gambled in oil and lost, matters were such that the boom benefited ordered society in Texas to the disadvantage of ordered society elsewhere. By the time Cook arrived in Fort Worth that city was headquarters for some 2,000 independent oil companies, each of which based their operations on two facts that had become evident over the years: that the public purchased oil stock because it was hungry to get rich; and that most of those people who invested in oil and failed to profit would continue to invest. Veteran promoters who had once sold stock by personal canvass were now working from "sucker lists" and directing nationwide mail-order campaigns in which the literature might read:

> DO YOU WANT TO GET VERY RICH? I BELIEVE THIS WILL MAKE YOU AN INDEPENDENT FORTUNE SOON. I am only asking $43,700. This is a very small amount. It will be barely sufficient for me to pay my acreage and drill my well, but I expect to make a fortune out of my share. To those who actually want to get rich, I say that if you will send me from $1.00 to $1,000 it is my uttermost conviction . . .

The target for such prose, meanwhile, was almost entirely ignorant of the situation in Texas, although if he had been more of a student of ordered society in his own area he would have caught on. He did not know that the company that had approached him might own only a one-eighth royalty in a drilling site, and that this one-eighth might have been split into 500,000 shares, so that even if oil came in, years would pass before he received a dividend of $5.00. He did not know that, possibly, he was being invited to purchase shares in a drilling site that, although large enough to support a derrick, lacked space for a commercial reservoir. He did not know that the man who was writing him might not own a single share in the company he was promoting. Nor did he know that some promoters were capable of forgetting to drill the well. In Texas 1,050 oil companies were organized in 1918 and 1919, but only seven paid dividends.

And so, entering Texas, Cook was once again smack in the middle of a situation where the possibilities for fraud were as large as the possibilities for genuine accomplishment.

In this hectic and greedy environment the independent oil man who was exploring for oil, but lacked a personal fortune, could only accept the conditions that existed within the industry. He financed himself by using other people's money, and played his hand in one of two ways. He could become a wildcatter, and using second-hand tools, a third-hand boiler, and promises to pay if and when, drill on a "poor boy" site. The alternative was to become an oil promoter, sell stock to the public, and after obtaining enough capital, drill in several choice locations almost simultaneously.

If he became a promoter, the business methods that independent oil men had developed since 1901, when oil was first discovered in Texas, were immediately available to him. These methods, including the built-in opportunities for trickery, were accepted by the industry and the community, both of which recognized that the search for oil was a form of sport, speculation at its wildest, certainly; and that it was also very expensive. To drill a well in 1919 cost between $35,000 and $40,000. Dry holes were the rule, oil the exception.

Sometime about the middle of 1919, Cook combined with two men whom he had known in Wyoming to organize the Texas Eagle & Refining Company. They paid $50,000 for a site at Burkburnett, and although oil was brought in, the quantity was slight. Then the economy slumped, oil became difficult to sell at any price, and only the big companies survived. Texas Eagle went into receivership and its assets were acquired by Revere Oil, a merging outfit that bought the assets of dying companies and gave the stockholders a choice of being frozen out or putting up more money to be merged.

Cook returned to being a geologist, and was employed by Tex Rickard, a boxing promoter, and by Marriner Eccles, who eventually became chairman of the Federal Reserve Board. The sites he selected for these men and others produced gushers, but the well that he drilled for himself on adjacent property came up a duster.

Around March 1, 1922, he organized the Petroleum Producers Association with himself as president and sole trustee. Like Revere, PPA was a merging outfit made up of companies whose financial position was weak but whose leases or land or machinery were assets against which stock could be sold to finance drilling. He planned, as he said later, "to amass a large operating fund, acquiring the choicest leases in several fields and carry out an extensive drilling campaign. *The oil was there.* I saw no reason why we could not strike it by a really thorough drilling campaign."[4]

He had now been in Texas for over three years, and he thought as he did because, as he would testify in 1923:

"The experience which I had with the Texas Eagle convinced me that if we could have raised $50,000 we could have saved that company with its properties. The fact that the Texas Eagle was combining with the Revere Oil Company, approved by the receiver and the order of the court, convinced me that that was a reasonable method under which many other companies of that type could be handled. There were many properties here in Texas being neglected, which were valuable if under a new head, under a combination, those properties could be renovated, could be developed, and I felt that the stockholders in the combined organization could be put into the position to make some money upon what otherwise could have been almost a lost hope."[5]

But rational explanations are sometimes incomplete explanations, particularly when they are put forward by obsessed men. He could have added that not every player in the oil game in Texas was a hard-headed businessman, and that not every promoter was an "oil trickster." He could have acknowledged that oil had its share of driven men, of romantics who were after more than just gobs of money, and that one of them was himself. He could have said as he would say when, so far as he was concerned, the mad gamble for oil was over: "I only had one dream, call me visionary if you will, but within me was an abiding desire to find an oil field that would remain a monument to my name and memory, and all the money I received was spent to that end."[6]

So that was what he was doing in Texas, where, once again, he was making the same tremendous effort that he had previously made elsewhere. The assault of Mount McKinley had been a charge. The assault of the North Pole had been a charge. Now he was charging oil.

He was fifty-seven years old, his hair was gray, combed back, and worn long on the neck. His face was furrowed and his body was older, softer, and smaller. A reporter described him as "a little gray man." But there was nothing gray about his enthusiasm. Even today the velocity of his charge remains astonishing.

As in his previous adventures, he did not attempt to change the environment. He adapted himself to it and became one of the largest, and perhaps the largest, oil promoter in Fort Worth. He merged 413 companies into the Petroleum Producers Association. He employed eighty-five secretaries. His offices occupied an entire floor of a bank building.

He hired four professional writers of promotional letters. One of them, S. E. J. Cox, had already served a jail sentence for oil fraud. Cook was not concerned about this. He was only interested in Cox's proven ability — Cox had previously sold $1,500,000 worth of stock for one company — as a writer of letters. "Mr. Cox was at no time directly concerned with our organization," Cook would testify, "except as rendering service in writing letters."[7]

When a sensational oil trade paper criticized PPA and several others, Cook contributed $1,000 to its purchase.

Anticipating that a well PPA was drilling would come in, and after a lease broker had informed him that he could get

Cook $40,000 for a property in Portola,[8] he declared a two-percent dividend.

Most of his time he spent in the field. Between March, 1922, and January, 1923, his letter writers sold $403,818 worth of stock.[9] Much of this money he used to buy leases and finance drilling operations. According to his field superintendent, T. O. Turner, the Petroleum Producers Association drilled nine wells in approximately one year; owned 170 acres in fee, 9,400 acres leased, and 120 royalty tracts, of which 32 produced oil; and had an interest in 174 wells.[10] In the field the Doctor traveled in an old twin-six Packard that could maneuver over sand and rough terrain. He was sometimes driven by his daughter Helene, who remembers the car as no beauty — "more like a truck that had gone 200,000 miles." In the car, or by rail, he moved about Texas and into Oklahoma, Arkansas, and New Mexico, at all times hunting for oil.

Some things, however, he did not do. The man who had signed a "no editorial guarantee whatever" contract with *Hampton's;* the man who had not locked his trunks when he loaned his hotel suite to Evelyn Briggs Baldwin; the man who had ignored huge offers of money in Copenhagen, did not keep his eye on what was going on in his office. Particularly, he did not attend to what was being said in the promotion letters, all of which were sent out over his name.

And he did not strike oil. Even today the search for petroleum is characterized by uncertainty, and in 1922 the drilling of an oil well was gambling at its wildest.

Meanwhile, the year remained 1922 and at the pinnacle of ordered society in the United States was President Warren G. Harding. On an adjacent peak, and in charge of law and order, was Attorney General Harry Daugherty, leader of what historians have identified as the notorious "Ohio gang." With persons of such caliber in possession, vigilance — vigilant men and vigilance across the land — was mandatory.

Herbert S. Houston was chairman of the National Vigilance Committee. He had previously been president of the Advertising Federation of America, and of the Associated Advertising Clubs of the World, which had conceived the National Vigilance Committee, itself a forerunner of the Better Business Bureau. Years earlier, at the University of South Dakota, Houston had been a member of Psi Upsilon. Now he was a cheerfully established New York clubman with a dapper white mustache. In New York one of Herbert S. Houston's mentors was Herbert L. Bridgman. (The relationship between Houston and Bridgman was such that when Bridgman died in 1924 Houston had an important role in the Psi Upsilon memorial service.[11])

In August, 1922, a representative of ordered society in New York arrived in Fort Worth to study ordered society there. He was Edward A. Schwab, special investigator for the National Vigilance Committee. Months later he told the Brooklyn *Eagle:* "I found it hard to get anything started. Everyone knew that fraudulent oil promotions were thriving . . . but the city . . . winked at what was going on. It meant money for the merchants . . . it was good business. . . . The banks and politicians were not zealous to put a stop to the common practice. . . . I called on Dr. Cook one day . . . and he was very cordial. 'I heard you were around,' he said, and then went on to assure me that everything was honest and above board in his business. . . . His apparent honesty was absolutely convincing. He was a likeable personality, was always affable, and seemed open and above board."[12]

In December, after persuading the Fort Worth *Press* to lead a campaign against the oil promoters, Schwab returned to New York. There, on January 10, 1923, during a meeting of the Associated Advertising Clubs of the World, Herbert S. Houston revealed the situation in Fort Worth. He was excited about the promoters as a group, but most of all he was excited about "our old friend Dr. Cook. He did not discover the North Pole, but we certainly have discovered him."[13]

By this time the public had learned that Secretary of the Interior Albert Fall had quietly leased the Navy's oil reserves at Teapot Dome to the Sinclair Oil Company. Although the fact that Fall had taken a $100,000 bribe for doing so had not yet been revealed, the Harding Administration was aware of a need to appear vigilant about oil. In March, 1923, Attorney General Daugherty signed a series of special indictments; and on April 2 ninety-seven Fort Worth oil promoters, representing some fifteen companies, were charged with using the mails to defraud. Among them were Cook and thirteen of his associates in PPA.

Soon afterward, representatives of the Advertising Clubs of Texas gathered at Fort Worth for a special meeting. "There has come to this conference," they resolved, "information which reveals that the sale of fraudulent stocks in Texas is of the most vicious character. . . . We . . . call on all Texas banks and bankers, all civic clubs, to inform the public regarding the flagrant character of the operations."[14]

Meanwhile, the District Attorney in Fort Worth had made a proposal to Cook: if the Doctor would plead guilty, he would only have to serve two years in prison. Through his lawyer, former U.S. Senator Joe Bailey, Cook replied that he had done nothing wrong, and rejected the idea. Of the ninety-seven men indicted, he was the only one to plead not guilty.

The trial of Frederick A. Cook took place in Fort Worth and began on October 16, 1923. He was charged with defrauding the public by exaggerating the prospects of the company to promote the sale of stock; with having used the U.S. Mails to do so; and with having done all of this deliberately. "Intent. That is the key note," the Fort Worth *Record* observed, "of the government's reliance for a conviction. Almost every witness has been placed on the stand to establish intent."

The case was given to the jury on November 20, 1923. After deliberating for twenty hours the jury returned a verdict of guilty.

It is contended here that Cook was not guilty. It is contended that he was an honest man who had exposed himself to the hazards of an extremely speculative industry during a period of great optimism. "The general plan for future activities, and the execution of the details thereof," he would say of PPA, "was in accord with the business methods and precepts of oil operation in newly discovered fields. At such times the boom spirit of growing oil towns enters into every phase of business enterprise. We were naturally imbued with this fire, but . . . sole purpose was to build . . . association into a strong profit-sharing organization acquiring and successfully developing oil properties."[15]

It is further contended that if the Harding Administration had warned him that the business methods traditionally employed by independent oil operators in Texas were now suspect, he would have obeyed the warning. But the Harding Administration could not afford to warn him or anyone else. "The attention of the inspectors," Cook wrote in Hearst's *American Weekly*, "was frequently called to the fact that ours was a new business venture developing along well-established precepts and principles in oil fields — that we were willing and ready to change our methods in line with any suggestions that they cared to make, but if the government chose to interfere with and regulate long-established business methods . . . the greatest good to the greatest number would suggest a helpful and not a destructive policy. I am certain that a few words from official sources at this time would have eliminated any need of prosecution and would have saved many thousands of dollars to the Government and the stockholders."

It is contended, also, that if the Harding Administration had not interfered with the operations of PPA, its stockholders would have profited, because Cook did have a nose for oil. On October 29, 1928, the New York *World* would carry a dispatch from Texas stating: "Dr. Cook's oil judgment in the lands to the west of Erath County, notably Winkler County, seems to have been thoroughly vindicated. Winkler is now one of the centers of oil production. Dr. Cook's interests had a block of 36,000 acres there." On November 4, 1928, the *World* would add: "That oil was flowing exactly where Dr. Cook believed it to be, is some vindication for him. . . . Recently drilled oil wells in Erath County, Texas, on former holdings of

Dr. Cook, are now flowing 100,000,000 cubic feet of gas daily, which is a good indication of oil. Howard County, where Dr. Cook operated, is now a rich oil-producing section." And on February 21, 1936, the San Angelo (Texas) *Times* would point out: "Down the Pecos River . . . is the Yates field, one of the world's greatest oil producers. It was in such territory that Dr. Cook sought to place the flag of oil production."

And finally it is contended, and above all else, that Cook was not a swindler. It is contended that he was, to a tremendous degree, a man of action; and it is acknowledged that as such he was an aggressor. Like the members of the Peary Arctic Club, he too was descended from the hunting hominoid; but unlike the club and its kind, Frederick A. Cook did not prey on people. He was an invader of the earth, a seeker of its prizes, an assaulter of the invisible.

Before presenting the evidence, produced at the trial, that supports the above contentions, it seems proper to call attention to a newspaper report on the original indictment of the ninety-seven Fort Worth promoters. "No doubt some of these companies," the New York *Times* said on April 7, 1923, "were started by men who hoped to strike oil and make money from the production, but in practically every case the promoters had laid their plans to profit from stock selling, regardless of the results of field operations. Seldom was it that a promoter invested his own money."

A complete presentation of Cook's financial situation is not possible today, but it is a fact, established during the trial, that Cook had not only invested his own money in PPA, he was the largest investor. Indeed, he had put almost everything he owned into his own company. Schwab, the Vigilance investigator, acknowledged that the Doctor and his family were living very modestly. "I do know that Dr. Cook was not a great spender," he told the *Eagle*. "He did not live on an extravagant scale; he made no splurge."

The proofs that Cook's intent was honest are not extensive, but they are very solid. They are:

During the trial it was established that in addition to putting his own money into his own company, Cook had given it a potentially valuable 121 acres. That he had done so came out when he was being interrogated by his lawyer:

Q. "Dr. Cook, what was the first piece of property acquired by the Petroleum Producers Association?"
A. "The first piece of property that was acquired, and it is so stated in the declaration of trust, was a block of 121 acres in La Salle County, Texas."
Q. "From whom did your company acquire that?"
A. "From myself."
Q. "They did not pay for it?"
A. "They did not pay me anything for it."
Q. "Did you receive anything from the company for it?"
A. "I received nothing and asked nothing."
Q. "You mean to tell the jury that you conveyed that without price?"
A. "I did."
Q. "What was the character of the title you had to that, lease or fee?"
A. "The land in fee."
Q. "Was there a mortgage on it of any kind?"
A. "None whatever; the title was clear."[16]

It was also established, during the trial, that Cook took no money out of the company for himself. From March, 1922, to January, 1923, PPA's total income was $413,641.00. As sole trustee of PPA Cook was legally entitled to one-eighth of all money received, or approximately $51,700. During the trial, when questioned by the prosecution, he was asked:

Q. "I believe you said you never drew any of that money that came in, one-eighth of which you were entitled to under this declaration of trust, didn't you?"
A. "Yes, sir."
Q. "But that you intended to exercise the privilege which this declaration of trust gave you?"

A. "I am not entitled to it until the company is on a good paying basis, and the stockholders have gotten a good return."
Q. "Well, the declaration of trust provides that you were entitled to one-eighth of the money coming in from any source, doesn't it?"
A. "It does."
Q. "But you did not take that?"
A. "I did not take it."
Q. ". . . You say you were not to get that until the company was on a good paying basis, is that right?"
A. "I did not say that I was not to get it; I said in my own judgment I did not think I ought to take it until the time the company was in good shape; in a well organized shape, and paying; I was entitled to take it any day that I wanted to, and the money was there."[17]

It was further established, during the trial, that Cook's statements were correct. The Federal Bank Examiner acknowledged, in sum:

That Cook was the largest investor by actual cash in the company and that he held no promotional stock.

That Cook had drawn no salary or commissions or profit of any kind.

That the books of the company balanced with no indication of embezzlement or missing funds.

In addition, the testimony of T. O. Turner, that PPA had drilled nine wells in less than a year, indicates that Cook was seriously engaged in exploring for oil.

And finally, the trial established that at the time of his indictment in April, 1923, Cook was drilling a well at Corsicana. In 1922 this field produced only 245,705 barrels of oil. In 1923 the same field, as a result of deeper drilling, produced 32,361,150 barrels.[18] T. O. Turner testified that PPA's Corsicana property was still good, "and that it was possible to drill 50 wells on the 216 acres the company had there."[19] It would appear, therefore, that PPA was very close to bringing in the gusher that would have enabled Cook to fulfill the statements made in the company's promotional letters. As former Senator Bailey said: "If a man sinks a well and finds oil, he is honored, banqueted, and rides around in a limousine. If he finds a dry hole he goes to jail. If Cook's company had found oil this suit would not be heard of."

He took the stand on November 9. "The Doctor sat in an easy, placid manner in the witness chair," the *Record* stated. On the third day of his testimony he got into trouble because of the content of some of the promotional letters that, although he did not sign them — did not even see many of them, being away in the field — were sent out over his name. He seemed particularly unaware of the contents of certain letters sent out by his chief writer, H. O. Stephens. These letters did not go as far as those sent out by other promotion outfits that "guaranteed" that their wells would come in. Nevertheless, the letters were so optimistic, and made such claims, that Cook's position became very uncomfortable.

"For hours the little gray man," the *Record* said, "sat in the witness chair and as the hours passed his face became more gray, the furrows between his eyes, already deep, grew deeper, and the lines around his mouth began to sag." On the stand he repudiated most of the later letters sent out by Stephens, who he declared must have been touched in the head.

Nevertheless, the judge ruled that Cook was responsible for all literature sent out from his office. The judge also ruled that Cook was responsible for all the acts of his subordinates.[20]

Ordered society's interests at the trial were guarded by Judge John M. Killits, who had been imported from Toledo, Ohio, where he sat on the Federal Bench of the Northern District of Ohio. Killits had acquired national prominence three years earlier while arbitrating a strike at Willys-Overland. Later, Killits had been considered, or at least mentioned, for appointment to the United States Supreme Court.

In 1918, according to his obituary in the New York *Times*, "proceedings were begun against Judge Killits in the United

States Supreme Court charging him with contempt for alleged failure to obey a court order forbidding suspension of sentences in criminal cases. The proceedings were withdrawn by Solicitor General Davis on April 5, who said that Judge Killits had complied with the order." The same paper also reported that Killits "was Prosecuting Attorney of Williams County, Ohio, from 1893 to 1898. During his term he was accused of juggling fees and was removed from office, to be later exonerated and reinstated, receiving his back salary."[21]

Killits was appointed to the federal bench in 1910. He retired in 1928 and died in 1938. During these years he received a total salary and pension of approximately $240,000.[22] At some time during his career the Ohio Savings Bank & Trust Company loaned Killits approximately $100,000.[23] That bank failed in 1931, and when Killits died he still owed it approximately $44,000 and had owed it such for at least seven years.[24] He left an estate of $3,097.[25] The estate of his wife, who died in 1952, was valued at approximately $82,000.[26] There is no indication that she had been independently wealthy.

By the time the case was given to the jury, Cook was resigned to a verdict of guilty. "I slept . . . fitfully," he wrote. ". . . Half waking, I reviewed my career in vivid dreams. I saw the flag and the snow hut at the Pole, the . . . mirages . . . the tall cliffs at Cape Sparbo . . . the walrus sprawled on the drifting pans."[27]

The next day, after the foreman of the jury had announced the verdict, and just before the sentence was pronounced, Killits turned to Cook. Throughout the trial it had been Killits's understanding, it seems, that anyone who was anybody operated about the way he himself appears to have operated. He therefore said to Cook:

"Now, Cook, you may stand up. What have you got to say as to why the Court should not pass judgment on you?

"This is one of the times when your peculiar and persuasive hypnotic personality fails you, isn't it? You have at last got to the point where you can't bunco anybody. You have come to the mountain and you can't reach the latitude: it's beyond you.

"First we had Ananias, then we had Machiavelli; the Twentieth Century produced Frederick A. Cook. Poor old Ananias, he is forgotten, and Machiavelli — we have Frederick A. Cook.

"Cook, this deal of yours, and this conception of yours, and this execution of yours, was so damnably crooked that I know the men who defended you, defended you with their handkerchiefs to their noses, rank, smelling to Heaven.

"I wish I could do with you as I might, the way I feel about you; I wish I were not circumscribed by some conventions, that I think are mistakes, yet until public sentiment is educated to a better respect for the law, we have got to respect them to some degree. I don't think you ought to run at large at all; you are too dangerous.

"Undoubtedly you have got those ill-gotten gains of yours laid away. Why, one of your counsel came to me this morning wanting to know what the . . . bond would be. . . . He said you could not give it, could not put it up. 'Why?' I asked him, as every sensible man would say to him, who wasn't under the hypnotic spell of your peculiar personality . . . like any man whose brains work, function normally. . . . The money you have taken in — right now you are holding money that belongs to poor people all over the United States. . . . I don't see how any living man who has any appreciation of the standards of decency or honesty, can suggest that you ought to hold a penny of it . . . because every penny of it was robbed from orphans and widows and credulous old people; people in the depth of poverty; people anxious to get money enough so as to insure a decent burial. . . .

"Oh, God, Cook, haven't you any sense of decency at all, or is your vanity so impervious that you don't respond to what must be calls of decency to you? Aren't you haunted at night? Can you sleep?

"What's the use of talking to you, your effrontery, vanity and nerve are so monumental, so cold-steel, so impervious, so adamantine to what I have got to say that I know I am voicing the feeling of the decent people of Texas without question; those of them that have brains enough not to fall for what some of these foolish people call your personality. I don't know where it is. They call it 'personality,' whether it is a poker face or a false face. . . . It is strange that the prosecuting officers have suggested to me that I be not quite so stiff with you. . . . It is my own disposition and my abhorrence for such a crook as you."[28]

He then sentenced Cook to fourteen years and nine months in prison. In addition, he fined Cook $12,000 and placed Cook's bond at $75,000.

It seems impossible that the fact that Cook had not been able to prove his North Pole and Mount McKinley assertions was not a factor in his indictment, trial, and sentence. Charles Stewart of the Central Press wrote: "While these weren't in themselves punishable offenses, the judge appeared to think they ought to have been."[29] Milton Miles Lory, a newspaperman, eventually informed Ralph Shainwald: "I was a witness for the government (although my sympathies were with him) at Dr. Cook's trial and know intimately how false the charges were against him. . . . It was quite apparent that the whole proceedings were directed at his discovery of the North Pole."[30]

But others thought differently. The Beaumont *Enterprise* observed that while it had taken the government "a quarter of a century to capture the oil stock swindlers . . . by succeeding so admirably in this conspicuous case, the effect will be increased a thousandfold." And *Oil Weekly* saw Cook's conviction as "a victory for truth in advertising."

Speaking from behind the bars of the Tarrant County Jail, Cook said: "I will appeal my case if I can raise the necessary funds, but it seems that an almost impossible burden has been placed on me. I have no money in spite of the charges by the judge and the United States Attorney that I have many dollars planted away. . . . To perfect the record will cost many thousands of dollars."[31]

Throughout the trial Marie Cook had been in attendance in

the courtroom. Because she and the Doctor had been divorced in February, her presence was a newspaper sensation. "There was the impression of great bitterness," the *Record* observed. "Yet . . . they were side by side . . . on the friendliest of terms." Now, in order to raise the money to perfect the court record, which ran some twelve thousand pages, Marie canvassed Fort Worth oil men, moving from office to office until she had raised the amount required. It was the same sum that Josephine Peary had collected years earlier to send a ship north for the Commander: $10,000.

In his cell, to move his mind away from grief, the Doctor took up embroidery. Each time his wife and daughter visited him they received very specific instructions as to what colors of thread they were to bring the next day.

Meanwhile, PPA had gone into receivership and its assets had been sold to the major oil companies for very nominal sums. "Not a penny was saved for the stockholders from the receivership wreck," Cook wrote. On June 7, 1924, Killits, writing to President Coolidge, recommended executive clemency for all PPA employees except Cook. It was granted immediately. On July 8 Cook petitioned as a pauper to be relieved of the costs of his appeal. Permission was granted but his bail remained high. His appeal was denied and he was taken from the Tarrant County Jail to Leavenworth Penitentiary in Kansas. "The rail journey . . . was faintly reminiscent of my lecture tours," he wrote. ". . . Fellow passengers pointed me out to each other with excited interest." On April 6, 1925 — it was the sixteenth anniversary of Peary's arrival at his North Pole — Frederick A. Cook entered Leavenworth and became Prisoner 23-118.

The 498 days that he had spent in jail in Fort Worth while his appeal was being processed were not considered part of his sentence.

So they had been right all along; just about as right as is humanly possible to be: the Peary Arctic Club, Edward N. Barrill, George Dunkle, the New York *Times*, August Loose, the National Geographic Society, Evelyn Briggs Baldwin. The party line had prevailed. "Just as he pretended to have reached the Pole when he never . . ." And since there had been so much talk about proof, well there was the proof — Prisoner 23-118. There, right there was proof of what sort of man Cook was. He was worse than Ananias, whoever *he* was. He was more dangerous than Machiavelli.

Ulysses was once identified as the most unfortunate man that ever lived. Of himself he said: "Think of the wretches who in your experience have borne the heaviest load of sorrow, and I will match my griefs with theirs." This statement, the creation of a great dramatic imagination, could be challenged by Cook, who was flesh and blood.

His first months in Leavenworth were horrible. "It was then that his health was in jeopardy," his daughter Helene has stated; ". . . the handwriting shows this, and then as he adjusted and put his energy to helping others he got his second breath." He was made night superintendent of the hospital. He organized a school for the prisoners. He became editor of the prison newspaper, *The New Era*, for which he wrote a series of inspirational messages that usually appeared on the cover. One read: "Did you ever see a boy in tears when he brought to his daddy his pet dog with a broken leg? Did you ever see a girl in tears when she brought to her mother a dying bird? That boy and that girl never need punishment by the rod. Their schooling is on a higher plane where sympathy, love and sublime duty rules. Those who fail to understand this lesson are entitled to all the pain and grief that comes their way."

Although he had requested no visitors, not even his daughters, one caller appeared whom he could not refuse.

"I had received and accepted an invitation to make an address," Roald Amundsen wrote in *My Life As an Explorer*, ". . . before the National Geographic Society. . . . My itinerary eastward from the Pacific coast took me . . . within a short distance of Leavenworth. Recalling . . . the two hazardous years of the *Belgica* . . . I felt I could do no less than . . . call upon my former benefactor. . . . Whatever Dr. Cook may have done, the Cook who did them was not the Dr. Cook I knew as a young man. . . . Some physical misfortune must have overtaken him to change his personality."

Amundsen called on January 20, 1926, at a time when the gentlemen of the Poles had not seen each other for seventeen years. The reunion of these two exceptionally apolitical men ("Some physical misfortune must have overtaken him"!) took place in the office of the warden and lasted for one hour. Afterward Amundsen, talking with reporters, described Cook as "the finest traveler I ever knew." On January 24, 1926, the New York *Times* reported: "Dr. Frederick A. Cook is a 'genius' in the estimation of Captain Roald Amundsen . . . and deserves the respect of the American people." The *Times* also quoted Amundsen as saying: "Dr. Cook may not have discovered the Pole, but Commander Peary also may not have, and the former has as good a claim as the latter." A day or so later the National Geographic Society notified Amundsen that his lecture had been canceled.

Although Cook could write only three letters a week, he received between ten and fifteen a day. One came from James R. Crowell of *American* magazine, who offered $20,000 for a "confession." Cook refused.

Meanwhile, some of the oil sites that he had lost when PPA was forced into receivership had been developed by their purchasers and were yielding immense profits. "It is . . . a fact," he wrote in 1936, "that the potential oil lands which I had acquired were not fully tested and were stamped as practically worthless by the prosecution. It is a fact . . . that some of the lands under question have since produced wealth of millions, far beyond the wildest assertions . . . made in literature and letters of the company. . . . I have never in my life taken a penny that did not belong to me, and I am convinced . . . that my judgment in regard to every phase of my oil development was sound."

In March, 1930, he became eligible for parole. Professor William H. Hobbs, a biographer of Peary, organized a protest.

"I hope you will be willing," Hobbs wrote Vilhjalmur Stefansson, "to protest the release of Dr. Cook now in progress . . . Act promptly . . . best done by telegram."

This final madness failed.

On the night before Cook's release, a dinner was given in his honor in the dining room of the prison hospital. Sixty prisoners attended. In *The New Era* his successor as editor wrote: "Perhaps no more noted prisoner was ever committed to a federal penitentiary. None was ever held in higher esteem by officials and inmates alike. . . . The world of freedom has reclaimed a man meek and loving, asking for nothing more than an even break from his fellow men. . . . His going is our loss."

On March 8, 1930, the Doctor — sixty-five years old and possessing only fifty dollars — walked out of the gate at Leavenworth and found the reporters waiting for him. He told them his refusal of Crowell's offer. "To a man in prison, $20,000 is a lot of money. It was indeed a fortune to me, since I am without funds."

13

WITH HIS LOSSES titantic and imperial, the Doctor lived on for ten years, a pauper supported by his daughter and his friends.

Part of his time he spent working on his manuscripts. He completed *Return from .the Pole*, which was published posthumously with an introduction by Frederick A. Pohl. In it the great explorer summed up his polar adventure by writing: "Our all-important discovery must be noted in that we found the greatest mystery, the greatest unknown, is not that beyond the frontiers of knowledge but that unknown capacity in the spirit within the inner man of self. In other words, all lasting good must be planted and nursed in that garden of life between the ears and behind the eyes. Therein is the greatest field for exploration." He also worked on a second manuscript, *Peeps into the Beyond*, which was to contain material about himself and a final chapter on explorers and exploration.

One Christmas he received a letter from Rudolph Franke: "Dear Doc, On this day, twenty-nine years ago, we celebrated Christmas in Annoatok. You and I did the best to make that day cheerful for one and another. That day, I made a pledge to go with you through thick and thin, with you always. I can say to myself honestly, that I kept that pledge and always will. . . . Your biggest fight is yet ahead. It isn't the fight about the North Pole, it is to remind the world how you have been wronged, and if you can do that, you will have done a great service, especially to the people of the U.S."[1]

It was good advice, but it was not really needed, because when he was not working on his manuscripts, or helping his daughter with the dishes, Cook was fighting his belittlers. When the historian Jeanette Mirsky described him as "a fiction writer," he sued immediately; sued and lost. When Donald B. MacMillan wrote, in *How Peary Reached the Pole:* "and now I must relate the history of the Dr. Cook episode, a story utterly discredited and unbelievable now," he sued and lost again. He also sued the Encyclopaedia Britannica, which contended that his claim to the Pole was "universally rejected." He lost that one too. He petitioned the American Geographic Society and requested that it review his case. His request was rejected.

At no time, in a world that, if it remembered him at all, remembered him as a comic and perhaps pathetic figure, did he fail to assert his identity.

Once in a while, something pleasant would happen to him. In 1936, for example, the International Mark Twain Society awarded him honorary membership. Cyril Clemens, the society's president, declared: "We do feel that it is probable that Dr. Cook really discovered the North Pole. . . . It is unjust to continue to regard him as a faker."*

And in 1937 the Danish Foreign Office prepared a memorandum which specifically stated that neither the University of Copenhagen nor the Royal Danish Geographic Society had withdrawn the honors awarded him in 1909 in Copenhagen.

No element in the North Pole controversy, not even the courage of Cook and Peary, contains even one single piece of good news for mankind. The absence of compassion for either explorer is particularly depressing. The only even mildly sensitive appreciation of Peary's plight was made in Brussels, when

* The link between Cook and Mark Twain is strong. As Cook is the foremost victim of ordered society, so is Mark Twain the most incisive critic of ordered society. See Maxwell Geismar, *Mark Twain, An American Prophet*, Boston, 1970; and *A Pen Warmed Up in Hell*, ed. Frederick Anderson, New York, 1972.

Adrien de Gerlache observed: "I understand the sentiments which Commander Peary must have felt in that tragic moment when . . . filled with the pride of having in a supreme effort realized the dream of his whole life, he suddenly found that it had been wrested from him." The only philosophically based estimate of Cook's assertion came from Rome: "The Pope expressed the opinion today that one must believe in the truthfulness of a man like Dr. Cook, whose character had been tried by such perils and who had faced death alone." The wisest observation made by anyone who might possibly be an American was made by Father Bernard Hubbard, S.J. It is worth repeating: "The important thing to remember is that anyone who accepted the challenge of the Arctic is worthy of the greatest consideration — whether he reached the Pole or not." The remainder of the record simply underscores the childhood of man in the universe.

Of the multitude of thick-headed statements made during the polar controversy, two are outstanding. Professor Thomas B. Chamberlin, the head of the geology department at the University of Chicago, declared: "Peary nailed the flag, while Cook buried it. That is a big point in Peary's favor." The other was contributed by Simeon D. Fess, president of Antioch College and Member of Congress from Ohio. During a long tirade against Cook in the House of Representatives, Fess said: "I shall voice my sentiments not only as a member of Congress but in the spirit of an educator — a college president, a teacher of history, and as a citizen jealous that there should be no perversions in our American history."

Sometime around the middle of February, 1931, a man named Shea received a letter written from Chicago. It read in part: "You probably have a higher opinion of this elusive quality which we call civilization than I can grasp. To me we have all overrated what we thought was progress. Our advance has been chiefly in tool making, not in essential brain culture nor in the physical [culture] of our bodies nor in social relations. After all, perhaps trouble will teach us more than ease . . . After all let us work with that delusion we call hope, beyond this there is an urge which may get us someplace. Sincerely, Frederick A. Cook."[2]

Matthew Henson continued to work at the Custom House in Manhattan. His salary was gradually increased to $2,000 a year. Donald B. MacMillan took an interest in him and he slowly received some recognition for his services to Peary.

In 1937 he was elected a full member of the Explorers Club of New York. He rarely visited the clubhouse, however, because he lacked the money to pay for his lunch.

In 1950 he was received by President Truman, who saluted him.

In 1954 he was congratulated, at the White House, by President Eisenhower.

Later, in his home state of Maryland, he was honored by a bronze tablet at the State House. On it he was identified as "Co-discoverer of the North Pole." It was an identification wrong in fact but correct in implication. Robert E. Peary provided the energizing desire for the polar dash, but he could not possibly have attained the Pole without Henson.

Matthew Henson died March 9, 1955, in New York City, at the age of eighty-eight.

Robert E. Peary, Rear Admiral (ret.), USN, died in Washington, D.C., on February 20, 1920, a victim of pernicious anemia. Two years later the National Geographic Society unveiled a monument at his grave in Arlington National Cemetery. The tablet on the monument specifically identified him as "the discoverer of the North Pole."

But in the larger world of less interested parties, the decision is no longer so absolute. The 1968 edition of the Encyclopaedia Britannica states: "The question of whether Peary or Cook, neither or both, actually reached this theoretical point on the moving ice is hard to prove or disprove; but until there is fresh documentary evidence or improved knowledge of the nature and movement of the ice in the Arctic ocean that supports a different interpretation of existing documents, Peary's claim seems the more valid one. At any event it was accepted by the U. S. Congress and geographical institutions in many lands."

For Robert E. Peary, actually, nothing has worked out quite right historically. This includes that item that he liked to consider on occasions, the monument over his grave.

"In the last year of his life, when he knew he would never be well again," his daughter told the New York *Times* in 1932, "he spent most of the summer lying in the sunshine on a musk-ox skin spread on the lawn of our island home in Maine. As he looked out to sea, directly in his line of vision was a rough stone monument on a nearby island, marking the ship channel. . . . It was his wish that a similar marker be set upon his grave."

A regulation limiting the height of monuments in Arlington precluded the accomplishment of his desire. It was carried out in spirit, however, in 1932, when his family and his friends chartered a ship and sailed to Cape York, where the real Arctic begins, and there established the monument he had desired. It is a triangular shaft sixty feet tall, made out of stone native to the region, and constructed on the spot, for $15,000, by masons from the state of Maine. Each of its three sides is decorated with a eight-foot hand-carved initial letter "P." It stands atop a headland 1,500 feet above the sea at a point 14° south of that magic spot that is itself without length, breadth, or thickness.

Frederick A. Cook, M.D., suffered a stroke and was taken to a hospital in a coma on May 3, 1940. He had maintained, during the three previous weeks, a day and night vigil at the bedside of the dying wife of Ralph Shainwald. While he remained in a semi-coma his friends petitioned President Franklin D. Roosevelt to pardon him as an act of mercy, that quality so uniquely denied him as long as he stood on his own two feet. A pardon was granted immediately, thus restoring Cook's rights as a citizen. He rallied slightly after being informed of this, but soon relapsed. He died in New Rochelle, New York, on August 5, 1940, at the age of seventy-five.

The North Pole was only one episode in the life of this fantastic man. Whether or not his attainment of it will ever be formally certified is unknown; but if not, then he stands, in the history of the American democracy, as its most uniquely grand and somehow royal person, its Prince of Losers. In this most powerful and careless of nations, that is the larger honor.

> Few men in all history, I am inclined to believe, have ever been made the subject of such vicious attacks, of such malevolent assailing of character, of such a series of perjured and forged charges, of such a widespread and relentless press persecution, as I; and few men, I feel sure, have ever been made to suffer so bitterly and so inexpressibly as I because of the assertion of my achievement.

Notes

I

1. Fitzhugh Green, *Peary, The Man Who Refused to Fail* (New York, 1926), p. 197.
2. New York *Times*, September 2, 1909.
3. Herbert L. Bridgman, *Independent*, September 9, 1909, p. 573.
4. Frederick A. Cook, *My Attainment of the Pole* (New York, 1913), p. 26.
5. Ibid.
6. W. T. Stead, "Dr. Cook, The Man and the Deed," *Review of Reviews* (American), October, 1909, p. 440.
7. Frederick A. Cook, *American Weekly*, July 19, 1925.
8. John Edward Weems, *Peary, The Explorer and the Man* (Boston, 1967), p. 52.
9. Green, *Peary, The Man Who Refused to Fail*, p. 33.
10. Weems, *Peary, The Explorer and the Man*, p. 84.
11. Frederick A. Cook, "Autobiographical Sketch," p. 3, The Stefansson Collection, Dartmouth College Library, Hanover, N.H.
12. Floyd Miller, *Ahdoolo!* (New York, 1963), p. 69.
13. Robert E. Peary, *Northward over the Great Ice* (New York, 1893), vol. I, p. 423.
14. New York *Herald*, September 28, 1909.
15. Eivind Astrup, *With Peary near the Pole* (London, 1898), p. 15.
16. Cook, "Autobiographical Sketch."
17. Brooklyn *Standard-Union*, July 11, 1893.
18. Stead, "Dr. Cook, The Man and the Deed."
19. Sydney (Nova Scotia) *Daily Post*, morning edition, September 21, 1909.
20. Roald Amundsen, *My Life as an Explorer* (New York, 1927), p. 28.
21. Cook, *American Weekly*, July 26, 1925.
22. Brooklyn *Eagle*, September 5, 1909.
23. New York *Times*, January 24, 1925.
24. Sydney *Daily Post*, September 21, 1909.
25. Robert E. Peary, *Nearest the Pole* (New York, 1907), p. 190.
26. Green, *Peary, The Man Who Refused to Fail*, p. 195.

27. Eliza Barker, "Peary as His Friends Portray Him," *Current Literature*, May, 1910, p. 497.
28. New York *World*, September 20, 1909.
29. John Edward Weems, *Race for the Pole* (New York, 1960), p. 44.
30. New York *Times*, October 2, 1895.
31. Peary, *Northward over the Great Ice*, Vol. I, p. xlix.
32. Bradley Robinson, *Dark Companion* (London, 1948), p. 134.
33. Andrew Freeman, *The Case for Doctor Cook* (New York, 1961), p. 64.
34. Peary, *Nearest the Pole*, p. 228.
35. Robinson, *Dark Companion*, p. 160.
36. Cook, "Autobiographical Sketch."
37. Cook, *American Weekly*, July 26, 1925.
38. Weems, *Peary, The Explorer and the Man*, p. 200.
39. Robinson, *Dark Companion*, p. 170.

2

1. Brooklyn *Eagle*, September 5, 1909.
2. New York *Times*, September 8, 1909.
3. Robert Dunn, *The Shameless Diary of an Explorer* (New York, 1907), p. 286.
4. Seward (Alaska) *Gateway*, June 30, 1906.
5. Russell W. Porter, "Arctic Fever," p. 87, The Stefansson Collection, Dartmouth College Library, Hanover, N.H.
6. Nellie Martin Wade, "To Mt. McKinley on Horseback," *Alaska*, June, 1972, p. 14.
7. Seattle *Post-Intelligencer*, November 10, 1906.
8. Ibid.
9. Frederick A. Cook, *American Weekly*, July 25, 1925.
10. New York *Herald*, October 24, 1909, affidavit of C. G. Bridgford.
11. Porter, "Arctic Fever," p. 88.
12. *Western News*, Hamilton, Montana, November 28, 1906.
13. Frederick A. Cook, *My Attainment of the Pole* (New York, 1913), p. 553 (footnote).
14. Civil Action No. 32, District Magistrate Court, State of Alaska, Seward.
15. *Western News*, November 28, 1906.
16. Edwin Swift Balch, *Mount McKinley and Mountain Climbers' Proofs* (Philadelphia, 1914), p. 10.
17. Norman Bright, *American Alpine Journal*, 1939.
18. Hudson Stuck, *The Ascent of Denali* (New York, 1914), p. 79.
19. Alfred Lindley, "Mt. McKinley, North and South Peaks," *American Alpine Journal*, 1932.
20. *Encyclopaedia Britannica*, 1960, Vol. 15, "Mountaineering," p. 96.
21. Information supplied by Helene Cook Vetter.

22. Balch, *Mount McKinley and Mountain Climbers' Proofs*, p. 100.
23. Edwin Swift Balch, *North Pole and Bradley Land* (Philadelphia, 1913), p. 36.
24. Bradford Washburn, "Dr. Cook and Mt. McKinley," *American Alpine Journal*, 1958, p. 8.
25. T. C. Longstaff, *Mountain Sickness and Its Probable Causes* (London, 1906), p. 55.
26. Filippo de Filippi, *Mt. St. Elias* (London, 1900), p. 218.
27. Frederick A. Cook, *To the Top of the Continent* (New York, 1908), p. 226.
28. Belmore Browne, *The Conquest of Mount McKinley* (New York, 1913), p. 335.
29. Cook, *To the Top of the Continent*, p. 226.
30. Francis Farquhar, *Sierra Club Bulletin*, June, 1950, p. 26.
31. Cook, *To the Top of the Continent*, p. 231.
32. Stuck, *The Ascent of Denali*, p. 96.
33. Filippi, *Mt. St. Elias*, p. 219.
34. Cook, *To the Top of the Continent*, p. 231.
35. Grant Pearson, *My Life of High Adventure* (Englewood Cliffs, N.J., 1962), p. 152.
36. Cook, *To the Top of the Continent*, p. 231.
37. Pearson, *My Life of High Adventure*, p. 152.
38. Balch, *Mount McKinley and Mountain Climbers' Proofs*, p. 122.
39. Cook, *To the Top of the Continent*, p. 233.
40. Pearson, *My Life of High Adventure*, p. 153.
41. New York *Times*, November 28, 1906.
42. Pearson, *My Life of High Adventure*, p. 152.
43. New York *Globe*, October 14, 1909.
44. Stuck, *The Ascent of Denali*, p. 105.
45. Alfred Lindley, *American Alpine Journal*, 1932, p. 41.
46. Washburn, *American Alpine Journal*, 1958, p. 17.
47. John R. Bradley, "My Knowledge of Dr. Cook's Polar Expedition," *Independent*, September 16, 1909.
48. Vilhjalmur Stefansson, *The Friendly Arctic* (New York, 1921), p. 31.
49. Brooklyn *Eagle*, September 5, 1909.

3

1. *Peary Arctic Club*, Lotus Press (New York, 1905).
2. Howard Beale, *Theodore Roosevelt and the Rise of America to World Power* (New York, 1962), p. 80.
3. Robert A. Bartlett, *The Log of Bob Bartlett* (New York, 1928), p. 203.
4. John Edward Weems, *Race for the Pole* (New York, 1960), p. 36.
5. New York *Times*, September 9, 1909.

6. John Edward Weems, *Peary, The Explorer and the Man* (New York, 1967), p. 239.
7. New York *Herald*, September 19, 1909.
8. John R. Bradley, "My Knowledge of Dr. Cook's Polar Expedition," *Independent*, September 16, 1909.
9. Frederick A. Cook, *My Attainment of the Pole* (New York, 1913), p. 74.
10. New York *Herald*, September 3, 1909.
11. Frederick A. Cook, "Preparations for Pole — Etah — July, 1907, February 18, 1908," unpublished notebook in the possession of Helene Cook Vetter.
12. New York *Herald*, September 2, 1909.
13. Ibid., September 25, 1909.
14. Brooklyn *Eagle*, September 10, 1909.
15. New York *American*, September 6, 1909.
16. New York *World*, October 14, 1908.
17. Weems, *Race for the Pole*, p. 40.
18. Andrew A. Freeman, *The Case for Doctor Cook* (New York, 1961), p. 111.
19. Bradley S. Osbon, "Cook and Peary," *Tourist*, October, 1910, p. 309.
20. Weems, *Race for the Pole*, p. 171.
21. New York *Herald*, September 13, 1909.
22. New York *Times*, September 16, 1909.
23. New York *Herald*, September 10, 1909.
24. Cook, *My Attainment of the Pole*, p. 229.
25. J. R. L. Anderson, *The Ulysses Factor* (New York, 1970), p. 20.
26. Guy R. L. Potter, "Peary and the North Pole," *Polar Notes*, October, 1970 (The Stefansson Collection, Dartmouth College Library, Hanover, N.H.), p. 16.
27. John Euller, *Arctic*, December, 1964, p. 220.
28. Boston *American*, July 17, 1910.
29. Donald B. MacMillan, *How Peary Reached the Pole* (Boston, 1934), p. 289.
30. Ibid.
31. New York *World*, September 20, 1909.
32. Weems, *Peary, The Explorer and the Man*, p. 193.
33. Boston *American*, July 17, 1910.
34. J. Gordon Hayes, *Robert Edwin Peary* (London, 1929), p. 91.
35. New York *American*, September 20, 1909.
36. Boston *American*, July 17, 1910.
37. Ibid.
38. Ibid.
39. Thomas F. Hall, *Has the North Pole Been Discovered?* (Boston, 1917), p. 367.
40. New York *Herald*, September 18, 1909.
41. New York *Herald*, October 1, 1909.
42. New York *World*, October 2, 1909.

43. New York *Herald*, September 18, 1909.
44. New York *Herald*, October 1, 1909.

4

1. Harry Whitney, "Hunting in the Arctic," *Outing*, December, 1909, p. 262.
2. New York *World*, September 28, 1909.
3. New York *Herald*, September 16, 1909.
4. Robert A. Bartlett, *The Log of Bob Bartlett* (New York, 1928), p. 149.
5. New York *Times*, September 29, 1909.
6. New York *Times*, October 1, 1909.
7. New York *Herald*, September 29, 1909.
8. Frederick A. Cook, *American Weekly*, August 9, 1925.
9. H. M. Lyon, "When Cook Came to Copenhagen," *Collier's*, September 25, 1909.
10. Brooklyn *Standard-Union*, September 5, 1909.
11. New York *Times*, September 6, 1909.
12. Letter, Frederick A. Cook to William E. Shea, May 20, 1927. In the possession of Helene Cook Vetter.
13. New York *Times*, September 7, 1909.
14. New York *Herald*, September 7, 1909.
15. Frederick A. Cook, *American Weekly*, August 9, 1925.
16. Letter, Frederick A. Cook, to William E. Shea, November 24, 1927. In the possession of Helene Cook Vetter.
17. New York *World*, September 20, 1909.
18. New York *World*, September 22, 1909.
19. Brooklyn *Eagle*, September 10, 1909.
20. Frederick A. Cook, *American Weekly*, August 9, 1925.
21. New York *Herald*, September 19, 1909.

5

1. New York *World*, September 22, 1909.
2. New York *World*, September 24, 1909.
3. New York *Times*, November 27, 1909.
4. New York *American*, December 10, 1909.
5. Brooklyn *Eagle*, September 22, 1909.

6

1. New York *Herald*, September 3, 1909.
2. New York *World*, September 9, 1909.

3. E. F. Hussey, "Dr. Cook's Pemmican," *Independent*, November 11, 1909, p. 1083.
4. Bradley Osbon, "Cook and Peary," *Tourist*, September, 1910, p. 211.
5. New York *World*, September 27, 1909.
6. Ibid.
7. New York *World*, October 1, 1909.
8. New York *World*, September 29, 1909.
9. New York *World*, October 4, 1909.
10. New York *World*, September 29, 1909.
11. New York *Herald*, September 29, 1909.
12. New York *Times*, October 13, 1909.
13. New York *World*, October 1, 1909.
14. New York *World*, October 4, 1909.
15. New York *World*, September 29, 1909.
16. Brooklyn *Standard-Union*, September 21, 1909.
17. Robert E. Peary, *The North Pole* (New York, 1910), p. 274.
18. Ibid., p. 288.
19. New York *World*, October 2, 1910.
20. New York *World*, October 3, 1910.
21. Robert A. Bartlett, *The Log of Bob Bartlett*, (New York, 1928), p. 196.
22. Theon Wright, *The Big Nail* (New York, 1970), p. 199.
23. Ibid.
24. J. Gordon Hayes, *Robert Edwin Peary* (London, 1929), p. 87 (chart).
25. Ibid., p. 214.
26. New York *American*, September 20, 1909.
27. Hayes, *Robert Edwin Peary*, p. 144.
28. Ibid., p. 87 (chart).
29. Ibid., p. 87 (text).
30. Wright, *The Big Nail*, p. 200.
31. Ibid., p. 199.
32. Hayes, *Robert Edwin Peary*, p. 255 (chart).
33. Wright, *The Big Nail*, p. 203.
34. Frederick A. Cook, *My Attainment of the Pole* (New York, 1913), p. 212, footnote.
35. Buffalo *Courier-Express*, October 21, 1949.
36. John Edward Weems, *Peary, The Explorer and the Man* (Boston, 1967), p. 274.
37. Donald B. MacMillan, *How Peary Reached the Pole* (Boston, 1934), p. 285.
38. New York *Times*, September 8, 1909.
39. John D. MacDonald, *The End of the Night* (New York, 1969; paperback edition), p. 145.
40. Edwin Swift Balch, *North Pole and Bradley Land* (Philadelphia, 1913), p. 30.
41. New York *Times*, September 3, 1909.
42. New York *World*, September 11, 1909.

43. New York *Times*, September 12, 1909.
44. Sydney (Nova Scotia) *Daily Post*, morning edition, September 21, 1909.
45. Cook, *My Attainment of the Pole*, p. 281.
46. Wally Herbert, *Across the Top of the World* (London, 1969), p. 165.
47. John Euller, *Arctic*, December, 1964, p. 220.
48. New York *World*, October 1, 1909.
49. Jeanette Mirsky, *To the Arctic* (New York, 1948), p. 331.

7

1. W. S. Laughlin, "The Importance of Hunting in Human Evolution," as quoted by Lionel Tiger, *Men in Groups* (New York, 1969), p. 170.
2. New York *World*, October 2, 1910.
3. Quoted in letter, Clark Brown, of Albany, N.Y., to E. C. Roost, April 28, 1914. Letter now in the possession of Helene Cook Vetter. According to Brown, Bridgman made the statement during a lecture in Albany. In "The Case for Doctor Cook," *The Platform*, the Lyceum and Chautauqua magazine, June 11, 1914, Fred High wrote: "Herbert L. Bridgman . . . admitted to Clark Brown . . . that $350,000 had been subscribed to 'see Peary through.' "
4. Thomas Beer, *Hanna, Crane and the Mauve Decade* (New York, 1941), p. 541.
5. Frederick Lewis Allen, *The Big Change* (New York, 1952), p. 73 (quoting Henry Clews).
6. "Official Souvenir of the Testimonial Tendered to Commander Robert E. Peary, U.S.N., by the Citizens of New York, Governor Hughes Presiding" (copy in possession of the Brooklyn Public Library, Brooklyn, N.Y.).
7. Brooklyn *Eagle*, September 7, 1909.
8. Henry S. Burrage, *Thomas Hamlin Hubbard* (Portland, Me., 1923), p. 46.
9. *Hampton's*, January, 1910.
10. Thomas H. Hubbard, *Legal Ethics* (Albany, N.Y., 1903), p. 26.
11. Burrage, *Thomas Hamlin Hubbard*, p. 46.
12. Bridgman died September 27, 1924. Beyond his obituary in the New York *Times* the main source of information on him is the memorial pamphlet *His Last Voyage*, Brooklyn *Standard-Union*.
13. Marie Peary Stafford, "Herbert L. Bridgman," The Stefansson Collection, Dartmouth College Library, Hanover, N.H.
14. Robert A. Bartlett, *The Log of Bob Bartlett* (New York, 1928), p. 200.
15. New York *Herald*, September 16, 1909.
16. Brooklyn *Standard-Union*, December 2, 1893.
17. *His Last Voyage* (Captain Riesenberg).

8

1. New York *Times*, February 20, 1913 (Letter to the Editor).
2. Brooklyn *Standard-Union*, September 21, 1909.
3. New York *Herald*, October 6, 1909.
4. New York *Times*, October 14, 1909.
5. *Daily Missoulian* (Missoula, Montana), September 26, 1909.
6. New York *Times*, October 14, 1909.
7. *Daily Missoulian*, September 26, 1909.
8. Ibid.
9. *Daily Missoulian*, September 9, 1909.
10. *Daily Missoulian*, September 26, 1909.
11. Frederick A. Cook, *My Attainment of the Pole* (New York, 1913), p. 566.
12. Bradley Osbon, "Cook and Peary," *Tourist*, November, 1910, p. 447.
13. Frederick A. Cook, *American Weekly*, August 9, 1925.
14. *Daily Missoulian*, September 26, 1909.
15. New York *Herald*, October 24, 1909.
16. Cook, *My Attainment of the Pole*, p. 292.
17. New York *Times*, October 30, 1909.
18. New York *Globe*, October 16, 1909.
19. New York *Sun*, October 16, 1909.
20. New York *Herald*, October 19, 1909.
21. Andrew A. Freeman, *The Case for Doctor Cook* (New York, 1961), p. 179.
22. New York *Globe*, October 15, 1909.
23. New York *Herald*, October 16, 1909.
24. Cook, *My Attainment of the Pole*, p. 505.
25. Walter Lonsdale, "The Real Story of Dr. Cook and the North Pole," *Travel*, June, 1910, p. 452.
26. New York *Sun*, September 6, 1909.
27. New York *Globe*, October 14, 1909.
28. Cook, *My Attainment of the Pole*, p. 13.
29. *Anaconda Standard* (Butte, Montana), October 28, 1909.
30. New York *Herald*, October 30, 1909, New York *Times*, October 30, 1909; Ravalli *Republican* (Hamilton, Montana), October 29, 1909; *Western News* (Hamilton, Montana), November 3, 1909.

9

1. New York *Times*, December 27, 1909.
2. Walter Lonsdale, "The Real Story of Dr. Cook and the North Pole," *Travel*, June, 1910, p. 425.

3. New York *Times*, November 28, 1909.
4. Ibid.
5. New York *Times*, November 27, 1909.
6. New York *Herald*, November 26, 1909.
7. New York *American*, December 22, 1909.
8. Frederick A. Cook, *My Attainment of the Pole* (New York, 1913), p. 504.
9. Lonsdale, "The Real Story of Dr. Cook and the North Pole," June, 1910, p. 427.
10. Brooklyn *Eagle*, December 19, 1909.
11. Lonsdale, "The Real Story of Dr. Cook and the North Pole," June, 1910, p. 427.
12. New York *Times*, December 27, 1909.
13. New York *World*, September 18, 1909.
14. New York *Times*, November 27, 1909.
15. New York *American*, December 9, 1909.
16. New York *American*, December 10, 1909.
17. Brooklyn *Eagle*, December 17, 1909.
18. New York *Herald*, December 10, 1909.
19. New York *Times*, December 10, 1909.
20. New York *Times*, December 9, 1909.
21. Cook, *My Attainment of the Pole*, p. 536.
22. New York *Times*, December 9, 1909.
23. Cook, *My Attainment of the Pole*, p. 537.
24. Ibid., p. 538.
25. Ibid.
26. New York *Times*, December 9, 1909.
27. Lonsdale, "The Real Story of Dr. Cook and the North Pole," *Travel*, May, 1910.
28. New York *American*, December 10, 1909.
29. Ibid.
30. Ibid.
31. New York *Times*, January 21, 1910.
32. New York *Times*, November 25, 1923.
33. Mark Twain, *Autobiography*, Paine edition, Vol. II, p. 7.
34. Brooklyn *Eagle*, December 10, 1909.
35. Ibid.
36. Lonsdale, "The Real Story of Dr. Cook and the North Pole," June, 1910, p. 451.
37. New York *Times*, December 9, 1909.
38. New York *Times*, December 8, 1909.
39. Aarbog for Kobenhavns Universitet, Indeholdende Meddelelser for det akademiske Aar 1909–1910, Copenhagen, 1914, p. 1247.
40. New York *Times*, December 21, 1909.
41. Brooklyn *Standard-Union*, December 21, 1909.
42. New York *American*, December 22, 1909.
43. New York *World*, December 22, 1909.

44. New York *World*, December 22, 1909.
45. New York *American*, December 22, 1909.

10

1. New York *Herald*, September 6, 1909.
2. Thomas F. Hall, *Has the North Pole Been Discovered?* (Boston, 1917), p. 237.
3. Private Calendar No. 733, 61st Congress, 3rd Session, House of Representatives, Report No. 1961, pp. 11–12.
4. Ibid., pp. 18–22.
5. Ibid., pp. 7–8.
6. New York *Times*, December 16, 1909.
7. Hall, *Has the North Pole Been Discovered?*, p. 215.
8. "Official Souvenir of the Testimonial Tendered to Commander Robert E. Peary, U.S.N., by the Citizens of New York, Governor Hughes Presiding" (copy in Brooklyn Public Library, Brooklyn, N.Y.).
9. Private Calendar No. 733, 61st Congress, 3rd Session, House of Representatives, Report No. 1961, p. 17.
10. Ibid., Helgesen's "Extension of Remarks," p. 275.
11. Cook, *My Attainment of the Pole*, New York, 1913, p. 4.

11

1. New York *World*, October 3, 1910.
2. New York *World*, December 10, 1909.
3. Andrew A. Freeman, *The Case for Doctor Cook* (New York, 1961), p. 222.
4. *Congressional Record*, 63rd Congress, 3rd Session, Vol. 52, Pt. 6, Appendix 1–5, p. 675, speech by Congressman T. H. Caraway.
5. Theon Wright, *The Big Nail* (New York, 1970), p. 274.
6. Affidavit of T. Everett Harré, in the possession of Helene Cook Vetter.
7. Harry Whitney, "Hunting in the Arctic," *Outing*, December, 1909.
8. Freeman, *The Case for Doctor Cook*, p. 218.
9. John Edward Weems, *Peary, The Explorer and the Man*, p. 294.
10. Marie Peary Stafford, "The Peary Arctic Club," The Stefansson Collection, Dartmouth College Library, Hanover, N.H.
11. New York *Times*, January 30, 1913.
12. San Diego (California) *Union*, March 27, 1912.
13. New York *Times*, December 28, 1913, December 29, 1913.
14. Ibid.

15. Ibid.
16. Ibid.
17. Letter, Ralph Shainwald to Senator Poindexter, December 31, 1913. Copy in the possession of Helene Cook Vetter.
18. Ibid.
19. Ibid.
20. New York *Times*, December 28, 1913.
21. Ibid.
22. Ibid.
23. Ibid.
24. New York *Times*, December 29, 1913.
25. New York *Times*, January 2, 1914.
26. Letter, G. W. Baker to Senator Poindexter, January 6, 1914. Copy in the possession of Helene Cook Vetter.
27. *Congressional Record*, March 4, 1915, "The North Pole Aftermath, Reply to Some Criticisms in the North Pole Controversy," Extension of Remarks of Honorable Henry T. Helgesen of North Dakota.
28. Pittsburgh *Sun*, April 3, 1914.

12

1. Court Record 2273, Frederick A. Cook, FRC 368994-8. On deposit in Federal Records Center, Fort Worth, Texas. Cook's testimony fills Vols. 23, 25, and 26.
2. Frederick A. Cook, "Autobiographical Sketch," The Stefansson Collection, Dartmouth College Library, Hanover, N.H.
3. Court Record 2273, Fort Worth, Texas.
4. Frederick A. Cook, *American Weekly*, August 9, 1925.
5. Court Record 2273, Fort Worth, Texas.
6. Fort Worth *Record*, November 24, 1923.
7. Court Record 2273, Fort Worth, Texas.
8. Fort Worth *Star-Telegram*, November 17, 1923.
9. Court Record 2273, Fort Worth, Texas.
10. Fort Worth *Star-Telegram*, November 15, 1923.
11. *His Last Voyage*, Brooklyn *Standard-Union*, 1924, p. 61.
12. Author has photocopy of article in a Sunday issue of Brooklyn *Eagle*. Exact date missing. Original in the possession of Helene Cook Vetter.
13. New York *Times*, January 11, 1923.
14. *Oil Weekly*, April 21, 1923.
15. Frederick A. Cook, Application for Executive Clemency, July 25, 1926. Copy in the possession of Helene Cook Vetter.
16. Court Record 2273, Fort Worth, Texas.
17. Ibid.
18. Andrew A. Freeman, *The Case for Doctor Cook* (New York, 1961), p. 244.

19. Fort Worth *Star-Telegram*, November 15, 1923.
20. Ibid., November 18, 1923.
21. New York *Times*, September 14, 1938.
22. Based on information supplied by the Administrative Office of the United States Courts, Washington, D.C.
23. Information supplied by Department of Commerce, Division of Banks, State of Ohio.
24. Information supplied by Probate Court, County of Lucas, Toledo, Ohio.
25. Ibid.
26. Information supplied by County Judges Court, County of Pinellas, Clearwater, Florida.
27. Frederick A. Cook, *American Weekly*, August 9, 1925.
28. Court Record 2273, Fort Worth, Texas.
29. East St. Louis *Daily Journal*, March 25, 1927.
30. Letter, Milton Miles Lory to Ralph Shainwald. Original in the possession of Helene Cook Vetter.
31. Fort Worth *Record*, November 24, 1923.

13

1. Letter, Rudolph Franke to Frederick A. Cook, December 25, 1936. Original in the possession of Helene Cook Vetter.
2. Letter, F. A. Cook to W. E. Shea, February 14, 1931. Original in the possession of Helene Cook Vetter.

Bibliography

Books: Primary

Roald Amundsen, *My Life as an Explorer* (New York, 1927).
Edwin Swift Balch, *Mount McKinley and Mountain Climbers Proofs* (Philadelphia, 1914).
———, *North Pole and Bradley Land* (Philadelphia, 1913).
Frederick A. Cook, *Through the First Antarctic Night* (New York, 1900).
———, *To the Top of the Continent* (New York, 1908).
———, *My Attainment of the Pole* (New York, 1911).
———, *Return from the Pole* (New York, 1952).
Andrew A. Freeman, *The Case for Doctor Cook* (New York, 1961).
Thomas F. Hall, *Has the North Pole Been Discovered?* (Boston, 1917).
J. Gordon Hayes, *Robert Edwin Peary* (London, 1929).
Robert E. Peary, *The North Pole* (New York, 1910).
John Edward Weems, *Peary, The Explorer and the Man* (Boston, 1967).
———, *Race for the Pole* (New York, 1960).
Theon Wright, *The Big Nail* (New York, 1970).

Books: Secondary

Frederick Lewis Allen, *The Big Change* (New York, 1952).
J. R. L. Anderson, *The Ulysses Factor* (New York, 1970).
Eivind Astrup, *With Peary near the Pole* (London, 1898).
Robert A. Bartlett, *The Log of Bob Bartlett* (New York, 1928).
Howard Beale, *Theodore Roosevelt and the Rise of America to World Power* (New York, 1962).
Thomas Beer, *Hanna, Crane and the Mauve Decade* (New York, 1941).
Lucas Bridges, *Uttermost Part of the Earth* (London, 1948).
Belmore Browne, *The Conquest of Mount McKinley* (New York, 1913).
Henry S. Burrage, *Thomas Hamlin Hubbard* (Portland, Me., 1923).
Robert Dunn, *The Shameless Diary of an Explorer* (New York, 1907).
Encyclopaedia Britannica, 1960, 1968.

Filippo de Filippi, *Mt. St. Elias* (London, 1900).
Fitzhugh Green, *Peary, The Man Who Refused to Fail* (New York, 1926).
Matthew Henson, *A Negro Explorerer at the North Pole* (New York, 1912).
Wally Herbert, *Across the Top of the World* (London, 1969).
T. C. Longstaff, *Mountain Sickness and Its Probable Causes* (London, 1906).
Donald B. MacMillan, *How Peary Reached the Pole* (Boston, 1934).
Floyd Miller, *Ahdoolo!* (New York, 1963).
Jeanette Mirsky, *To the Arctic* (New York, 1948).
Grant Pearson, *My Life of High Adventure* (Englewood Cliffs, N.J., 1962).
Robert E. Peary, *Nearest the Pole* (New York, 1907).
————, *Northward over the Great Ice* (New York, 1893).
Bradley Robinson, *Dark Companion* (London, 1948).
Hudson Stuck, *The Ascent of Denali* (New York, 1914).
Vilhjalmur Stefansson, *The Friendly Arctic* (New York, 1921).

Magazines

American Alpine Journal
American Weekly
Arctic
Collier's
Current Literature
Hampton's
Independent
Oil Weekly
Polar Notes (occasional publication of The Stefansson Collection, Dartmouth College Library, Hanover, N.H.), October, 1970.
Review of Reviews (American)
Rosary
Sierra Club *Bulletin*
Tourist
Travel

Newspapers

Anaconda Standard, Butte, Montana
Boston *American*
Brooklyn *Eagle*
Brooklyn *Standard-Union*
Daily Missoulian, Missoula, Montana

Fort Worth *Record*
Fort Worth *Star-Telegram*
New York *American*
New York *Globe*
New York *Herald*
New York *Sun*
New York *Times*
New York *Tribune*
New York *World*
Pittsburgh *Press*
Pittsburgh *Sun*
Ravalli *Republican*, Hamilton, Montana
San Diego *Union*
Seattle *Post-Intelligencer*
Sydney *Daily Post*, Sydney, Nova Scotia
Western News, Hamilton, Montana

Miscellaneous

Russell W. Gibbons, "An Historical Evaluation of the Cook-Peary Controversy," Department of History, Ohio Northern University, 1956 (a 129-page bound typescript).

Ted Leitzel, "The Untold Story of the Cook-Peary Polar Controversy," (a collection of magazine articles by Leitzel from *Real America*, October, 1935–January, 1936, reprinted by Russell W. Gibbons in April, 1965, for the Dr. Frederick A. Cook Society).

Peary Arctic Club (brochure).

"Legal Ethics" (Lecture by Thomas H. Hubbard at Union University)

His Last Voyage (Memorial to Herbert L. Bridgman)

Official Souvenir of the Testimonial Tendered to Commander Robert E. Peary by the Citizens of New York, Governor Hughes presiding.

Frederick A. Cook, seven pocket-size polar notebooks and diaries in the possession of Helene Cook Vetter.

Unpublished Material in the Possession of The Stefansson Collection, Dartmouth College Library, Hanover, N.H.

Frederick A. Cook, "Autobiographical Sketch."
F. J. Pohl, "Defense of F. A. Cook."
Russell W. Porter, "Arctic Fever."
Marie Peary Stafford, "Herbert L. Bridgman."
_____, "The Peary Arctic Club."

Index